English Archives
An Historical Survey

English Archives

An Historical Survey

Richard Olney

LIVERPOOL UNIVERSITY PRESS

First published 2023 by
Liverpool University Press
4 Cambridge Street
Liverpool
L69 7ZU

Copyright © 2023 Richard Olney

Richard Olney has asserted the right to be identified as the author of this book in accordance with the Copyright, Designs and Patents Act 1988.

All rights reserved. No part of this book may be reproduced, stored in a retrieval system, or transmitted, in any form or by any means, electronic, mechanical, photocopying, recording, or otherwise, without the prior written permission of the publisher.

British Library Cataloguing-in-Publication data
A British Library CIP record is available

ISBN 978-1-80207-841-1 cased
ISBN 978-1-80207-770-4 limp

Typeset by Carnegie Book Production, Lancaster
Printed and bound by CPI Group (UK) Ltd, Croydon CR0 4YY

An independent voice for archives

The British Records Association (BRA) is a charity promoting the preservation, understanding, accessibility and study of our recorded heritage for the public benefit: the nation's records preserved, accessed and interpreted for the benefit of all

It initiates, encourages and supports projects that:

- contribute to their appropriate preservation.
- increase their accessibility for research.
- enable the exchange of views and information.
- influence public opinion and policymakers.

Please join us to help us continue our work. Member benefits include a twice-yearly peer-reviewed journal *Archives* and a regular digital newsletter, discounted rates for the annual conference and other events, such as visits to sites of recordkeeping interest, and opportunities to broaden networks and contacts within the broader archival community (encompassing users, archivists and owners), such as the annual Maurice Bond Lecture. Increasing our membership also enables the Association to contribute more to major initiatives such as saving collections which are at risk, and advocating for the importance of archives and records.

The Association also awards the prestigious Janette Harley prize which recognises the best/most original piece of work that has promoted the preservation, understanding, accessibility or study of archives.

To join us, please email subscriptions@liverpool.ac.uk or telephone +44 (0)151 795 1080

Time which antiquates Antiquities, and hath an art to make dust of all things, hath yet spared these *minor* Monuments.

Sir Thomas Browne, *Hydriotaphia: Urn-Burial*

Preface

England is a country rich in archives – the records that are accumulated at every level of society, by governments, national and local organisations, families and individuals. They grow almost by a kind of natural process, as the bodies that create them go about their business. But that does not mean that they are dull and bureaucratic. They can tell us about the lives of men and women from every walk of life, from those who petitioned their sovereign in the Middle Ages or took their marital troubles to the Church courts, to the citizens of a more recent period who appear in the returns of the census enumerators. In other words, they are an indispensable source for political, administrative, religious, economic, social and cultural history.

English archives have a continuous history stretching over several centuries. In some cases – the records of the State, ecclesiastical organisations, old-established charities, landed families – individual archives have their origins in the Middle Ages, and remain functioning entities today. In that respect they are outstanding not only in national but in European terms. Yet it is only comparatively recently that their importance as part of the national heritage has come to be more generally recognised. The use of archival sources, or 'original documents', is now part of the academic historian's training, and there is a growing interest in questions such as the use of archives for political purposes, or their significance as cultural objects in their own right. Since the mid-twentieth century England has also had an archival profession, and there is a small but growing literature on the history of record-keeping, for instance, and the development of national policies towards archives.

What has been lacking until now, however, is a general history of English archives, from the Anglo-Saxon period down to the late twentieth century. That is what this book attempts, however summarily, to provide. It treats a wide range of individual archives as entities in their own right, tracing their origins, their changing fortunes and in some cases their eventual loss or destruction. But it also places them in their historical context, discussing the reasons for the emergence of certain kinds of archive at different periods, and identifying those times when they were especially vulnerable to change or disturbance.

The author hopes that this book will be of use to both historians and archivists, as well as of interest to the non-specialist. It is also hoped that it may stimulate further research in areas of the subject that are as yet thinly covered. Its appearance, furthermore, may be timely, since, despite many advances in recent decades, English archives are more vulnerable today than they have been for some time past.

* * *

Although this book is the product of work in retirement it could not have been written without knowledge and experience gained as a member of staff first of the Lincolnshire Archives Office (now Lincolnshire Archives) and then of the Historical Manuscripts Commission. To my successive employers, and to colleagues and friends at both places, I owe a considerable debt. I am also grateful for much help and encouragement received during the preparation of the volume. Among those who kindly answered my enquiries or gave advice on particular points were Simon Bailey, Peter Brears, James Collett-White, Christopher Currie, Stephen Freeth, Robin Harcourt Williams, Kate Harris, Liz Hart, Penny Hatfield, Eleanor Hoare, Christopher Hunwick, Giles Mandelbrote, Tom Mayberry, Matthew Payne, Kate Peters, David Prior, Nigel Ramsay, Anthony Smith, Elisabeth Stuart, James Toye, Christopher Wright and Geoffrey Yeo. My thanks, too, for help generously given and gratefully received from archivists and librarians at The National Archives, the British Library, the London Library, the Society of Antiquaries and London University's Institute of Historical Research.

Dr Elizabeth Hallam Smith, Professor Paul Harvey, Dr Christopher Kitching and Professor Dame Jinty Nelson read sections of an earlier version of the book and made invaluable comment and corrections, all I trust transferred to the revised and somewhat re-ordered text. Dr James Parker and Sir John Sainty very kindly read the whole book in draft and gave much-appreciated advice. Needless to say, any errors or inadequacies that remain are entirely my responsibility. At Liverpool University Press my warm thanks are due to Alison Welsby, its editorial director, for her interest in the book and her patience during its long gestation; and to all those who so expertly saw it through the press. The book, however, would not have been published had it not been for the generosity of the British Records Association. I am most grateful to its officers and Council, and especially to its honorary editor Dr Ruth Paley, for her unstinted interest and help during the publication process.

My greatest personal debt, however, is to my wife Ruth, who not only lived with this book for several years but gave much wise advice along the way.

Contents

Preface vii
List of Abbreviations xiii
Glossary xiv

Introduction 1
    A Few Definitions – The Scope and Arrangement of the Volume – A Note on Sources

I The Age of the Administrator c675–1530

1 Archives before the Norman Conquest 9
    Introduction – Monastic and Cathedral Archives – Royal Government – The Laity

2 Post-Conquest Archives 1066–1190 25
    The Church – Royal Government – The Laity

3 The First Great Age of Archive Creation 1190–1300 35
    Introduction – Royal Government – Local Administration – The Church – The Laity

4 The Later Middle Ages 1300–1530 51
    Introduction – Royal Government – Local Administration – The Church – Institutional Archives – Estate and Personal Archives – The Peasants' Revolt

5 Archival Furniture in Medieval England 81

II The Age of the Antiquary 1530–1830

6 Dissolution and Reformation 1530–1560 91

7 Early Modern Archives 1560–1640 — 101
   Central Government – Local Government – The Church of England – Charitable Foundations – The Archives of Landed Society – Business Archives – The Personal Archive – The Antiquaries

8 Civil War, Commonwealth and Protectorate 1641–1660 — 121

9 The Later Seventeenth Century 1660–1700 — 129
   The Archives of Government – Religious Archives – Institutions and Organisations – Estate and Business Archives – The Personal Archive – Historians and Antiquaries – The Great Fire of London

10 The Long Eighteenth Century 1700–1830 — 143
   Central Government – Local Government – Religious Archives – Other Institutional Archives – Estate and Business Archives – The Personal and Family Archive

III The Age of the Archivist 1830–1980

11 Archives in an Age of Reform 1830–1900 — 173
   Introduction – Central Government and the Public Records – Local Government – The Established Church – Institutions and Organisations – Business and Estate Archives – Personal and Family Papers

12 Twentieth-Century Challenges 1900–1980 — 205
   Introduction – Public and Other Governmental Records – Local Government – The Established Church – Institutions and Organisations – Estate and Business Archives – Personal and Family Papers – Towards a National Policy for Archives – Losses in the Second World War

Postscript — 237

Select Bibliography — 239

Index — 245

Abbreviations

AHR	*Agricultural History Review*
Arch Soc	Archaeological Society
BIHR	*Bulletin of the Institute of Historical Research*
BL	British Library
BRA	British Records Association
EHR	*English Historical Review*
HMC	Historical Manuscripts Commission (more formally the Royal Commission on Historical Manuscripts)
IHR	London University Institute of Historical Research
JSA	*Journal of the Society of Archivists*
NRA	National Register of Archives
PRO	Public Record Office
Rec Soc	Record Society
RHS	Royal Historical Society
TNA	The National Archives
TRHS	*Transactions of the Royal Historical Society*
VCH	Victoria County History

Glossary

This is a list of words associated with archives and record-keeping, with the meanings attached to them in this volume. For words that have changed their meaning over time, see also the index. Other technical and legal terms are glossed on their first appearance in the text. Cross-references are italicised.

abstract of title	a compilation of summaries or copies of *evidences* relating to a property
act book	a record of proceedings, especially ecclesiastical
aerary	a *muniment room* (Latin aerarium, a treasury)
archive	the *documents* or *records* accumulated by an organisation in the course of its everyday business (see also the Introduction). Can also be applied to the records of a family or individual. Earlier, a place where records were kept (L. archivum)
archivist	a custodian of archives (French archiviste). A usage uncommon before the twentieth century
ark	a chest (L. arca)
armariolum	a cupboard for storing records
artificial collection	a collection of material gathered from various sources, in contradistinction to an *archive* (see the Introduction)
bull, papal	a papal *document* with a lead seal (L. bulla)
calendar	a list of documents arranged by date and summarised rather than fully transcribed
cartulary	a compilation of copies of *charters*, usually in volume form (L. cartularium.) See also *register*

charter	a grant or conveyance written on a single leaf of *parchment* (L. carta)
chirograph	a *document* written in duplicate or triplicate on one sheet and divided into parts that could later be matched to validate a transaction. Originally simply a written document (from the Greek)
coffer	a chest for documents (L. coffra, cophina)
custumal	a collection of the customs of a manor or borough
deed	a legal instrument, usually a conveyance of property. Originally the act of delivery, or seisin, evidenced by the document
despatch	an official letter relating to foreign affairs, and treated as a *public record*
diploma	a *charter*, etc. Originally a folded *document*
diplomatic	the study of records, 'including their forms, language, script and meaning' (Peter Beal, *A Dictionary of Manuscript Terminology 1450–2000*, Oxford 2008)
docket	an endorsement on a document
document	an item (until recent times normally a manuscript item) that furnishes evidence or information. The basic unit of an archive (L. documentum, a proof)
enrolment	the process of entering copies of documents on a roll
evidences	charters, deeds, court rolls, etc that supply evidence or proof (L. evidentia)
exemplification	an attested copy or transcript of a document
extent	a (manorial) survey and valuation
file	a group of documents held (not bound) together. Originally the thread on which they were strung (L. filum)
formulary	a volume containing examples of standard documents. A precedent book
guarding	mounting and protecting documents, usually in association with filing
hanaper	a basket or hamper for holding documents
hutch	a chest or coffer, especially one raised off the floor by end panels extended below its base

indenture	a deed or similar document. Originally so called because the sheet of parchment on which it was written had been cut with a wavy or indented line (cf *chirograph*)
journal	a narrative of daily occurrences. In accounting, a day book, recording transactions chronologically. A record of parliamentary proceedings
ledger	a volume of accounts arranged by debtors and creditors
letter book	a volume of copies of letters (usually out-letters)
letters patent	an open *writ* or letter. A document issued over the Great Seal (see also *seal*)
limbo repository	a store for records awaiting sorting and evaluation (mainly used of the public records)
muniment room	a record repository (now mainly of colleges, cathedrals, etc)
muniments	documents 'whereby a man is enabled to defend the title of his estate' (Blount's *Law Dictionary and Glossary*, 1717 edn) (L. munimenta, defences)
order book	a minute book, especially of justices of the peace
ordinances	regulations, for charitable foundations, etc
palaeography	the study of the handwriting of documents
papyrus	documentary medium made from the plant Cyperus papyrus, from which the word paper also derives
parchment	documentary medium made from the skin of a calf, sheep or goat (L. pergamentum, from Pergamum in Asia Minor (see also *vellum*)
press	a large cupboard, usually with shelves
public records	records created by Government, as defined by legislation. Formerly records in which the public had an interest
pyx	a deed box or money box, especially for specimen coins of the realm (L. pyxis)
pyxides	small boxes made to fit inside drawers or chests

Glossary xvii

quire	a gathering of leaves, for binding as part of a volume
record, court of	a court of law whose records have the status of legal evidence
record office	an office that keeps archives and makes them available to searchers. Formerly used mainly in the context of the public records
records	documents that preserve the evidence of facts or events (L. recordare, to remember) Any group of archival documents (see the Introduction)
recto	the front of a leaf of manuscript
register	a volume containing records of acts of an archive – creating authority, or copies of documents issued by it (late L. regesta, matters recorded). A compilation of *charters* and other documents
registrar	the keeper of a register (sometimes formerly called a register or registrary)
repertory	a list or catalogue (L. repertorium)
respect des fonds	the preservation of the integrity of an archive, by sorting and arranging records in accordance with their administrative provenance and original order
scrinie	small boxes
seal	a figure or device impressed in wax and attached to a document to authenticate it. It can be pendant, as in *letters patent*, or used to fasten or close it, so that only the recipient who breaks the seal can read it (as in letters close). The original device used to make the impression is called the matrix
skippet	a box of turned wood for keeping documents
standard	a large chest
tally	a wooden stick with notches and writing on it, split in such a way that the two parts can later be matched in the manner of a *chirograph*
terrier	an estate survey (L. terrarius)
till	a small box or compartment inside a larger box or chest

vellum	high-quality parchment made from calfskin
verso	the back of a leaf of manuscript
voucher	a receipted bill, kept in connection with the auditing of accounts
writ	a document conveying an instruction or message, usually sealed

Introduction

A Few Definitions

In the Preface the reader will already have encountered the words archive, record and document. These are all part of everyday language and might therefore seem in no need of further explanation. But they have various meanings in common parlance, and since they occur frequently in the following pages it may be helpful to define more narrowly how they are used in this book.

The word archive is the most important of the three, but also the most troublesome, since it has come to be used for almost any collection of materials, however brought together. As most often used by professionals, however, it is a collective noun for all the documents or records assembled by an organisation during the transaction of its business. (See the Glossary, which also gives brief definitions of the terms document and record.) Within an organisation different individuals or departments may be responsible for keeping their own records, but such records are constituent parts of the institutional archive as a whole. Examples of the organisations dealt with in this volume include government departments, units of local administration, ecclesiastical dioceses and many institutions and societies. The types of record kept vary with the organisation, but may include minutes of meetings, accounts, correspondence, subject files and so on.

This book, however, expands the strict definition a little to embrace the archives of families and individuals. Family archives may contain deeds and legal papers, estate papers and business papers, but they may also include personal papers of family members, sometimes amalgamated with the papers of other relatives and covering more than one generation. Single individuals more usually maintain their own separate archives, often featuring personal letters and diaries as well as papers of a business nature.

Even the institutional archive, though utilitarian in origin, may as it matures be preserved for a more complex mixture of reasons. It may come to represent the status and venerability of its creating body and help to define its corporate identity. At a later stage, historical criteria may come into play. The more ephemeral documents may be culled, but others may be judged worthy of preservation for their historical interest. It might be decided to store this section of the archive separately from the more recent and current records. Eventually the organisation may cease to exist and may lack a successor body to assume responsibility for its archive. Its fate might then depend on whether it is thought to be sufficiently valuable historically to merit permanent preservation.

The words document and record also have various modern meanings. In terms of archival history, however, they have more specific usages, and in this respect they antedate the word archive in its modern definition. In origin the word document refers to a piece of writing on parchment or paper that affords evidence or proof of an event or transaction. In a similar way a record is a document made with the purpose of providing a written memorandum of an event or process that would otherwise have had to be recalled by memory alone. Documents have a particular authenticity when they form part of the archive of a Court of Record, giving them the status of legal evidence. In this book, however, the word document is most frequently used to mean simply an item that has been created as part of an archive. The word record, given its possible ambiguity, is generally avoided in the singular. In the plural it is used to mean a group of archival documents. Such a group may form a section or subdivision of an archive, as in 'accounting records' in a business archive, but the word is also used more broadly, as in 'the public records' or 'records relating to foreign policy'.

In current usage the word records also occurs in the phrase records management. This is fundamentally no different from archives administration, but in practice the term records management is normally used in connection with archival material of recent origin. There are now two professional organisations, one for archivists and one for records managers. The word archivist, however, is itself of fairly recent origin in the English language: before the modern era the usual term was 'keeper of records', and the word archive referred for many centuries to a place where records were stored rather than to the records themselves. The older word for archives was muniments (see again the Glossary): the term muniment room, meaning an archive repository, is not yet extinct.

The Scope and Arrangement of the Volume

This book is about the creation, maintenance and preservation of archives at different periods of English history. As already stated in the preface, individual archives have their own histories, and these histories unfold in individual ways. In the case of the longer-lived institutions, the archives that they create and preserve may originate in one period, flourish in a succeeding one, and come to an end in one later still. But archives, like the people and organisations that create and shape them, have never existed in a vacuum, and have always been influenced by wider contemporary developments. Thus the reader of this volume will encounter discussions of broad themes such as the changing relations of Church and State, the spread of literacy and the impact of the industrial revolution. Attention is also paid to episodes or periods of particular archival significance – the Peasants' Revolt, the dissolution of the monasteries, the Civil War, the Great Fire of London and the Second World War.

Nevertheless, the book does not claim to provide a comprehensive account of its subject, nor could it do so within the limits of a manageable volume. It is, for instance, a history of archives rather than a history of record-keeping. It does not ignore topics such as the emergence and development of different types of record, from the medieval charter to the computer print-out. Nor does it neglect the history of archival storage, from the chest to the file and from the treasury to the record repository. But in general these matters are dealt with as they occur in successive chapters. There is, however, one exception to this, and that is the discussion of medieval archival furniture, which has a chapter to itself. This is an area where it is difficult in the present state of knowledge to establish a precise chronology, and where a division of the account into shorter periods would have meant unnecessary repetition.

Another limitation is that the book is concerned more with the creation and preservation of archives than with their use. Of course the two subjects cannot be totally separated. An archive is, after all, created in order to be used, and what is kept and what is thrown away at a later stage in its life may be influenced by various factors – not only how administratively valuable the records may still be but also what political or cultural uses they are perceived to have. At the Dissolution, for instance, some monastic documents were abandoned as useless, some destroyed as popish relics, but others saved for their historical or aesthetic value. In recent times there has been a growth in interest in a much wider range of topics, to do, for instance, with the use of archives as political weapons or how they have been made to serve the purposes of imperialist projects. But, fascinating and important though such questions are, they fall outside the scope of the present study.

At the risk of appearing chauvinist, it was decided to concentrate on English records, to the virtual exclusion of those of Wales, Scotland and Ireland. This was partly to keep the volume within manageable bounds, but it is also the case that the archives of these countries diverge from those of England in various ways, although some of them eventually came together among the records of the United Kingdom.

In terms of chronology the book is not so constrained. It begins with a late seventh-century document, the earliest surviving one for which a continuous archival pedigree can be convincingly claimed. The main part of the volume ends thirteen centuries later, in the late 1970s, although a postscript carries the story in brief outline down to the present day. The last half-century has been a period of very rapid change, and to do it full justice would have lengthened the volume considerably. Besides, it is not an easy matter to write an objective history of one's own times.

The narrative is divided into three main sections, corresponding with the medieval, early modern and modern periods. Within these the book is divided into chronological chapters, which vary in length according to the amount of ground to be covered. The Anglo-Saxon period, for which material is sparse, is dealt with in a single chapter, whereas the period of the Dissolution and Reformation (1530–60) has a chapter to itself. As a rule the chapters follow a similar pattern, beginning with the public records and continuing with the archives of local government, the Church, secular institutions and organisations, businesses, landed estates, families and individuals.

A selection of archival terms, as used in the text, is given in the Glossary. Other terms are glossed where appropriate in the text and may be referenced in the index. The index may also help in tracing individual archives or broader themes from chapter to chapter.

A Note on Sources

The select bibliography includes the more general studies and reference works that have been found most useful in the research for the book. For the much more extensive printed literature relating to individual archives and the institutions that produced them the reader is referred to the footnotes to each chapter. They include the publications of national and local record societies, and numerous articles in journals such as *Archives* (the journal of the British Records Association) and the *Journal of the Society of Archivists* (now *Archives and Records*).

The primary source, however, for any history of archives is the archives themselves. During the preparation of this book I have visited a number of record repositories and corresponded with archivists and historians. I have also drawn on over half a century's personal experience of working on archival collections both as an archivist and as an historian. But, needless to say, to have attempted to base the work entirely on fresh research of that kind would have been an impracticable undertaking. There is nevertheless another rich, if uneven, source in the corpus of printed and typescript lists and catalogues that are publicly available for many archives. Some repositories, such as the British Library's Department of Manuscripts and the Bodleian Library, Oxford, have published detailed catalogues of their holdings. The volumes of the List and Index Society cover many of the records held by The National Archives. Other lists reside on the shelves of search rooms and reading rooms all over the country, but many are also available as 'reports' supplied to the National Register of Archives maintained by the Historical Manuscripts Commission. The Commission merged in 2003 with The National Archives (TNA), formerly the Public Record Office. An increasing number of these reports can therefore now be found, together with indexes to them, on the TNA website.

I

The Age of the Administrator, *c*675–1530

It was in the greater Anglo-Saxon religious houses that the medieval English archive emerged. The Benedictine monks were responsible for the importance given to written documents, and to the preservation of those documents as muniments of title. Their most valuable records were accorded a quasi-sacred status, but the monks also pioneered the creation and preservation of the more mundane records necessary for the efficient administration of their estates.

To the years after 1066 belong the fuller development of the monastic archive, but also the emergence of the archives of royal government, for which there is so little pre-Conquest evidence. A characteristic of the entire medieval period was the overlap between clerical and lay archive-creators: at the highest level they were often the same people. The institutions of government, notably the Exchequer and Chancery, took over clerical documentary forms such as the charter, but they also evolved their own forms of record-keeping based on documents such as the writ, the court roll and the account roll.

In the thirteenth century, described here as the first great age of records creation, the State may be said to have taken over the lead from the Church in archival matters. The secular influence is shown in the establishment of archives of a more local nature, such as those of manors and boroughs. From the fourteenth century dates the more frequent appearance of institutional archives such as those of colleges, hospitals and other charitable foundations. Towards the end of the Middle Ages, with the spread of English as a written language and the more widespread use of paper rather than parchment, they were joined by family, estate, business and personal archives.

Around the time of the Norman Conquest the archive of a major religious institution might fill one chest. By 1500 it might take up a whole room. The later medieval record-keepers were the first to have to grapple with two consequent problems – how to store their expanding archives securely, and how to manage their use. The period saw the development of the specialised record repository from the earlier general treasury, and the deployment of that characteristic medieval device the cartulary or register.

1

Archives before the Norman Conquest

Introduction

The habit of keeping written records, that is, of accumulating archives, is characteristic of any literate society. In the Ancient World the Assyrian empire had established a central archive at Nineveh by around 700 BC. The Egyptians were assiduous archivists and influenced later Roman practice. As the power of Rome grew and its reach extended it must have relied increasingly on its archives, not only at the centre but also in the provinces. A far-flung outpost such as Britain could not have been governed without literate soldiers and officials.[1]

Following the collapse of the Roman empire, however, the central archive in Rome itself was lost. In Britain the government had no literate successor and all trace of its archive must quickly have disappeared. But the longer-term fate of archives also depends to some extent on the durability or otherwise of the materials of which they are composed. In the case of the Assyrians their chosen medium had been the clay tablet, which had the advantage of being resistant to fire: in fact the heat baked it harder. Thus, when the archive building at Nineveh was burnt to the ground its contents were buried but not destroyed. Imperial Rome on the other hand used the much more fragile medium of papyrus (see the Glossary) for its more important documents. It was light and flexible, but vulnerable to that great enemy of archives, damp.

---

[1] See Ernst Posner, *Archives in the Ancient World*, Cambridge MA 1972; and, for a study of mainly pre-Roman archives informed by more recent scholarship, Geoffrey Yeo, *Record-Making and Record-Keeping in Early Societies*, London 2021. See also Warren C Brown *et al*, eds, *Documentary Culture and the Laity in the Early Middle Ages*, Cambridge 2013, pp17ff.

For more ephemeral documents the Romans used wax tablets. A thin layer of wax was spread on small wooden boards, sometimes hinged, and a stylus used to incise a message, note or calculation in the wax, which could later be erased simply by scraping it off. The chances of the wax surviving for more than a very short period were nil. But the wood, if buried in the right anaerobic conditions, might survive undecayed for many centuries. If therefore the stylus had scratched through into the wood of the tablet some trace of the message might remain. Remarkably, some tablets from the Roman occupation of Britain have been discovered and partially deciphered. The Vinolanda tablets, from a station near Hadrian's Wall and dating from about 120 AD, are well known. Even more remarkably, a recent excavation in the City of London has revealed a collection of tablets from the early days of the settlement of Londinium following the Claudian invasion of 43 AD. These tablets came from the same room and appear to represent a small business archive.[2]

Monastic and Cathedral Archives

There followed a dark age of English archival history that lasted over five-and-a-half centuries, until Augustine and his fellow monks landed in Kent in 597. They too came from Rome, but their mission was one of conversion rather than conquest. They were of course highly literate, and the creation and preservation of documents was an important part of their work. In fact they created a new type of document that owed more to secular Italian than to papal practice. This was the grant or charter. Written on a single sheet – hence the Latin name *carta* – it was evidence of a grant of land or privileges. It was the written record of a public ceremony or transaction and supplemented the memory of those who had witnessed it. (The word record comes from the Latin *recordare*, to remember.) For the monks the significance of the charter was that it provided them with evidence of title to their possessions, by recording the endowment

---

[2] Alan K Bowman and J David Thomas, *Vinolanda: the Latin Writing Tablets*, London 1983; *Guardian*, 26 June 2013. For the only known writing tablet to survive from Anglo-Saxon times, see Claire Breay and Joanna Story, eds, *Anglo-Saxon Kingdoms: Art, Word, War*, London (BL) 2018, p218. It is made of whalebone rather than wood.

of their religious houses with land and other forms of property. At a period when royal and other prominent benefactors were illiterate, or lacked regular scribes of their own, the monks drew up these charters themselves.

They appear very early on to have decided on another important innovation, this time relating to the medium rather than the content of their documents. Rejecting as locally unsuitable the use of papyrus (to which the papacy was to remain attached for a few centuries to come), they chose instead to use parchment (see the Glossary) for their charters, correctly judging that it was tough and damp-resistant enough for the English climate. It had already been introduced to the West in book production, and although not cheap could be produced wherever flocks and herds were grazed. It was to establish itself as the medium of choice for the more important documents of the Middle Ages and has still not quite gone out of use today.

It is, however, a recurring theme of archival history that the earliest years of individual archives are often the least well documented, either in the archives themselves or in contemporary sources. Today no genuine Anglo-Saxon charter is known to exist before 679. In that year the king of Kent made a grant to the abbey of Reculver, and this is thought to be 'the oldest extant Anglo-Saxon charter with a sustainable claim to authenticity and integrity', that is, not a later copy or forgery.[3] There are various possible reasons why no original charter exists for the years between 597 and 679. The monks may have used papyrus for a time before abandoning it for parchment; the charter may have been

---

[3] Pierre Chaplais, 'The Origin and Authenticity of the Royal Anglo-Saxon Diploma', *JSA*, vol 3 (1965–9), pp49–54; PH Sawyer, *Anglo-Saxon Charters: an Annotated List and Bibliography*, London (RHS) 1968, p72 (no 8); David Howlett, *Sealed from Within: Self-Authenticated English Charters*, Dublin 1999, p13; Breay and Story, *op cit*, pp190–1. Probably originally attached to a gospel-book, it is likely to have moved with other records from Reculver in 949 when that house was taken over by Christ Church, Canterbury, and to have remained at Canterbury until the Dissolution, after which it found its way into the great manuscript collection of Sir Robert Cotton. It is now BL Cotton MS Aug.ii.2. A grant of 675 to St Augustine's Abbey, Canterbury has some claim to be an authentic text, but it survives only in a fifteenth-century copy. SE Kelly, ed, *Anglo-Saxon Charters Vol 4: Charters of St Augustine's Abbey, Canterbury, and Minster-in-Thanet*, Oxford (British Academy) 1995, plxxiii and no 6; Sawyer, *op cit*, no 7.

introduced not by Augustine but by a later mission from Rome in 669; or – perhaps the most likely explanation – all the charters from the earlier part of the seventh century may have fallen victim to those unstable and unsettled times.[4]

By 1066, in contrast with the situation three-and-a-half centuries earlier, England was a nation State under a single monarch, and there are indications that archives were being kept by the government itself and by important lay people. But, as shown later in this chapter, the evidence is fragmentary. What is certain is that the most coherent and substantial archives of the Anglo-Saxon period were ecclesiastical rather than lay. Despite later vicissitudes and discontinuities, enough records from those archives have survived to enable the historian to form a picture of how they developed between the seventh and the eleventh centuries. Of the ecclesiastical archives, moreover, by far the most substantial were produced by the greater Benedictine monasteries. Most were generously endowed, and not a few had royal connections. Christ Church, Canterbury, a cathedral priory, and St Augustine's Abbey, Canterbury, were only the earliest of these foundations. By 1066 they had been joined by many more, some of them revivals or new foundations of the tenth century. Unlike all or most secular institutions they occupied substantial stone buildings, and they came to represent continuity and stability in a society prone to political and dynastic upheaval.

Such features were favourable to record-keeping, but the monasteries owe their place in English archival history to two factors above all. They were centres of literacy and learning, with *scriptoria* that produced devotional and other manuscripts as well as archival documents. And keeping records was embedded in their way of life. As already described, they relied on their archives to supply the title to their properties, and to protect them from external threats and challenges. For archives they used the word *munimenta*, meaning defences. Secondly, their archives represented the purpose and justification of their institution, its

---

[4] Pierre Chaplais, 'Who Introduced Charters into England? The Case for Augustine', *JSA*, vol 3 (1965–9), pp526–42; Susan (SE) Kelly, 'Anglo-Saxon Lay Society and the Written Word', in Rosamund McKitterick, ed, *The Uses of Literacy in Medieval Europe*, Cambridge 1990, pp40–1; Charles Insley, 'Archives and Lay Documentary Practice in the Anglo-Saxon World', in Brown *et al*, *op cit*, p343n.

sacred mission to forward God's work and 'sustain belief'.[5] This was reflected in the reverence accorded to individual documents. At Christ Church, Canterbury about 750, a charter was laid on the high altar as part of a grant-making ceremony. The same ritual is recorded in 959 and again in 1018.[6] Another practice was to copy important documents into gospel-books or service books, as happened at Durham and St Augustine's, Canterbury.[7] A royal grant to Christ Church in 949 claims that it was written by St Dunstan 'with his own fingers', a helpful circumstance for the monks who were busy fostering the cult of that highly record-conscious saint.[8]

One might expect these great monasteries to have created and preserved not just their evidences of title but documents relating to the administration of their estates and the management of their finances. But it is only from the last century or so of the Anglo-Saxon period that we have evidence that abbeys and cathedral priories were keeping documents such as leases and descriptions of estate boundaries. At Worcester the monks were concerned to keep track of the cathedral's properties by recording the leases for lives on which many of their older estates were let.[9] From the early eleventh century houses such as Bury St Edmund's and Peterborough appear to have kept a more varied range of records.[10] They were not, however, intended for long-term preservation, and their survival has been accidental and fragmentary. The monks of Ely, for instance,

---

[5] Francesca Tinti, *Sustaining Belief: the Church of Worcester from c870 to c1100*, Farnham 2010, p13.

[6] N Brooks, *The Early History of the Church of Canterbury: Christ Church from 597 to 1066*, Leicester 1984; Janet Backhouse *et al*, *The Golden Age of Anglo-Saxon Art*, London (BL), pp163–4. The practice seems to have been revived more recently. At the consecration of a south London church in 1881, the conveyance of the site was laid on the altar during the service. Richard Olney, *Church and Community in South London: St Saviour's Denmark Park 1881–1905*, Studley 2011, p41n.

[7] Kelly, *Charters of St Augustine's Abbey*, pxxv; David N Dumville, *Liturgy and the Ecclesiastical History of Late Anglo-Saxon England*, Woodbridge 1992. At St Augustine's, two tenth-century (vernacular) documents were entered in a sixth-century gospel-book.

[8] Brooks, *op cit*, pp232–6.

[9] Tinti, *op cit*, pp61, 85.

[10] SE Kelly, ed, *Anglo-Saxon Charters Vol 14: Charters of Peterborough Abbey*, London and Oxford (British Academy) 2009.

used a parchment leaf to make some jottings relating to farm and estate management. After the Dissolution this leaf was cut into three strips, all of which, astonishingly, are extant today. Two were used for the binding of a sixteenth-century book that remains in a Cambridge college library, while the third survived in a private collection.[11]

Where did the monks keep their archives? Unfortunately there is a dearth of evidence as far as England is concerned, and the same is true of continental monasteries.[12] We have suggested that monastic buildings were relatively substantial and secure, but the buildings themselves have not survived, and there are few clues as to what spaces in them may have been designated for the storage of records. It is likely, however, that the quantities involved were small, at least before the tenth century, and that they were lodged in general treasuries along with other valuables. Some very valuable charters may have been kept on the altars on which they had originally been placed, alongside gospel-books and service books, but if this was a regular practice it cannot have been a very convenient one.[13] The Rule of St Benedict included no detailed advice, and probably there was no standard practice. One account refers to a church near the east end of Canterbury Cathedral that was used to store books and documents as well as for its original purpose as a baptistery, but this is thought to have been a unique case.[14]

What is more certain is that the possession of consecrated and comparatively secure premises did not guarantee the survival of Anglo-Saxon monastic archives. There were plenty of occasions when records fell victim to the destruction and looting that accompanied civil wars and foreign invasions. Some of Canterbury's earliest records may have been lost in *c*796–8, when a rising against Mercian rule after the death of King Offa forced the archbishop to flee.[15] On a much larger scale, the north and east of England were settled by Scandinavian incomers following the invasions of the 850s and 860s. Records creation and preservation seem to

---

[11] Backhouse *et al*, *op cit* (note by MAF Borrie); Breay and Story, *op cit*, pp376–7. The three strips are now reunited as BL Add MS 61735.

[12] Brown *et al*, *op cit*, p155.

[13] Brooks, *op cit*, p267.

[14] *Ibid*, pp40, 51; J Blair, *The Church in Anglo-Saxon Society*, Oxford 2005, p202.

[15] Brooks, *op cit*, p167.

have been comprehensively disrupted, and when they resumed in the mid-tenth century they reflected not the older traditions and practices of those parts of the country but the political and legal system of the Danelaw.[16] There were further attacks in the early eleventh century. At Canterbury the cathedral was sacked in 1011, although on that occasion the books and archives largely escaped destruction.[17] Peterborough was attacked in 1010 and 1013, and farther north the losses were greater still.

Over the long Anglo-Saxon period, however, archives were also a prey to less dramatic vicissitudes. In the early tenth century, for instance, charters were issued for the New Minster at Winchester to replace 'documents recently lost, stolen, burnt or water-soaked'.[18] At the same period, houses such as Glastonbury (under Dunstan) and Christ Church, Canterbury were busy revising or replacing their evidences.[19] Periods of laxity and neglect could thus be followed by spasms of record-keeping activity, something that was to become a recurring theme of English archival history.[20]

What have we been left with? A survey of Anglo-Saxon documents in existence in the 1960s – and the situation will not have altered much since then – produced a total of just over sixteen hundred. This included documents such as leases and wills, but the majority were charters. Many of the charters were later copies, although thought to be of genuine originals, but that still left just under three hundred originals, mostly, as one would expect, royal and other grants to monastic institutions.[21] This must represent a small fraction of the number that were created, but it is nevertheless an impressive figure considering all the hazards that they must

---

[16] CR Hart, *The Early Charters of Northern England and the North Midlands*, Leicester 1975, pp14–15.

[17] Brooks, *op cit*, p285; Nigel Ramsay, 'The Cathedral Archives and Library', in Patrick Collinson, Nigel Ramsay and Margaret Sparks, eds, *A History of Canterbury Cathedral*, Oxford 1995, p345.

[18] FM Stenton, *The Latin Charters of the Anglo-Saxon Period*, Oxford 1955, p52.

[19] Brown *et al*, *op cit*, pp344, 358.

[20] Brooks, *op cit*, p308.

[21] Sawyer, *op cit*. The great majority of Carolingian land grants were similarly 'made for churches'. Janet L Nelson, 'Alfred's Carolingian Contemporaries', in Timothy Reuter, ed, *Alfred the Great: Papers from the Eleventh-Centenary Conference*, Aldershot 2003, p306. For losses after the Conquest, see the next chapter.

have survived in the Anglo-Saxon period itself, let alone during the following nine centuries.

* * *

Although Anglo-Saxon record-keeping was dominated by the monasteries the monks did not hold a complete monopoly. Some cathedrals were served not by monks but by secular (that is, non-monastic) clergy, but their muniments fared less well than those of the monasteries. Cathedrals, for one thing, were less stable. Selsey, for instance, was moved to Chichester and Sherborne to Old Sarum.[22] St Paul's, London remained on its early site, and seems to have had a more continuous archival history, but its Anglo-Saxon charters were later lost.[23]

By the eleventh century the bishops, whose seats these cathedrals were, had become a powerful body in the counsels of the realm, and in some cases notable magnates in their own right. But their standing, and their administrative control over their dioceses, had increased only slowly over the preceding centuries.[24] Their duties included the ordination of clergy and the visitation of various bodies within their jurisdictions, but the evolution of systems for the creation and maintenance of records relating to those functions were slow to evolve. In 1066 the establishment of diocesan archives of any substance and permanence was still more than a century in the future. One major reason for this was that bishops, unlike monasteries, were not corporate bodies with a continuous existence. Gaps could occur between the death or translation of one bishop and the appointment of his successor. A bishop also moved around his diocese, occupying a number of episcopal residences or palaces in turn, a life not conducive to regular record-keeping. His seat (*cathedra*) was in the cathedral itself, but he was not in charge of the cathedral buildings,

---

[22] MA O'Donovan, ed, *Anglo-Saxon Charters Vol 3: Charters of Sherborne*, London and Oxford (British Academy) 1988, pxix.

[23] Kathleen Edwards, *The English Secular Cathedrals in the Middle Ages*, 2nd edn 1967, pp1–21; SE Kelly, ed, *Anglo-Saxon Charters Vol 10: Charters of St Paul's, London*, London and Oxford (British Academy) 2004, pp47, 51.

[24] Blair, *op cit*, pp73, 116, 497. Their dioceses had also been subject to periodic boundary changes. Nicholas Orme, *The History of English Cathedrals*, Toronto 2017, pp16–17.

and if he kept his charters within their precincts he did so with the consent of the relevant dignitaries. As for those charters, they did not at this period even form a distinct group of records within the cathedral muniments, and in some cases this was to cause continuing archival confusion in the years after the Norman Conquest.

Royal Government

Turning now to the archives of the Anglo-Saxon kings and their governments, the first thing to say is that not a jot of them survives at the present day. In the absence of direct evidence it is possible to argue either that all trace of them was destroyed by their Norman successors, or that there never were such archives at all, which of course makes it unnecessary to try to account for their disappearance. To explore the question further, however, it might be helpful to look at what *might* have been the machinery of Anglo-Saxon government, and what kings might have kept in the way of more personal records.

Medieval kings had various responsibilities – to preserve the peace of their dominions, and to protect them from enemies both within and without; to define and administer their laws; and (in the absence of adequate means of their own) to raise funds for these purposes by some form of taxation. Unless they were controlling only a very small territory it is hard to see how they could do all this without some rudimentary structure of servants and officials. But, at least in the earlier half of the Anglo-Saxon period, it is likely that much royal business was conducted by word of mouth, with a subsequent reliance on memory rather than any written record. We know that on solemn occasions, perhaps in an assembly or *witenagemot*, kings issued charters, because some of these charters survived in monastic archives,[25] but at a time when there were probably few literate men at court it was simplest to rely for their production on the services of monastic scribes.[26]

---

[25] Stenton, *op cit*; Sawyer, *op cit*; Simon Keynes, *The Diplomas of King Æthelred the Unready 978–1016: a Study in their Use as Historical Evidence*, Oxford 1980; Nicholas Brooks, 'Anglo-Saxon Charters: the Work of the Last Twenty Years', *Anglo-Saxon England*, iii (1974), pp211–31.

[26] For the debate on literacy in Anglo-Saxon England, see CP Wormald, 'The Uses of Literacy in Anglo-Saxon England and its Neighbours', *TRHS*, 5th S vol 27 (1977), pp94–114; Kelly, 'Anglo-Saxon Lay Society', pp36–62; Simon

One might think that royal government had developed beyond that point by the late ninth century. Wessex under Alfred was after all a kingdom with substantial and well-established institutions. The Crown lay at the centre of a system of local administration, defence and fiscal arrangements. Alfred himself was a great promoter of literacy and must have employed a group of scribes. Yet it has been remarked that 'So far as surviving documents take us, ninth-century England was notably, strikingly, less well documented than were lands across the Channel.'[27] Much evidence, particularly that preserved in monastic archives, must have been lost in the destruction wreaked by subsequent Viking raids. But it is also likely that Alfred did not feel the need to keep a regular archive. As one historian reminds us, Wessex was small enough to allow 'relatively close and frequent contacts between the king and the elite', and Alfred's personal style was one of 'intimacy and directness' rather than bureaucratic detachment.[28]

Alfred did not of course rule over anything like the whole of England. The possibility of the creation of an embryo governmental archive increases in the tenth century, but any progress under Athelstan (924–39) and Edgar (959–75) may have been reversed during the following periods of instability and strife. A definite change, however, may be detected in the last few decades before the Norman Conquest, a period during which the English realm reached a degree of sophistication, especially in the organisation of its defences and finances, which made it the envy of other European states. When in 1016 Æthelred was succeeded by the Danish Cnut, the latter seems to have taken over the English government rather than dismantled it, in a somewhat similar way that on the Continent the Roman and later the Carolingian bureaucracies had been adopted by their successors.[29]

Keynes, 'Royal Government and the Written Word in Late Anglo-Saxon England', *ibid*, pp226–57; and for a Continental comparison, Janet L Nelson, 'Literacy in Carolingian Government', *ibid*, pp258–96.

[27] James Campbell, 'Placing King Alfred', in Reuter, *op cit*, p5. The comparison is particularly with the Carolingian dominions (*ibid*, p22).

[28] Nelson, *ibid*, pp307, 309.

[29] FM Stenton, *Anglo-Saxon England*, Oxford 1943, p390; Nicholas Everett, 'Lay Documents and Archives in Early Medieval Spain and Italy', and Matthew Innes, 'Archives, Documents and Landowners in Carolingian Francia', in Brown *et al*, *op cit*.

By this date the royal writ had become part of the machinery of government. (Precisely when it had evolved is unclear – most probably some time in the tenth century.) Unlike the charter, it was addressed by the king to specified individuals, often including the chief official of a shire (the shire reeve or sheriff), who saw to it that it was read out in the shire court. Again unlike the charter it was sealed, to ensure that it was read only by the person or persons to whom it was directed. (Some writs, however, came to serve the function of charters, in that they were grants to particular institutions, and passed into the custody of those institutions once they had been read out in the shire court. Writs indeed were sometimes used in conjunction with rather than instead of charters.)[30]

What, however, were the implications for record-keeping and the formation of archives? To create a writ meant to employ a scribe to draft it and then make a fair copy of it, and somebody to keep the royal seal whose impression was affixed to it, yet it is unclear who might have been available for such duties. Did the king have his own embryo bureaucracy, or, more likely, did he rely on clerks attached to his household, to the royal chapel or to a nearby institution such as the bishopric of Winchester? In whatever way these documents were produced, however, there is no evidence that they were systematically kept. Even if some original writs were returned in due course to the royal officials they were probably not regarded as requiring long-term storage. As with charters, most Anglo-Saxon writs survive because they ended up in ecclesiastical archives, but even the monks seem to have regarded them as generally less worthy of preservation than charters. As we shall see, the systematic registration or enrolment of documents issued by a regular department – a Chancery under the direction of a Chancellor – did not begin until a century after the Conquest. It

---

[30] TAM Bishop and Pierre Chaplais, eds, *Facsimiles of English Royal Writs to AD 1100*, Oxford 1957; Florence Harmer, *Anglo-Saxon Writs*, 2nd edn Stamford 1989; Pierre Chaplais, 'The Anglo-Saxon Chancery: from the Diploma to the Writ', in Felicity Ranger, ed, *Prisca Munimenta: Studies in Archival and Administrative History Presented to Dr AEJ Hollaender*, London 1973, pp43–62. For the 'writ-charter', see Richard Sharpe, 'Address and Delivery in Anglo-Norman Royal Charters', in Marie Therese Flanagan and Judith A Green, eds, *Charters and Charter Scholarship in Britain and Ireland*, Basingstoke and New York 2005, pp32–52.

seems therefore reasonable to suppose that, even though on the eve of the Conquest Edward the Confessor had a more sophisticated government machine at his disposal than had many of his predecessors, it was still a small and relatively informal one.[31]

One factor above all militated against the formation and maintenance of a coherent royal archive. Like the bishops, kings were usually on the move, and their courts, including any clerics called on to write documents, were also peripatetic. While on his travels the king probably kept current records close to him in his chamber – Edward the Confessor was reputed to have stored them under his bed – or in the adjacent room or closet that came to be known as the Wardrobe, along with clothes, money and other valuables.[32] Alternatively, documents might be temporarily deposited in a monastic house with royal connections: there is evidence that Eadred (946–55) used Glastonbury for that purpose.[33]

In the later Anglo-Saxon period, however, the need must have grown for a more permanent repository where the king could leave not only valuables such as regalia and relics but also manuscript items that were to become the standard occupants of the later medieval royal treasury – royal wills, treaties and diplomatic correspondence such as letters from the Pope. We know that important documents could be drawn up in duplicate, so that one copy could be lodged in such a repository; and less obviously archival manuscripts such as law codes, significantly compiled in Old English rather than Latin, might also have been kept there. From the last years of the regime comes evidence to suggest that such a treasury, or *haligdom*, was established at Winchester, by then the principal seat of government.[34] But none of the documents that

---

[31] For the debate about the antecedents of Chancery, see Brooks, 'Anglo-Saxon Charters', pp217–19; Chaplais, 'The Anglo-Saxon Chancery', pp49–53, 60–1; Keynes, 'Royal Government and the Written Word', pp256–7; Keynes, *The Diplomas of King Æthelred*, pp145, 153n; Keynes, 'Church Councils, Royal Assemblies and Anglo-Saxon Royal Diplomas', in Gale R Owen-Crocker and Brian W Schneider, eds, *Kingship, Legislation and Power in Anglo-Saxon England*, Woodbridge 2013, pp50–1; Alexander R Rumble, 'Anglo-Saxon Royal Archives: their Nature, Extent, Survival and Loss', *ibid*, pp185–99.

[32] For the legend of the documents under Edward's bed, see Hubert Hall, *The Antiquities and Curiosities of the Exchequer*, London 1891, pp5–6.

[33] Keynes, *Diplomas of King Æthelred*, p148; David Knowles, *The Monastic Order in England 934–1216*, Cambridge 1940, p39; Rumble, *op cit*.

[34] Stenton, *Anglo-Saxon England*, p414.

would have been lodged there survived in the longer term. Even had they reached the custody of the Conqueror he would have had little use for such relics of a defeated dynasty.

Finally, from the very last years before the Conquest, some shadowy evidence emerges for the keeping of some records of taxation. It is likely that the Norman compilers of Domesday Book made use of hidage lists and records of shire and borough farms passed to them from their Anglo-Saxon predecessors.[35] In the twelfth century it was to be the financial records of government (kept in the Exchequer) that were formalised before the records of Chancery, so it would not be surprising if under Edward the Confessor the accountants had been leading the way. Furthermore, these records may well have been kept in the Winchester treasury. Once, however, they had passed into the hands of William's men it is unlikely that they would have been kept for more than a few decades. Tax records soon go out of date, and the fact that they were written in the rapidly obsolescent vernacular would no doubt have hastened their demise. Latin was the official language of the new regime, and from about 1070 William ceased to issue writs routinely in Old English.[36]

In the absence of a central royal archive it would be unrealistic to expect to find records of Anglo-Saxon local government. London had by 1066 a long tradition of governing itself, and had become the largest commercial centre in England, if not yet its undisputed capital. But its history had been a chequered and often violent one, and nothing in the way of an archive survives for it prior to the Conquest. In the provinces there was by 1066 a structure of administrative units, some of them of ancient origin, regularly used for the collection of taxes and the implementation of the law; but business was transacted in meetings of which no formal record was kept. The shire reeves were among the recipients of royal writs, and by the eve of the Conquest their responsibilities might well have entailed the keeping of some records in the short term. In these areas, then, the transition from oral to written process was already

---

[35] Sally PJ Harvey, 'Domesday Book and Anglo-Norman Provenance', *TRHS*, 5th S vol 25 (1975), p178.

[36] MT Clanchy, *From Memory to Written Record: England 1066–1307*, 3rd edn Chichester 2013, p24. Nevertheless, a few diplomas and writs were written in the vernacular even after 1100. See David AE Pelteret, *Catalogue of English Post-Conquest Vernacular Documents*, Woodbridge 1990.

under way, but the beginnings of consistent archive-making at shire or county level were still some centuries in the future.

The Laity

There is evidence that from the ninth century legal documents were beginning to feature in the affairs not just of ecclesiastical landowners but also of the major lay proprietors. Such documents might include evidence of land held by charter (or bookland) or by lease from another owner, wills (made in the vernacular) and documents relating to exchanges or disputes.[37] Laymen needed to be familiar with the purport of such records and, like the monasteries, to keep them for future reference in case of challenges or disputes. One clear evidence of this is the development of the chirograph, a document made in duplicate or triplicate so that each party to a transaction could keep a copy.[38]

Nothing, however, that can be called an archive survives for the laity of pre-Conquest England. Many archives of landed estates in existence today contain large numbers of medieval deeds, but of these archives only four are thought to contain original Anglo-Saxon charters. In three cases they are remnants of monastic archives acquired after the Dissolution, and in the fourth, the Winchilsea papers, they are part of an artificial collection within the archive. (There is a fifth, but very doubtful, case, a mid- or late eleventh-century writ of one of the earls of Northumbria in the Lonsdale collection. Its provenance is obscure and it is in any case uncertain whether it dates from before 1066.)[39]

---

[37] For wills, see Linda Tollerton, *Wills and Will-Making in Anglo-Saxon England*, York and Woodbridge 2011.

[38] KA Lowe, 'Lay Literacy in Anglo-Saxon England and the Development of the Chirograph', in P Pulsiano and EM Traherne, eds, *Anglo-Saxon Manuscripts and their Heritage*, Aldershot 1992, pp161–204. The leaf used for making a chirograph was cut into separate portions after the word *chyrographum* had been written across the line of the cuts. 'Later in the Middle Ages the cut became a wavy or indented one, hence its common name of indenture' (*ibid*, pp170–1). For triplicate chirographs, see Rumble, *op cit*, pp192–4. For a royal will drawn up as a chirograph, see Breay and Story, *op cit*, pp358–9.

[39] HMC *Principal Family and Estate Collections*, Guides to Sources ... 10 and 11, 2 vols London 1996, 1999. For the Lonsdale writ, see Harmer, *op cit*, pp419–24, and Woodman, *Charters of Northern Houses*, pp363–7. The new French overlords

Where there *is* more helpful evidence it usually emerges, as might be expected, from monastic archives. There is not much of it, possibly because in many monasteries documents in the vernacular appear to have been weeded out during the twelfth century, mirroring a similar process that we have postulated for the royal archive.[40] But some instructive examples remain. In the early tenth century a West Saxon noble called Ordlaf wrote, or had written for him, an account of a legal dispute involving the Fonthill estate in Wiltshire. The dispute was between laymen, but the property ended up with the bishop of Winchester. The memorandum, however, came to rest in the archive of Christ Church, Canterbury, possibly taken there by a bishop promoted from Winchester to the archbishopric. At Canterbury it was later marked *inutile* (of no use) by a monk who nevertheless did not destroy it.[41] To take another example, in the early years of the eleventh century, Wulfric Spot, a wealthy Mercian landowner, left a large property to Burton Abbey in Staffordshire, and with it a group of deeds that must once have formed a coherent section within the abbey's archive. Almost all the originals were later lost, but not before they had been copied into a cartulary, or collection of evidences.[42]

Such groups of deeds, however, may have been rare even at that comparatively late period. It was not unusual for a charter or landbook to be passed down with the property to which it related, obviating the need to prepare a new document each time it changed hands.[43] There is no English equivalent of the eleventh-century cartulary compiled for the Frankish counts of Falkenstein.[44] It may also be noted that in England very few documents indeed of the kind we have been describing survive for lands north of the Trent.

would have had little interest in retaining the Old English evidences relating to their possessions. Clanchy, *op cit*, p32.

[40] Tollerton, *op cit*, pp11–18, 37–8.

[41] Insley, in Brown *et al*, *op cit*, pp336–7, 344–8; Breay and Story, *op cit*, pp190–1. Ordlaf's narrative has been called 'the earliest surviving letter in the English language' (*ibid*).

[42] Insley, *op cit*, pp352–4; Stenton, *Latin Charters*, pp83–4. Continental monasteries such as Cluny also inherited pre-foundation archives of a similar kind.

[43] Kelly, 'Anglo-Saxon Lay Society', p46.

[44] Elisabeth Noichl, *Codex Falkensteinensis*, Munich 1978; J Freed, *The Counts of Falkenstein: Aristocratic Consciousness in Twelfth-Century Bavaria*, Philadelphia 1983. The late Prof Benjamin Arnold drew my attention to this cartulary.

As already mentioned, there was widespread devastation in the North, both before and after the Conquest, but it is also likely that the use of written documents had been less common in that part of the country.[45]

Finally, there is the matter of where lay landowners might have kept their evidences. Where their own dwellings were insufficiently secure or fireproof, might they not have followed the royal example and used a monastic house such as Abingdon or Glastonbury or a priory such as Worcester as a place in which to lodge deeds and other valuables for safe keeping? (They certainly did so in later centuries.) Such a practice may explain why monastic archives sometimes contain charters that appear to have no connection with the house's own properties. But appearances can be deceptive, and it is not always possible to be sure that such deeds did not arrive as part of a bundle of evidences of prior title to a monastic estate. When, moreover, documents *were* deposited for safe keeping it may for the most part have been on a temporary basis, at times of unusual insecurity.[46]

---

[45] Kelly, *Charters of Peterborough Abbey*, p79; DA Woodman, ed, *Anglo-Saxon Charters Vol 16: Charters of Northern Houses*, London and Oxford (British Academy) 2012, p6; Insley, *op cit*, pp359–61.

[46] Insley, *op cit*, pp356ff.

2

Post-Conquest Archives 1066–1190

The Church

William the Conqueror has been accorded a prominent place in English archival history, largely on the strength of Domesday Book (for which see below). That, however, belongs to the final phase of his reign, and it was a reign that began badly from the archival point of view. As we saw in Chapter 1, any Anglo-Saxon governmental records that survived the Conquest may not have been preserved for more than a few years. The Anglo-Saxon system of local government was longer-lived, but in the shires there would also have been major upheavals, as the Anglo-Saxon ruling class was largely replaced by a Norman one. Then there was the 'Harrying of the North', William's revenge for the resistance of the northern parts of the country that left large areas devastated.[1] There was more continuity, however, among ecclesiastical archives, and it is with them that this chapter begins.

The English dioceses were not immune from disturbance. The largest of them had its seat transferred from its southern edge at Dorchester-on-Thames to Lincoln; and following the Harrying of the North York had to rebuild its cathedral. The bishops as a body retained their high status, as influential figures in the counsels of the realm, but their administrative archives were to stay in a rudimentary state until the early thirteenth century, and their estate muniments remained in some cases entangled with those

---

[1] FM Stenton, *The Latin Charters of the Anglo-Saxon Period*, Oxford 1955, p32; DA Woodman, ed, *Anglo-Saxon Charters Vol 16: Charters of Northern Houses*, London and Oxford (British Academy) 2012. For Lincolnshire, only five pre-Conquest charters survive, of which four derive from Burton or Peterborough abbeys, both outside the county. Peter Sawyer, *Anglo-Saxon Lincolnshire*, Lincoln 1998, pp1, 148, 231–4.

of their cathedral chapters. The chapters themselves had varied post-Conquest experiences. Those comprised of secular canons were given new constitutions, which meant fresh starts in some areas of record-keeping. The cathedral priories, however, were less systematically disturbed, as were the religious houses more generally. Many monasteries survived the Conquest, and they were joined by some important new foundations. It could in fact be said that the Conquest was a stimulus to religious record-keeping. The new houses had of course to start their archives from scratch, but the older ones needed to ensure that the change of regime had not adversely affected their title to their possessions. One way to do this was to modify existing documents such as foundation charters to fit the altered circumstances. Another, more radical, way was to fill perceived gaps in the evidence by creating new documents that purported to be old ones. Forgery, in plain terms, was to become a commonplace of medieval record-keeping. It could be prompted by a sudden loss of archival material, such as that caused by the Crowland Abbey fire of 1091, or perhaps by the exigencies of a lawsuit.[2]

As the numbers of charters and other documents held by the monasteries grew, so did the need to manage them in a more sophisticated way. This is the background to the introduction and spread of the cartulary, which became a notable feature of medieval English record-keeping. It had been known in parts of Europe since the ninth century, but did not appear in Western Francia, Southern Gaul and England until the eleventh.[3] It was essentially a collection of copies or summaries of charters entered in or made up into a bound volume.[4] This format made it a convenient tool for ready reference, being easier to leaf through than a bundle of loose charters. It also helped to preserve the documents themselves, which, together with their seals, could be damaged each time a chest was rummaged through in order to find a particular item. In

---

[2] For the Crowland Abbey fire, see CR Hart, *The Early Charters of Eastern England*, Leicester 1966, p11.

[3] Matthew Innes, 'Archives, Documents and Landowners in Carolingian Francia', in Warren C Brown *et al*, eds, *Documentary Culture and the Laity in the Early Middle Ages*, Cambridge 2013, p175.

[4] Strictly speaking, a cartulary contains only copies of deeds and charters, whereas a register may include copies or summaries of other documents. Sometimes, however, the monks called their cartularies registers, as at Norwich.

the longer term, too, it had a better chance of survival than a file or bundle of loose leaves. Today a significant number of cartularies survive in archives or library collections, whereas the original documents from which they were compiled have in many cases long since perished.[5]

It is noteworthy that a particularly early cartulary, from the early years of the eleventh century, was produced at the cathedral priory of Worcester, which already had an exceptionally good archive. Nearly a century later one of the Worcester monks, Hemming, compiled another cartulary, at least partly with the aim of distinguishing the priory's properties from those of the bishop.[6] Later the compilation of a cartulary, like the renewal or re-creation of the charters themselves, might be associated with a damaging fire, as at Peterborough in 1116, or a lawsuit (or another fire), as at Bath Abbey in 1130.[7]

Early cartularies, although created for utilitarian purposes, could nevertheless be accorded a semi-sacred status, as in the Anglo-Saxon period, and bound up with sacred or liturgical works. Thus a late eleventh-century bishop of Worcester attached a cartulary to a large and ancient bible, and half a century later the monks of Sherborne created a composite volume that was half deed register and half liturgical book.[8] The Cistercians and some other orders favoured the compilation of 'foundation histories' that combined the reproduction of key charters with an historical narrative.[9]

---

[5] See GRC Davis, *Medieval Cartularies of Great Britain: a Short Catalogue*, 2nd edn, ed Claire Breay *et al*, London (BL) 2010; Trevor Faulds, 'Medieval Cartularies', *Archives*, vol xviii no 77 (Apr 1977), pp3–35; David Walker, 'The Organisation of Material in Medieval Cartularies', in DA Bullough and RL Storey, eds, *The Study of Medieval Records: Essays in Honour of Kathleen Major*, Oxford 1971, pp139–50; R Ian Jack, 'An Archival Case History: the Cartularies and Registers of Llanthony Priory in Gloucestershire', *JSA*, vol 4 (1970–3), pp370–83.

[6] Francesca Tinti, *Sustaining Belief: the Church of Worcester from c870 to c1100*, Farnham 2010, pp61, 91, 134–5.

[7] Janet D Martin, *The Cartularies and Registers of Peterborough Abbey*, Northants Rec Soc, vol xxviii (1978), pxii; SE Kelly, ed, *Anglo-Saxon Charters Vol 13: Charters of Bath and Wells*, London and Oxford (British Academy) 2009, p25.

[8] Tinti, *op cit*, pp4–5, 125–6, 135; MA Donovan, ed, *Anglo-Saxon Charters Vol 3: Charters of Sherborne*, London and Oxford (British Academy) 1988, ppxv, xvii.

[9] J Burton, *The Foundation History of the Abbeys of Byland and Jervaulx*, York (Borthwick Texts and Studies vol xxxv) 2006.

At Worcester, Hemming did not just compile a cartulary. As part of his work on the archive, he tells us, 'he had a new lock put on the muniment chest and ... diligently repaired all the original documents that were torn or damaged by damp'. According to the historian (and former archivist) VH Galbraith, this entitles him to be regarded as the earliest English archivist.[10] It is interesting to note, however, that in Hemming's day the Worcester cathedral archive could still be contained in a single chest.[11] Clearly such a receptacle would not require a room to itself but could be stored in a treasury along with vestments and other valuables. A treasury might alternatively be called a vestry or sacristy, but however named it would be sited in or very near the conventual church. At Winchester in the late 1150s, part of the arcade on the west side of the south transept of the Norman minster was infilled in order to make a sacristy, perhaps with a sacrist's dwelling above it.[12] At Christ Church, Canterbury the same period saw the building of a room specifically designed as a vestry or sacristy. Originally entered from St Andrew's chapel, near the east end of the cathedral as consecrated in 1130, it may have taken over the function of a treasury from the chapel itself. Certainly its construction, entirely of stone and raised over an undercroft, with narrow windows and easily controlled access, would have made it entirely suitable as a repository. It was erected during the time of the energetic Prior Wibert, and remarkably is shown on a drawing of c1158. Around that date the cathedral acquired a treasurer as a central accounting officer, and it is possible that Wibert intended his vestry to hold the treasurer's accounts as well as charters and vestments.[13] More

---

[10] VH Galbraith, *Historical Research in Medieval England*, 1952, p32.

[11] For chests and other archival receptacles, see below, Chapter 5.

[12] John Crook, ed, *Winchester Cathedral: Nine Hundred Years 1093–1993*, Chichester 1993, p148.

[13] Robert Willis, *The Architectural History of the Cathedral Buildings of the Monastery of Christ Church in Canterbury*, London (Kent Arch Soc) 1869; RAL Smith, *Canterbury Cathedral Priory: a Study in Monastic Administration*, Cambridge 1943, pp14–15; Peter Fergusson, *Canterbury Cathedral Priory in the Age of Beckett*, New Haven CT and London 2011, pp125–6. The drawing, showing a scheme for supplying water to the monastic premises, labels the building a *vestiarium* rather than a *thesaurus*. It survived in a psalter now in the library of Trinity College, Cambridge. See also Francis Woodman, *The Architectural History of Canterbury Cathedral*, London 1981, pp28, 80.

remarkably still, this handsome room survives today, and after a long period of use as a record store is now again a vestry. Other monasteries may have had similar, if less impressive, rooms, but even among cathedral priories many buildings were lost at the Dissolution, and generally any evidence for as early as the twelfth century is likely to have been obliterated by subsequent demolition or rebuilding programmes.[14]

Royal Government

Domesday Book as it exists today is the foundation document of the English governmental archive. It was the product of an impressively detailed fact-finding exercise and involved the condensation of a large number of returns from all over the country into a consistent summary. In archival terms it is what may broadly be called a survey – an inventory of the King's possessions and those of other landholders, together with a great deal of financial information arranged topographically. Although it did not lead to any major overhaul of the tax system at the time, it was clearly of great fiscal value to the Crown and has always been treated as an Exchequer document.[15]

Although it was such an impressive administrative achievement it had no comparable successor, and it and its small group of associated documents occupy an isolated position in English archival history. It was not until the earlier part of the twelfth century that an office of royal finance, a bureau producing records on a regular basis, began to emerge. It was headed by a Treasurer (literally the officer responsible for the king's treasure), but the office became known as the Exchequer, from the chequered cloth that, in the days before the adoption of Arabic numerals, was used as an accounting aid.[16] It had two departments. The superior one consisted of the officials sitting to audit the royal accounts, and

---

[14] As at Norwich. See Barbara Dodwell, ed, *The Charters of Norwich Cathedral Priory*, Pipe Roll Soc, vol lxxviii (NS vol xl), 1974, introduction.

[15] See Elizabeth M Hallam, *Domesday Book through Nine Centuries*, London 1986. For the Exchequer, see below.

[16] Hubert Hall (*The Antiquities and Curiosities of the Exchequer*, London 1891, pp114–22) explained how the cloth worked. It was renewed periodically down to the early nineteenth century.

to hear cases arising from the operation of the fiscal regime. (The medieval mind was nothing if not legalistic, and by the end of the Middle Ages there was virtually no government department that had not acquired its own court.) The lower part of the office was where the incoming moneys were received and stored, a department in other words more akin to the Anglo-Saxon royal treasury.

A key factor in the establishment of a regular Exchequer archive was the fact that the office itself ceased to travel with the king but came to rest in permanent quarters. They were in the royal palace of Westminster, next to the Abbey. Westminster lay just to the west of the City of London and had begun to supersede Winchester as the pre-eminent seat of government. This development was influenced by wartime conditions: when the king was in the field it was important to have a central office for the collection of funds and their onward transmission to the royal headquarters. The regular communication that was necessary between Exchequer and Household placed an additional premium on efficient record-keeping.

For the late twelfth-century Exchequer we know not only approximately where it sat but how it worked. It occupied a two-storey building on the east side of Westminster Hall, the Court or audit chamber occupying the upper storey and what became known as the Exchequer of Receipt the lower.[17] We have a good idea of what went on in these premises thanks to a treatise written in the late 1170s by the Treasurer Richard Fitz Nigel, when the Exchequer was already taking on the aspect of a mature institution. In it he particularly mentioned Domesday Book and the king's Exchequer seal, but also referred to a group of records that needed to be kept for reference, including the 'great yearly rolls of account', the 'writ of farms' (the account of the revenue due from the king's own possessions in each county, no doubt the successor of a similar late

---

[17] HM Colvin, gen ed, *The History of the King's Works Vol 1: the Middle Ages*, London 1963, pp538–41. The medieval quarters of the Exchequer of Receipt, a building of the late eleventh century though later much altered, survived until the early nineteenth century. See Howard Colvin, ed, 'Views of the Old Palace of Westminster', *Architectural Historian*, vol 9 (1966), esp fig. 23. It is uncertain whether the Receipt occupied this building from the start or moved into it some decades later. From the mid-thirteenth century the Court of the Exchequer and associated offices were located on the other, western, side of the Hall.

Anglo-Saxon record), and original writs returned by the sheriffs as part of the auditing process.[18]

Of these records the most important were the 'great yearly rolls of account', the fair-copy annual audit rolls. They came to be known as the Pipe Rolls, after the pipes or sheets of parchment on which they were written. Each rotulet, or pair of parchment membranes, was fastened at the top to its fellows, resulting in a kind of book with rolled-up pages. The earliest pipe roll to survive, though certainly not the first to be made up, dates from 1130.[19] After that there is a gap for the turbulent years of Stephen's reign, but from the reign of Henry II the series continues almost unbroken until its abandonment in 1833. It is a mystery, however, why this format was chosen. Rolls had not been a prominent feature of ecclesiastical record-keeping, and the Continent afforded few if any precedents.[20] Rolls are more awkward to use than records in volume form. On the other hand they may have been easier than bound volumes to pack into chests, and somewhat lighter to transport.[21] What is nevertheless clear is that the parchment roll was an earnest of record-keeping intent. The pipe rolls and their companions the receipt rolls, also referred to by Fitz Nigel, formed uniformly maintained series to be retained for future reference. The whole Exchequer system in fact depended on the creation of accurate records and the maintenance of their integrity by careful preservation.[22]

Another group of records, again well-established by Fitz Nigel's time, was the tallies. They were made not of parchment but of wood and consisted of notched and inscribed sticks. They served as a kind of voucher and were the financial equivalent of the chirograph (for which see Chapter 1), in that they were split in such a way that they could later be married up as evidence of a transaction. Striking the

---

[18] Charles Johnson, ed, *Dialogus de Scaccario, the Course of the Exchequer by Richard Fitz Nigel*, 2nd edn Oxford 1963.

[19] Mark Hagger, 'A Pipe Roll for 25 Henry 1', *EHR*, vol 122 (2007), pp133–40.

[20] Continental governments preferred books or registers; see, for instance, the series of papal registers starting in 1198.

[21] MT Clanchy also notes (*From Memory to Written Record: England 1066–1307*, 3rd edn Chichester 2013, p143) that the individual membranes of an Exchequer roll could be of different sizes, and compiled separately by different clerks, whereas the pages of a quire, to be made up later into a volume, would need to be uniform.

[22] Adrian Jobson, ed, *English Government in the Thirteenth Century*, Woodbridge 2004, p2; Hall, *op cit, passim*.

tallies was part of the duties of the Deputy-Chamberlains of the Exchequer, and was carried out in the Tally Court, a room in the Exchequer of Receipt. Like the chequered cloth, the tallies belonged to an era before the introduction of Arabic numerals; like the pipe rolls they were astonishingly long-lived. They were finally discontinued in 1826, and it was a decision to burn a heap of them in 1834 that led to the destruction by fire of a large part of the Palace of Westminster.[23]

The pipe rolls exist today as the earliest example of regular enrolment in English archival history, but for the twelfth century they stand virtually alone, with only fragments to indicate what else might once have existed. This is true even of the more important subsidiary records in the Exchequer described by Fitz Nigel, including the receipt rolls and the returned writs.[24]

The royal treasury had a longer history than the Exchequer, as discussed in Chapter 1, but its contents and whereabouts in the first century and more after the Conquest are problematic. The word treasury indicated a store for regalia, relics and other valuables that might or might not have been used also for record storage. There was more than one treasury, and it seems that the principal treasury at Winchester was only gradually superseded by the one at Westminster. There is in any case no surviving collection of most of the kinds of document that might have been of treasury provenance – royal wills, treaties and the like – and that date from the twelfth

---

[23] *Guide to the Contents of the Public Record Office Vol 1*, 1963; Hilary Jenkinson, 'Exchequer Tallies', *Archaeologia*, vol lxii (1911), pp367–80; Clanchy, *op cit*, pp125–6. Jenkinson worked on several hundred tallies that escaped the fire of 1834 and were found in the Chapel of the Pyx in the early twentieth century.

[24] Richard Fitz Nigel noted that the Exchequer was keeping copies of writs 'in testimony of the writs having been made', but they do not seem to have been *systematically* preserved. See David Carpenter, 'In Testimonium Factorum Brevium', in Nicholas Vincent, ed, *Records, Administration and Aristocratic Society in the Anglo-Norman Realm: Papers Commemorating the 800th Anniversary of King John's Loss of Normandy*, Woodbridge 2004, p20. See also Richard Sharpe, 'Address and Delivery in Anglo-Norman Royal Charters', in Marie Therese Flanagan and Judith A Green, eds, *Charters and Charter Scholarship in Britain and Ireland*, Basingstoke and New York 2005, p33. It should be noted that at first the routine work of the Exchequer was performed by scribes on an *ad hoc* basis: only later did specific official posts emerge. JC Sainty, *Officers of the Exchequer*, List and Index Soc Special Series vol 18 (1983), pp1–3, 58 *et passim*.

century. The coronation charter of Henry I, for instance, survives only in copies.[25]

Given the established nature of the Exchequer treasury by the late twelfth century it is unsurprising that the practice grew up of depositing documents of treasury status such as treaties and papal bulls with the Exchequer of Receipt, and it must have been decided at some point that they, or some of them, needed a more secure place of deposit separate from the Exchequer building itself. For once, Fitz Nigel provides no help, but it can be suggested that around his time a suitable room was found within the precincts of Westminster Abbey. It was part of a stone-vaulted undercroft beneath the monks' dormitory, near the chapter house. It was secured with a stout door, and its status as a repository enhanced by making it a chapel. This room was certainly in use in the later Middle Ages, and was known as the Chapel of the Pyx, from the pyx or coffer containing specimen coins of the realm that was kept there along with selected documents. The room can still be seen, with its stone altar and a few ancient chests *in situ*, today.[26] But its use as early as the late twelfth century must remain conjectural: the first written reference to it as an Exchequer treasury dates only from the early fourteenth century.[27]

---

[25] Judith A Green, '"A Lasting Memorial": the Charter of Liberties of Henry 1', in Flanagan and Green, *op cit*, pp53–69.

[26] For the Pyx Chapel, see Simon Bradley and Nikolaus Pevsner, *The Buildings of England: London 6, Westminster*, New Haven CT and London 2003, p193; Warwick Rodwell, *Chapter House and Pyx Chamber, Westminster Abbey*, London (English Heritage) 2002; Warwick Rodwell and Tim Tatton-Brown, eds, *The Art, Architecture and Archaeology of the Royal Abbey and Palace of Westminster*, 2 vols Leeds 2015, i.72. Ecclesiastically, the pyx is the vessel in which the consecrated Host is kept. In the early fourteenth century the Chamber was given a new entrance from the Abbey cloisters, with two heavy doors, one behind the other, making it 'one of the most secure treasuries in England' (Rodwell, *op cit*, p16). See also Jeremy Ashbee, 'The Royal Wardrobe and the Chapter House of Westminster Abbey', in Warwick Rodwell and Richard Mortimer, eds, *Westminster Abbey Chapter House: the History, Art and Architecture of 'a Chapter House Beyond Compare'*, London (Society of Antiquaries) 2010, pp113–17.

[27] PRO *Guide*, i.109. Henry II directed copies of his will to be lodged in St Augustine's Abbey, Canterbury, the Winchester treasury and his own coffers ('coffris suis'). Nicholas Vincent, 'Why 1199? Bureaucracy and Enrolment under John and his Contemporaries', in Jobson, *op cit*, p27. So in the late 1180s the situation was still one of almost Anglo-Saxon fluidity.

The Laity

It is likely that by the mid- or late twelfth century the greater nobility – the king's tenants-in-chief – were beginning to accumulate their own archives. They needed, like the monasteries, to keep their evidences or muniments of title; like any bishop or religious house they had to administer the estates from which they drew their income; and like the king himself they maintained large households that required their own administration. Very little, however, of these archives survives from before, say, 1150. For the great Mowbray family, for instance, the main source of information is charters preserved by religious houses, a situation familiar to the Anglo-Saxon historian.[28] The troubled times of the twelfth century militated against continuity in the great landed families. The heads of those families were to a considerable degree peripatetic, and the castles between which they moved were designed for military occupation rather than as more settled administrative centres.

This chapter concludes with a most unusual document that once formed part of a late twelfth-century *personal* archive. Master David of London was a canon of St Paul's, and in the 1170s was employed by the bishop of London on missions to Rome. He kept a register or letter book of his correspondence for that period, and in it are references to papers that he directed to be kept 'with my charters' back in London. The significance, however, of this unique archival survival is hard to assess. Although David was close to government his register would seem to align him more with ecclesiastical methods of keeping records, and it is significant that it is now preserved as part of a composite volume in the Vatican Library in Rome.[29]

---

[28] DE Greenway, ed, *Charters of the Honour of Mowbray 1107–1191*, Oxford (British Academy Records of Social and Economic History, New S no 1) 1972, pxxxiii.

[29] ZN Brooke, 'The Register of Master David of London and the Part He Played in the Becket Crisis', in HWC Davis, ed, *Essays in History Presented to Reginald Lane Poole*, Oxford 1927, pp227–45; Clanchy, *op cit*, pp47–8.

3

The First Great Age of Archive Creation 1190–1300

Introduction

The thirteenth century was a period of considerable change in English society. At the national level, the reach of government was extended, and the king's courts became busier. At the local level, there was a growth in the urban population and an expansion of the money economy. At all levels of society, the lives of subjects were increasingly affected by the workings of officialdom. Closely linked with these changes was, if not a dramatic increase in literacy, at least an increase in the number of people available locally to assist the citizen in dealing with the demands of bureaucracy. More documents were being created, and more clerks were needed both to prepare them and to interpret them to those to whom they were addressed. Documents proliferated not only in number but in type, from deeds, wills and records of court proceedings to accounts and memoranda of every description. The thirteenth century was also, and not merely coincidentally, when the Church lost its primacy in archival matters to the State.

Royal Government

In royal government the start of the great expansion in record-keeping can be dated more precisely to the last decade of the twelfth century, with the new initiatives of the reign of Richard I. The earliest records of the *Curia Regis*, the king's court, date from 1194. From it in the early thirteenth century emerged two distinct courts, King's Bench and Common Pleas, each with its own set of records. They dealt with criminal and civil cases respectively and were supplemented by courts held by the king's justices in eyre (on circuit).

Hubert Walter, Richard's Justiciar (or chief justice) from 1193, was a great innovator in archival matters. To him, for instance, is due that long-lived document the final concord. It was already a well-established practice for copies of agreements made in the king's courts to be made in the form of duplicate indentures, one for each party to the suit. In 1195 Hubert began the practice of creating these indentures not in duplicate but in triplicate. The third or bottom copy was retained by the court and eventually lodged in the Exchequer Treasury. These 'feet of fines' acted as a kind of registration scheme for subjects who lacked secure places in which to keep their own copies, and they continued to serve this purpose until 1833.[1] In 1192 he had already incorporated the use of triplicate chirographs into a scheme for supervising the financial transactions of the Jews. It was directed from Westminster but administered by local officials who have been described as 'the first recorded local public archivists in England'. The relevant documents were lodged in public *arca*, or chests, in those towns where there were Jewish communities. This arrangement did not, however, last as long as the scheme for final concords: it ended with the expulsion of the Jews in 1290.[2]

Of far greater long-term significance was the emergence of Chancery. By the reign of Edward the Confessor there must, as we saw in Chapter 1, have been a system for the production of royal writs, but it was small and informal, and its head, the Chancellor, was a comparatively minor official. After the Conquest it was the Exchequer, not Chancery, that led the way in archival matters (see Chapter 2). But by 1200 Chancery had evolved into a regular bureaucracy, and the Chancellor had become one of the great officers of State. In that year Chancery embraced the principle of enrolment and initiated what soon became three major series of records, the patent rolls, for letters patent or open letters from the king, the close rolls, for royal letters addressed to particular individuals, and the charter rolls. In one respect Exchequer precedent was not followed: Chancery rolls were made up from sheets of parchment attached end to end rather than gathered together at the top, creating

---

[1] PRO *Guide to the Contents of the Public Record Office*, 2 vols 1963, i.16.
[2] HG Richardson, *The English Jewry under the Angevin Kings*, London 1960, pp147, 264–7; MT Clanchy, *From Memory to Written Record: England 1066–1307*, 3rd edn Chichester 2013, pp73, 168.

The First Great Age of Archive Creation 1190–1300   37

documents that in some cases became very long indeed. The patent rolls, though no longer in roll form, are still maintained today. It has been argued that Chancery enrolment began a few years before 1200, the earliest rolls having been subsequently lost, but there is a good case for attributing its introduction to Hubert, who became Chancellor in 1199.[3]

Chancery, like the Exchequer, soon evolved its own court of law. The writs, returns and other subsidiary records that it began to accumulate were sorted into to two principal series, those relating to the king's business and those that concerned his subjects. They came to be known by the names of their original receptacles, documents relating to the first-named being placed in a 'petty bag', and those relating to the second consigned to a somewhat more capacious 'hanaper', or basket. (For archival furniture see also below, Chapter 5.) By the time these two series were finally abandoned in 1921 they occupied 'some one thousand files, bundles and sacks', and the immense task of sorting and cataloguing them is still in progress.[4]

The Exchequer also saw a great growth in records creation in the thirteenth century. Some of the pipe rolls from late in the reign of Henry III are 'nearly double the size of those from the start',[5] and they were joined by series such as the memoranda, receipt and plea rolls. (The receipt and issue rolls, recording payments in and out of the Exchequer, were kept by the Clerk of the Pells, the word pell signifying a skin or roll of parchment.) Yet another series, the originalia rolls, were extracts from the fine rolls of Chancery, recording offers of money to the Crown, and were sent to the Exchequer to help co-ordinate the work of the two departments.[6] The growing number of records produced by the

---

[3] See Adrian Jobson, ed, *English Government in the Thirteenth Century*, Woodbridge 2004. Enrolment was begun in the French chancery at a similar date.

[4] PRO *Guide*, i.10. The growth in records creation by Chancery clerks in the second half of the thirteenth century has been gauged from their greatly increased consumption of sealing wax (Clanchy, *op cit*, p63). It has been claimed that the Chancery records as a whole have been 'preserved ... with a completeness unrivalled anywhere else in medieval Europe'. Vincent, 'Why 1199?' in Jobson, *op cit*, p19.

[5] David Crook and Louise J Wilkinson, eds, *The Growth of Royal Government under Henry III*, Woodbridge 2015, p4.

[6] Paul Dryburgh, 'The Form and Function of the Originalia Rolls', *ibid*, pp30–43. The series begins in 1226–7 and is nearly complete from 1235.

Exchequer Court led to the creation of two posts, those of Lord Treasurer's Remembrancer and King's Remembrancer, whose job it was to follow up the decisions of the Court, and whose archives are reflected in the arrangement of the Exchequer records in The National Archives today.

Despite these remarkable survivals we have today nothing like a complete thirteenth-century royal archive. That century was notable more for the fertility of its archive creation than for the efficiency of its record-keeping. Many of the loose items that originally supported the great series of enrolments must later have been accidentally destroyed or weeded out as being unworthy of longer-term preservation.[7] Some accidental survivals give us a glimpse of the kind of material that has been lost. Letters, for instance, exist between Bishop Burnell, the late thirteenth-century Chancellor, and the heads of other departments. In more recent times they were identified among heaps of miscellaneous documents in the Public Record Office and placed in the artificial class called Ancient Correspondence.[8]

The main gaps, however, are in the area of the royal household. In the thirteenth century its most prominent institution, the Wardrobe, had already developed into a major department responsible for military clothing and supplies, with substantial buildings at Baynard's Tower (in the City) and the Tower of London. But it failed to develop an 'articulate departmental tradition', due perhaps to a sense that 'the king's business was essentially secret'.[9] Records for the issue of warrants under the Privy Seal (or private royal seal as distinct from the Great Seal kept by the Chancellor), a late twelfth-century innovation, were a Wardrobe responsibility, but they were either subsequently lost or not systematically kept in the

---

[7] Vincent, 'Why 1199?' in Jobson, *op cit*, pp27–9; HG Richardson and GO Sayles, *The Governance of Medieval England from the Conquest to Magna Carta*, London 1963, p171.

[8] Richard Huscroft, 'The Correspondence of Bishop Burnell, Bishop of Bath and Wells and Chancellor of England', *Archives*, vol xxv no 102 (Apr 2000), pp16–39. See also Jeanne Stones and Lionel Stones, 'Bishop Ralph Neville, Chancellor to Henry III, and his Correspondence: a Reappraisal', *Archives*, vol xvi no 71 (Apr 1984), pp227–57.

[9] VH Galbraith, *An Introduction to the Use of the Public Records*, Oxford 1934, p32; TF Tout, *Chapters in the Administrative History of Medieval England: the Wardrobe, the Chamber and the Small Seals*, 6 vols Manchester 1928, i.23, 34–5.

first place. Where Wardrobe accounts *have* survived it is because they were passed to the Exchequer or through some other chance.[10]

Even more highly valued records were not always safe, particularly when they were on the move. Domesday Book was lucky to escape destruction with John's baggage train in The Wash, perhaps because he had left it in the temporary keeping of Reading Abbey.[11] Records were lost in France, possibly in the early, certainly in the late, thirteenth century. The Scottish campaigns of Edward I necessitated the despatch of cartloads of documents to his temporary seat of government at York, where some of them languished for several years.[12]

Back at Westminster there were other hazards. Medieval bureaucrats had not previously had to face problems of record storage on such a scale, and they were not best placed to solve them. The Exchequer in particular had become a complex organisation by 1300, with officials in each sub-department responsible for managing their own archives. They were generally appointed for life and could act by deputy; their income might depend partly on the fees that they could charge for searching their records; and the finding aids that they compiled were regarded as their own property, and could be removed by them when they left office. It was a system, if such it can be called, that was to persist into the early nineteenth century. Nevertheless, Exchequer officials valued their more important and venerable documents as sources of constitutional precedent as well as for more immediate and practical reasons.[13] The chief problem was a lack of oversight and planning for records accommodation in the Palace of Westminster as a whole. It was a problem due only to worsen in the centuries

---

[10] For occasional survivals now in the Chancery Miscellanea, see Galbraith, *op cit*, p34. For the Wardrobe, see also PDA Harvey, 'Maps of the World in the Medieval English Wardrobe', in Paul Brand and Sean Cunningham, eds, *Foundations of Medieval Scholarship: Records Edited in Honour of David Crook*, York 2008, pp51–5.

[11] Elizabeth M Hallam, 'Nine Centuries of Keeping the Public Records', in GH Martin and Peter Spufford, eds, *The Records of the Nation: the Public Record Office 1838–1988, the British Record Society 1888–1988*, Woodbridge 1990, p25.

[12] Dorothy M Broome, 'Exchequer Migrations to York in the Thirteenth and Fourteenth Centuries', in AG Little and FM Powicke, eds, *Essays in Medieval History Presented to Thomas Frederick Tout*, Manchester 1925, pp291–300. The records were packed for transportation in chests, coffers and wine casks.

[13] *Ex inf* Dr Hallam Smith.

that followed, and that would be tackled effectively only with the eventual creation of a public record office.

From time to time, when space ran out, it became necessary to find out-stores, or in modern archival parlance 'limbo' repositories. These were places to which records no longer in day-to-day use could be transferred while those responsible for them determined, or failed to determine, their ultimate fates. During the thirteenth century the Exchequer increasingly used the Tower of London, which may have served as a royal treasury in the early years of its existence, and whose great Norman keep, the White Tower, contained a chapel that could be used for storage. It was certainly secure enough. Chancery on the other hand favoured the premises of the Knights Templar, a facility that was also used to a lesser extent by the Wardrobe and the Exchequer. The Templars, an order of military knights, were closely connected with the Crown, and played an important role in government finance. They must have had secure and well-protected buildings, and their site, the New Temple, which lay between the Thames and the Strand, was nearer to Westminster than the Tower.[14]

Local Administration

All this activity at national level might lead the historian to expect a similar expansion in the locally based administration of England, but the archival evidence at local level is sparse. The medieval county, for instance, was the successor of the Anglo-Saxon shire, and in many cases it is still an essential part of the modern structure of local government. Yet of the archives of the medieval counties not a shred remains in the hands of their present-day successors. In the thirteenth century the most important county official was still the sheriff, who must have kept the proceedings of his shire court, along with rating lists and records of his dealings with the king's government at Westminster. He probably housed these documents in a royal castle,

---

[14] Agnes Sandys, 'The Financial and Administrative Importance of the London Temple in the Fourteenth and Fifteenth Centuries', in Little and Powicke, *op cit*, pp147–62. The actual repository may have been the Temple Church itself. Helen J Nicholson, 'At the Heart of London: the New Temple in the Middle Ages', in Robin Griffith-Jones and David Park, *The Temple Church in London: History, Architecture, Art*, Woodbridge 2010, pp6, 13.

The First Great Age of Archive Creation 1190–1300   41

with one of which most counties were furnished. In Surrey, Guildford Castle acquired in 1247 a court house and chamber that must have provided secure archival accommodation.[15] In the 1290s Barnwell Priory in Northamptonshire instituted a search for documentary evidence at Cambridge Castle in connection with a lawsuit.[16] But it is likely that some or most of the sheriff's accounts and other records were never intended for long-term preservation locally, some being discarded and others forwarded to Westminster. Later in the Middle Ages these castles were subject to neglect and decay, and the office of the sheriff itself declined in importance. The county coroner, another prominent county officer in the thirteenth century, also left no archival trace locally: his court rolls were regularly handed over to the king's justices and lodged in the royal archive.[17]

The hundred was a territorial unit that formed the second layer of county government. Its executive official was a bailiff responsible to the sheriff, but again there is a general dearth of records for the medieval period. Most hundred courts lacked their own premises – their meetings were traditionally held in the open air – and in later centuries their importance waned. Where records survive it is usually where the hundred was a 'private' one, that is, where its jurisdiction had been granted to an individual or an institution. Thus the Hampshire hundred of Crondall, belonging to the bishop of Winchester, has surviving records for the period 1281–1307.[18]

* * *

The manor was not part of the system of local government in the same way as the county or the hundred. It varied in nature and size,

---

[15] Mabel H Mills, 'The Medieval Shire House (Domus Vicecomitis)', in J Conway Davies, ed, *Studies Presented to Sir Hilary Jenkinson*, London 1957, pp254–71; Clanchy, *op cit*, p168.

[16] Clanchy, *op cit*, p173.

[17] RF Hunnisett, *The Medieval Coroner*, Cambridge 1961, pp96 *et passim*. For Hubert Walter's role in the institution of coroners' rolls, see Clanchy, *op cit*, pp72–3.

[18] See Helen M Cam, *The Hundred and the Hundred Rolls: an Outline of Local Government in Medieval England*, London 1930 (repr 1963). What are known as the hundred rolls are the returns made to a very thorough government enquiry in 1275–6, and are to be found, again, in the public records.

could be larger or smaller than the parish, and did not uniformly cover whole counties; but it did represent the smallest unit of England's judicial structure as it evolved during the Middle Ages. It was not only a judicial unit, however, but also an economic one, and as such could function independently or as part of a larger ecclesiastical or lay estate. Indeed its economic role preceded the judicial, and in consequence gave rise to the earliest manorial records. The place of these records in estate archives, however, is mentioned later in this chapter: here the focus is on the records of the manorial court.[19]

In its judicial aspect, and in the records it kept, the manor was influenced by the government at Westminster. The manorial court was a court of record, that is, its proceedings could be cited as legal evidence. This meant that they had to be compiled on parchment, maintained in series in the form of rolls, and carefully preserved. It is noteworthy that as the manor developed during the thirteenth century local practice came to follow a uniform pattern, in types of document and in their format and content. Nevertheless, the major period of growth seems to have been the second half of the century. Discounting earlier fragments, the earliest court roll is that for some English manors of the French abbey of Bec. It starts in 1246 and was the work of the efficient prior of the bailiwick of Ogbourne (Wiltshire), William de Guineville.[20] After 1250 more manors began to keep regular records, reflecting a more general spread of record-consciousness around the country. Another stimulus may have been the desire of some owners of lordships to resist the encroachments of the Crown, by keeping in their own hands cases that would otherwise have gone to the royal courts.[21] But, as with the records

---

[19] For medieval and later manorial records generally, see PDA Harvey, *Manorial Records*, BRA Archives and the User no 5, rev edn 1999, pp15–53, and for the distinction between the court baron and the court leet, see pp44–5.

[20] The court roll is now in the archive of King's College, Cambridge. (See the Manorial Register maintained by the HMC at The National Archives. My grateful thanks to Liz Hart in this connection.) The English properties of the abbey of Bec were given in the early fifteenth century principally to King's, Eton College and St George's Chapel, Windsor: related records survive in all three archives. Marjorie Morgan, *The English Lands of the Abbey of Bec*, Oxford 1946, pp4–5.

[21] Paul Brand, 'Stewards, Bailiffs and the Emerging Legal Profession in Later Thirteenth-Century England', in Ralph Evans, ed, *Lordship and Learning: Studies in Memory of Trevor Aston*, Woodbridge 2004, pp139–53; Ralph Evans,

of central government, it is the main series of court rolls that have tended to survive, subsidiary records for this period having been almost entirely lost.

About seventy-six manors have preserved three or more court rolls from before 1300.[22] They are found in twenty-five or so English counties, but of those only four are north of the Trent. The eastern counties of Norfolk, Suffolk, Cambridge and Essex account for more than a third of the total. The lords of two-thirds of these seventy-six manors were institutions, with Glastonbury and Ramsey abbeys and Merton College, Oxford prominent among them. The remaining third were lay owners both large and small, although closer analysis would probably reveal a preponderance of the larger estates.

* * *

Unlike the county and the hundred, the borough was not part of the pre-Conquest pattern of local administration, and in fact stood apart from it. Some towns that became boroughs had Anglo-Saxon origins as urban settlements, but they were created boroughs by charter, and this had important archival consequences. They were set up with constitutions and privileges that made them akin more to religious houses or other chartered bodies than to the counties in which they were situated. They kept records of their administrative and judicial proceedings, their finances and their properties. They also fostered their corporate traditions, keeping sets of ordinances that embodied their regulations and customs – customs that in some cases had been inherited from the guilds merchant that had preceded the boroughs themselves.

A number of medieval boroughs have survived into modern times, and their records, some remarkably early, with them. Leicester has preserved guild merchant rolls from 1196, and Shrewsbury similar documents from 1209. At Ipswich, the townsmen, prompted by the grant of a royal charter in 1200, compiled a custumal that they called their Domesday Book, together with a roll containing

---

'Whose Was the Manorial Court?' in *ibid*, pp155–68; Z Razi and RM Smith, 'The Origins of the English Manorial Court Rolls as a Written Record: a Puzzle', in Razi and Smith, *Medieval Society and the Manor Court*, Oxford 1996, p41.

[22] See the survey by Judith A Cripps and Janet Williamson, *ibid*.

the ordinances of their guild merchant, although both survive only in later copies. The distinction of being the only borough to hold a court roll dating from before 1250 is claimed by the small Berkshire corporation of Wallingford, where the earliest plea roll of the burghmote court dates from 1231–2. After 1250 more court rolls appear – those for the City of London (the Hustings Court) from 1252, Ipswich from 1255–6 and Leicester from about 1260. Altogether twenty-two English boroughs retain records for before 1300, a tally that bears favourable comparison with the cities of continental Europe.[23] As one might expect, the City of London boasts an impressive series of medieval records. As well as the hustings court records it holds charters and deeds from before 1100 and custumals from 1274.[24] Not surprisingly an official with municipal record-keeping responsibilities soon emerged, in the person of the town clerk. Leicester and Ipswich had salaried common clerks in the 1270s, and other boroughs followed. In 1272 Ipswich's clerk absconded, taking records with him, and prompting the elders of the town to introduce a new record-keeping system shortly afterwards.[25]

Borough administrators, unlike those of the counties, were anchored to one spot, which made it easier to ensure the safe keeping of their archives. Leicester acquired its first permanent headquarters in the 1270s.[26] Earlier the records of the much smaller borough of Wallingford may have been kept in the adjacent castle of its lord, Richard, Earl of Cornwall. The borough of Halesowen (Shropshire, later Worcestershire) was the creation of the next-door abbey, which may help to account for the preservation of an unusually full run of court rolls from 1272.[27]

---

[23] See eg Geoffrey Martin, 'The Origins of Borough Records', *JSA*, vol 2 (1960–4), pp147–53.

[24] Philip E Jones and Raymond Smith, *A Guide to the Records in the Corporation of London Record Office and the Guildhall Library Muniment Room*, London 1951; Geoffrey Martin, 'Records and Record-Keeping in Medieval London', in MV Roberts, ed, *Archives and the Metropolis*, London 1998, pp11–21.

[25] Geoffrey Martin, 'The Governance of Ipswich I, from its Origins to c1550', in David Allen, comp, *Ipswich Borough Archives 1255–1835, a Catalogue*, Suffolk Rec Soc, vol xlvii (2000), pxxi.

[26] AKB Evans, 'The Custody of Leicester's Archives from 1273 to 1947', *Leics Arch and Hist Soc Trans*, vol lxvi (1992), pp105–20.

[27] RH Hilton, 'Small Town Society in England before the Black Death', in

The Church

By the early thirteenth century the work of England's diocesan bishops was increasing, and they began to look to improved record-keeping as a way of keeping track of their multifarious responsibilities. Prominent among them was the ordination of clergy and their induction to benefices, or livings, and this led to a major archival innovation. Around 1214–15, the archbishop of York and the bishop of Lincoln, both with large dioceses to look after, began to keep registered copies of their acts. Both Walter de Gray at York and Hugh of Wells at Lincoln were also senior civil servants, and in beginning to keep records in the form of parchment rolls they must have been influenced by government practice. Their example was followed only slowly by their episcopal colleagues, but by the end of the century registration had become standard practice, although by then most had converted to volumes rather than rolls.[28] Along with the register appeared a new official, the registrar, who took over the archival responsibilities previously assigned to the bishop's chancellor.[29]

Once adopted, the register became the key component of the diocesan archive, and so it remains today. Lincoln's medieval registers are complete from 1214 to 1215, changing from rolls to volumes in 1290, and Worcester's from 1268. But there are large gaps for the thirteenth century in some other dioceses, and in most dioceses there is a dearth of subsidiary records. Ordination lists, for instance, were probably compiled from the 1240s, but they were not preserved.[30] Various factors militated against the survival of diocesan records in bulk during the Middle Ages. The bishops, like the king, were frequently on the move. Unlike kings, however, they

Richard Holt and Gervase Rosser, eds, *The English Medieval Town: a Reader in Urban History 1200–1540*, London and New York 1990, pp71–96.

[28] See David M Smith, *Guide to Bishops' Registers of England and Wales: a Survey from the Middle Ages to the Abolition of Episcopacy in 1646*, London (RHS) 1981. The introduction of registers may also have been influenced by the chancery reforms of Pope Innocent the Third.

[29] At Canterbury the office of registrar emerged in the mid-fourteenth century. Irene Josephine Churchill, *Canterbury Administration: the Administrative Machinery of the Archbishopric of Canterbury Illustrated from Original Records*, 2 vols London 1933, i.22.

[30] William J Dohar, 'Medieval Ordination Lists: the Original Record', *Archives*, vol xx no 87 (Apr 1992), pp17–35.

did not succeed each other immediately but after an interregnum during which registers and other documents could disappear. They were also slow to acquire permanent repositories for their archives, both those relating to their spiritual duties and those needed for the management of their temporal possessions.[31] That applied also to the archives of the church courts, although in 1300 they were still in an early phase of their evolution. Some letters and other documents of Hubert Walter relating to his provincial court, that is, the court for his province of Canterbury rather than the diocese, are a unique early survival, but they are more personal than official in character.[32]

In marked contrast are the cathedrals. Among those administered by secular canons rather than monks there were some that had already accumulated substantial archives by 1200. Around 1220, a cartulary compiled for the dean and chapter of Lincoln, the *Registrum Antiquissimum*, concentrated on the charters relating to the Common Fund, that is, the endowments supporting the chapter as a whole rather than individual dignitaries: it dealt with about 1,225 documents in all. These and other records were carefully preserved, and in the 1250s a new home was provided for them, a three-storey building attached to the south-east transept of the cathedral. Its crypt was probably used as a treasury, the chamber above as a vestry, and the room above that, originally vaulted, as a muniment room.[33] There was a similar arrangement at Salisbury Cathedral, the by-product of another major mid-century building programme. There the former muniment room – it ceased to hold archives only in 1970 – has a tiled floor, a vaulted wooden roof and small barred windows with internal shutters and is approached from the room below by a staircase and three lockable doors.[34]

---

[31] See below, Chapter 4.

[32] Norma Adams and Charles Donahue Jnr, eds, *Select Cases from the Ecclesiastical Courts of the Province of Canterbury c1200–1301*, Selden Soc, vol xcv for 1978–9, p3. They were preserved among the Dean and Chapter records.

[33] CW Foster, ed, *The Registrum Antiquissimum of the Cathedral Church of Lincoln*, Lincoln Rec Soc, vol 27 (1931), pxxxiii; Dorothy M Williamson, *The Muniments of the Dean and Chapter of Lincoln*, Lincoln 1956, p6; Lesley Milner, 'Lincoln Cathedral Treasure House', *Antiquaries Jnl*, vol 97 (2017), pp205–9.

[34] Thomas Cocke and Peter Kidson, *Salisbury Cathedral: Perspectives on the Architectural History*, London 1993, p7 and plate 15; Tim Tatton-Brown, with photographs by John Crook, *Salisbury Cathedral: the Making of a Medieval*

As for the administrative records of the chapters, they tended to follow a similar line of development to those of the dioceses. By the end of the thirteenth century the office of chapter clerk had emerged. He was responsible to the chapter as a whole, and recorded their proceedings in an act book, the equivalent of the bishop's register. Act books formed the principal series of documents in chapter archives from around 1300 and continue to do so today.

* * *

During the thirteenth century many monasteries increased their property holdings, and expanded the administration of their estates. By 1300 the endowments of Westminster Abbey, to take a prominent example, stood at around 38,000 acres, in widely scattered estates whose customs and forms of tenure varied from district to district.[35] The trend was towards the direct exploitation of demesnes (the lands kept in hand rather than let to customary tenants), which meant closer supervision and more sophisticated accounting methods. Monasteries began to employ more, and more specialised, people – reeves, bailiffs, stewards, receivers; and some of the larger houses had their own private or local jurisdictions. Within the houses themselves administration also became more complex, with monks appointed to specific offices such as sacrist or cellarer. These officers, known as obedientiaries, often had their own endowments, as did the head of the house. All officers had to produce accounts, but some houses, following the example of Christ Church, Canterbury, also appointed a chief accountant in the form of a treasurer or bursar. Peterborough did so in 1247, and Durham around 1260.[36]

Masterpiece, rev edn London 2014, pp69–74. My thanks also to the staff of the cathedral.

[35] See Barbara Harvey, *Westminster Abbey and its Estates in the Middle Ages*, Oxford 1977.

[36] Barbara Harvey, *The Obedientiaries of Westminster Abbey and their Financial Records c1275 to 1540*, Woodbridge 2002; Alistair Dobie, *Accounting at Durham Cathedral Priory: Management and Control of a Major Ecclesiastical Corporation, 1083–1539*, Cambridge 2015, p29; DA Postles, 'Heads of Religious Houses as Administrators', in WM Ormrod, ed, *England in the Thirteenth Century: Proceedings of the 1989 Harlaxton Symposium*, Stamford 1991, p45.

As a result, the monasteries were by 1300 generating records on a scale quite different from a century before – not only charters and cartularies but estate and financial documents such as rentals, inventories, accounts and manorial court rolls. Little survives, however, from before 1250, and indeed accounts and related material are not preserved in any substantial quantity from before 1300.[37] (A notable exception is the accounts for Christ Church, Canterbury, which begin in 1198.) Although records of some kind were probably being created before 1250 they may not yet have assumed a consistent serial form, and it seems likely that only in the latter half of the century did systematic records creation, as well as preservation, begin.[38]

Whether the records once created were preserved must have depended at least partly on the provision of proper accommodation. As already noted, Christ Church, Canterbury had a very early repository, but elsewhere evidence is hard to come by. There is an early thirteenth-century reference to a papal privilege kept in the treasury at Peterborough, but no clue as to where within the abbey precincts it was located. Durham had a medieval muniment room, the Spendement, in the north-west corner of the cloister, with an inner room used as a muniment room or treasury and an outer one that functioned as an exchequer and chancery, but it is unclear whether this arrangement went back to the thirteenth century. Thirteenth-century monks, however, well understood that library books should be kept in dry, well-ventilated and secure rooms, and there is no reason to suppose that their muniments were not accorded the same level of care.[39]

Westminster Abbey may have the unique distinction of containing a mid-thirteenth-century monastic record repository that is still in

---

[37] For Norwich, see Barbara Dodwell, 'The Muniments and the Library', in Ian Atherton et al, *Norwich Cathedral: Church, City and Diocese 1096–1996*, London and Rio Grande OH 1996, pp325–38; and for Ely, Peter Meadows and Nigel Ramsay, eds, *A History of Ely Cathedral*, Woodbridge 2003, p164.

[38] At Westminster the earliest accounts are late thirteenth-century. By 1300 the obedientiaries were 'not only making accounts but beginning to preserve them as records', but it seems that they were not regularly transferred to the muniment room until after 1350. Harvey, *Obedientiaries*, pplxvii–liii.

[39] Janet D Martin, *The Cartularies and Registers of Peterborough Abbey*, Northants Rec Soc, vol xxviii (1978), pxiv; Michael Stansfield, 'The Archive', in David Brown, ed, *Durham Cathedral: History, Fabric and Culture*, New Haven CT and London 2015, pp423–33; WA Pantin, *Report on the Muniments of the Dean and Chapter of Durham*, pr 1939.

use for its original purpose today. The muniment room occupies part of a gallery in one of the transepts, a space created as part of Henry III's great rebuilding of the abbey. It is open to the church on two sides, but with its stone vaulting above and below and its narrow access it is a very suitable area for record-keeping. It is not known for certain how it was originally intended to use the space, and there is no positive evidence that it was a record store until the mid-1390s, but its archival furniture (discussed in Chapter 5) suggests a very early date for its adoption as a muniment room.[40]

The Laity

It was not only the king himself, the bishops and the great religious houses that held extensive landed estates in the Middle Ages. There were also many substantial lay owners, of whom the most prominent were the earls and barons who were close to the Crown, and who as tenants-in-chief could claim the feudal allegiance of lesser men. In some cases they built up estates by piecemeal purchases, as did the Fitzalans at Arundel (Sussex), but more commonly they acquired already formed estates en bloc, either by royal grant or through the operation of marriage or inheritance. As these great families rose the administration of their estates became more complex, involving stewards or accountants at the level of the manor, the honour (or regional group of estates) and the central administration. It was a similar story with noble households, as they became larger and more elaborate.

As with other individuals and institutions, the larger landowners began to increase their rate of record creation in the thirteenth century. In this they were influenced both by monastic practice and by developments in the government at Westminster. Of course they had to keep their deeds and related papers, the records of their jurisdictions, and surveys and other estate documents, but it was their financial records that appear to have proliferated at this period. Every official, from the bailiff to the receiver-general, was expected to produce regular accounts, and these were as regularly audited. A

---

[40] See also Paul Binski and Emily Guerry, 'Seats, Relics and the Rationale of Images in Westminster Abbey', in Warwick Rodwell and Tim Tatton-Brown, eds, *The Art, Architecture and Archaeology of the Royal Abbey and Palace of Westminster*, 2 vols Leeds 2015, i.182.

fine series of audited accounts survive for that wealthy thirteenth-century widow Isabella, Countess of Norfolk and Aumale.[41] It seems that, as with manorial court records, household accounts were also drawn up in increasing quantities after 1250.[42]

Survival rates, however, are low before 1300, and with a few exceptions substantial series of accounting records have been preserved because they passed at some point into the custody of the State, rather than remaining with the families that created them.[43] As noted in Chapter 2, nobles were peripatetic, and their castles were not always the most document-friendly of storage places. Families, moreover, could fail for want of heirs, or come to an abrupt end in times of civil strife. At the lower level of the gentry, even more has been lost, but two interesting survivals can be noted. In the mid-thirteenth century Thomas Hotot of Clopton (Northamptonshire), a member of a middling gentry family, took a personal hand in compiling a two-volume cartulary-cum-estate book. (Only the estate book now survives in the original, in the British Library, but the companion volume survives in an eighteenth-century copy.) The Hotots were proud of their Norman ancestry, but perhaps of more significance in explaining their record-mindedness is their close connection with Peterborough Abbey.[44] The Kniveton Leiger was a Derbyshire cartulary begun in the late thirteenth century but maintained by the family with various additions until the early sixteenth.[45] Completed at least partly as a guide for future generations, such a volume was consciously intended to become part of a family archive.[46]

---

[41] See N Denholm-Young, *Seignorial Administration in England*, Oxford 1937.

[42] CM Woolgar, ed, *Household Accounts from Medieval England Parts I and II*, Oxford (British Academy Records of Social and Economic History, New S xvii, xviii) 1992, 1993; CM Woolgar, *The Great Household in Medieval England*, New Haven CT and London 1999.

[43] As happened with the accounts of Countess Isabella, cited above.

[44] 'Estate Records of the Hotot Family', in Edmund King, ed, *A Northamptonshire Miscellany*, Northants Rec Soc, vol xxxii (1983), pp1–58; Edmund King, 'Estate Management and the Reform Movement', in WM Ormrod, ed, *England in the Thirteenth Century*, Stamford 1991, pp1–14. Richard Hotot was probably the brother of William Hotot, abbot of Peterborough.

[45] Avrom Saltman, ed, *The Kniveton Leiger*, Derbys Arch Soc Record Series, vol 7 (1977).

[46] For the cartulary as a 'didactic device', see Trevor Faulds, 'Medieval Cartularies', *Archives*, vol xviii no 77 (Apr 1987), pp29–30.

4

The Later Middle Ages 1300–1530

Introduction

As the archives of State and Church matured, but continued to grow in size and complexity, so the task of managing them became ever more demanding. At the same time, more recently established archives emerged as a prominent feature of English record-keeping. They included the archives of colleges, hospitals and other charitable foundations; manors, boroughs and later parishes; landed estates and mercantile enterprises. The creation and preservation of records became characteristic of local as well as national society, and part of the lives of ordinary citizens as well as the elite. This is illustrated by the part played by archival documents in the Peasants' Revolt. A century later, however, it was the State that led the way towards the early modern period of English record-keeping.

Royal Government

By the end of the thirteenth century it was becoming apparent to government that more extensive record-keeping was creating its own problems. It was increasingly difficult to locate and retrieve documents needed for political and administrative purposes. Thus, in 1291, Edward I ordered a chest of Chancery rolls at the New Temple to be searched in connection with his claim to the overlordship of Scotland, and in 1300 a search relating to forest rights was made in the archives of both Chancery and the Exchequer.[1] As so often, however, it was trouble abroad that caused

---

[1] MT Clanchy, *From Memory to Written Record: England 1066–1307*, 3rd edn Chichester 2013, pp154–5. Chancery records were being consulted for legal purposes from the mid-thirteenth century (*ex inf* Dr Hallam Smith).

the most acute difficulties. During the 1290s records for Gascony that had been kept at Bordeaux were largely lost, and back at home searches for documents to help fill the gap were instituted both at the Treasury of Receipt, where Chancery had become accustomed to send important diplomatic and other documents, and at the Tower of London, which by 1300 was housing some Exchequer and Wardrobe records.[2]

This led in the early 1320s to a more general sorting and calendaring of Exchequer and other records. It was masterminded by the Treasurer, Bishop Stapledon, and known as his 'Array', or setting in order. His calendar, completed in 1323, concentrated on the most significant documents in the royal archive, those that concerned the royal prerogative rather than the financial administration or the operation of the courts. They included treaties, papal bulls, evidences relating to Crown lands, royal wills, and records relating to Welsh, Scottish, Irish and continental affairs. Each section of the calendar was given a marginal sign or symbol, suggesting its subject matter, and the same signs were attached to the receptacles containing the documents themselves. The sorting operation took place in the Tower, and at its conclusion the calendared records were either returned to Westminster, where they were presumably lodged in the Treasury of Receipt or the Chapel of the Pyx, or retained at the Tower, where the chapel in the White Tower was fitted out as a repository for them.[3]

Stapledon's Array helped to ensure that the Tower of London would continue to have an important role in governmental record-keeping, a role it maintained until the mid-nineteenth century. But

[2] GP Cuttino, *English Diplomatic Administration 1259–1339*, 2nd edn Oxford 1971, pp112–26.

[3] VH Galbraith, 'The Tower as an Exchequer Record Office', in AG Little and FM Powicke, eds, *Essays in Medieval History Presented to Thomas Frederick Tout*, Manchester 1925, pp231–47; Elizabeth M Hallam, 'The Tower of London as a Record Office', *Archives*, vol xiv no 61 (1979), pp1–10. Stapledon has been described as 'the first great English record-keeper'. Elizabeth M Hallam and Michael Roper, 'The Capital and the Records of the Nation: Seven Centuries of Housing the Public Records in London', *London Jnl*, vol 4 no 1 (May 1978), p74. For his calendar, see Sir Francis Palgrave, *The Antient Kalendars and Inventories of the Treasury of His Majesty's Exchequer*, 3 vols London 1836, i.1–155. For the use of signs and symbols, see also MT Clanchy, *From Memory to Written Record: England 1066–1307*, 3rd edn Chichester 2013, pp174–9. For the significance of the Array in terms of record storage, see below, Chapter 5.

it never became a comprehensive government record office. For a time some Exchequer records continued to be sent to it, but in 1360 the White Tower was needed to accommodate a royal prisoner, King John of France, and its archival contents were moved to the Wakefield Tower. There they remained for many years, and when the White Tower again began to take in records they tended to be from Chancery rather than the Exchequer.[4]

Back at the Palace of Westminster, administrative and judicial records continued to accumulate. During the reign of Edward III (1327–77) the king and his justices became more permanently anchored in the royal capital, a process not unconnected with the start of the Thirty Years War in 1337–8. Within the Palace, a clearer demarcation emerged between the part occupied by the king and his household and the area around the great Hall, which was given a splendid new roof in the 1390s.[5] It was in the Hall itself that the royal courts sat, and around it that a miscellaneous group of buildings grew up, some of them occupied by government offices. It was inevitable that archives should accumulate close to where they were created, for the convenience of officials but also, increasingly, for that of members of the public with an interest in the proceedings and decisions of the courts.[6]

In the later Middle Ages it remained the great traditional organs of government, the Exchequer and Chancery, that contributed most to Westminster's ongoing storage problems. The Exchequer in particular took to disposing of its semi-current records in attics, basements, towers and gatehouses, in short in any space that was available.[7] Chancery did things rather differently. In the thirteenth century it had made use of the New Temple, but when the Knights Templar were suppressed in 1315 the Chancery clerks had to search for a new home. They found one a few hundred yards to the north,

---

[4] See Hallam, *op cit*.

[5] Tout, 'Beginnings of a Modern Capital', in *The Collected Papers of Thomas Frederic Tout*, 3 vols Manchester, 1934, iii.257ff.

[6] VH Galbraith, *Studies in the Public Records*, London 1948, p85.

[7] For the gatehouses of the Palace of Westminster, see successive volumes of HM Colvin, gen ed, *The History of the King's Works*, 6 vols London 1963–82, and Mark Collins, 'The Topography of the Old Palace of Westminster 1510–1834', in Warwick Rodwell and Tim Tatton-Brown, eds, *The Art, Architecture and Archaeology of the Royal Abbey and Palace of Westminster*, 2 vols Leeds 2015, ii.206–56.

where they took over the *Domus Conversorum*, a foundation for Jewish converts. These premises became known as the Rolls House and the Rolls Chapel, and from 1377 the post of Master of the House was formally combined with that of Keeper, later Master, of the Rolls.[8] It was on this site that the Public Record Office was to be erected in the mid-nineteenth century.

* * *

It is not surprising that the major part of the fifteenth century, with its periods of weak government and civil strife, should have been a low time in government record-keeping. By contrast, the years 1485–1530 were ones of vigorous royal rule and administrative innovation. Efforts were made to increase the king's revenue, and to tighten collecting and auditing procedures. The king's chamber, long a kind of domestic exchequer, now took the lead in this rather than the Exchequer. Accounts for the Treasurer of the Chamber survive from the late fifteenth century. There is evidence of the reforming activities of that trusted royal servant Sir Reginald Bray,[9] and the personal involvement of Henry VII should not be underestimated. Closely linked with these changes was the development of what can be termed the prerogative courts, of which the most important in record-keeping terms was the Court of Augmentations, set up to deal with the monastic properties that came into the king's hands at the Dissolution.[10] In the latter part of Henry VIII's reign this court superseded the Chamber as 'the chief national treasury'.[11]

In terms of the machinery of conciliar government, the period 1485–1530 saw two important archival developments. They both related to institutions that had earlier medieval origins, but that would acquire greater constitutional and political importance in the seventeenth century. The king's great council faded from view

---

[8] Hallam and Roper, *op cit*, p75. The office of Keeper of the Rolls is first referred to in 1286, but it had probably been in existence for a considerable period before that. Sir John Sainty, *The Judges of England 1272–1990: a List of the Judges of the Superior Courts*, London (Selden Soc) 1993, p143.

[9] WC Richardson, *Tudor Chamber Administration*, Baton Rouge LA 1952; *King's Works*, i.538–43.

[10] See below, Chapter 6.

[11] Richardson, *op cit*, pviii.

in the fifteenth century, but a smaller body, the Privy Council, had already emerged under Edward III, meeting in a room near the north-east corner of Westminster Hall known as the Star Chamber. From 1485 it kept registers of its proceedings, including those of a judicial nature.[12]

The other institution, Parliament, was an even older body, having emerged in the thirteenth century. It has not previously featured in this volume, however, since its archive properly so called begins only in the late fifteenth century. The earliest rolls of Parliament now form what is strictly speaking an artificial collection, having been assembled from relevant Chancery and Exchequer documents. It was Chancery that was responsible for keeping such records as were deposited with it at the conclusion of each parliament. From 1497, however, the Chancery clerk who enrolled the parliamentary proceedings also kept the original engrossments or fair copies from which the rolls were made up, and his successor as Clerk of the Parliaments had his own office independent of Chancery. For the House of Lords there is a series of original Acts from 1497, and a series of journals, which came to be recognised as the official record of proceedings, from 1510. Otherwise not a great deal survives for the Lords before the seventeenth century, and it was not until then that the House of Commons began to keep its own records.[13]

None, however, of these changes under the early Tudors amounted to a 'revolution in government' from the record creation point of view. The newer institutions had to coexist with Chancery and the Exchequer, and Tudor methods of managing the royal estate were 'almost entirely adaptations of medieval manorial practices'.[14] The Court of Augmentations was influenced by Duchy of Lancaster methods, with which Bray as its one-time Chancellor would have been thoroughly familiar. It would be equally wide of the mark to describe the record-*keeping* conventions of the royal government as undergoing any radical change in the early sixteenth century. Separate record stores, all more or less unsatisfactory, were still being maintained or created for the King's Bench, Common Pleas, King's Remembrancer, Lord Treasurer's Remembrancer, Clerk of

---

[12] For the Court of Star Chamber, see below, Chapter 7.
[13] HG Richardson and GO Sayles, 'The Early Records of the English Parliaments', *BIHR*, vol 5 (1927-8), pp129-54; Maurice F Bond, 'The Formation of the Archives of Parliament 1497-1691', *JSA*, vol 1 (1955-9), pp151-8.
[14] WC Richardson, *op cit*, p396.

the Pells and Auditor of Receipts.[15] They were fortunate not to be destroyed in a major fire at the Palace of Westminster in 1512.

* * *

The foregoing account has left out of consideration two important institutions, the Duchies of Lancaster and Cornwall. Both represented major sources of royal income, and both, together with their archives, have survived until the present day. Henry Bolingbroke's estates as duke of Lancaster were kept separate from the Crown lands when he took the throne as Henry IV in 1399 and have always been separately administered. They have descended without a break from sovereign to sovereign, and this continuity, exceptional for a great estate, helps to explain the richness of its archive. The extensive survival of its fifteenth-century records is particularly remarkable. Although essentially an estate archive, it includes the records of a great franchise or exempt jurisdiction, the county palatine of Lancaster, which have always been preserved as a more or less distinct section of the archive.[16]

The Duchy of Cornwall is an older foundation, having been established in its present form by Edward III in 1337 for the support of his son the Black Prince. Its archive, however, has had a less straightforward history, arising from the fact that when there is no eligible male heir to succeed to the duchy on the attainment of his majority the estates revert to the Crown. The Duchy maintains its own archive, but it has gaps for the periods when there was no separate duke of Cornwall, and when in consequence relevant material has to be sought among the public records. The incompleteness of the archive, of considerable interest and value though it is, is also due in part to losses during the Civil War.

Local Administration

For the period 1300–1530, as for the thirteenth century, no locally kept shrievalty records survive in official custody in any English

---

[15] Hallam and Roper, *op cit*, p76.
[16] Robert Somerville, *History of the Duchy of Lancaster Vol 1: 1265–1603*, London 1953, pix.

county, but from the fourteenth century onwards there is a very small but increasing chance that such documents have been preserved in private collections. Thus Edmund Stonor (d1382) left a personal archive that included two county court rolls relating to his shrievalty of Oxfordshire and Berkshire in 1377–8. A Bedfordshire plea roll for 1332–3 and a Wiltshire sheriff's notebook for 1465 similarly passed into family collections. In the first and third of these cases, however, the documents are now to be found among the public records, having entered public custody for legal reasons at a later date.[17]

By 1400 a new system of county government appears to have become firmly established as a supplement to the royal and county courts, and that was the jurisdiction exercised by magistrates in quarter sessions. These magistrates or justices were appointed by royal commission, but they served without fee or salary. They met to transact their most important business quarterly (hence the name), and were assisted by an official at county level, the Clerk of the Crown or Clerk of the Peace. Above this clerk was the *Custos Rotulorum*, or keeper of the rolls of the county, but he normally delegated his archival responsibilities to the clerk of the peace.[18] It was this clerk who kept the court records and produced them at the sessions.

Again, however, no quarter sessions records survive locally for the medieval period, and our knowledge of the workings of these courts is based largely on the records of cases that were referred to the king's justices at the Assizes, and that in consequence found their way into the public records.[19] The magistrates were often

---

[17] Christine Cooper, ed, *Kingsford's Stonor Letters and Papers 1290–1483*, Cambridge 1996, pp94–105, 449–50; C Hilary Jenkinson and Mabel H Mills, 'Rolls from a Sheriff's Office of the Fourteenth Century', *EHR*, vol xliii (1928), pp21–32; RF Hunnisett and JB Post, eds, *Medieval Legal Records, Edited in Memory of CAF Meekings*, London 1978, pp409–28 (a Wiltshire shrievalty notebook edited by MM Condon).

[18] Later the office of Custos Rotulorum was usually combined with that of Lord Lieutenant.

[19] See eg Elizabeth G Kimball, 'Rolls of the Gloucestershire Sessions of the Peace 1361–1398', *Trans Bristol and Gloucs Arch Soc*, vol 62 (for 1940). Some mid-fourteenth-century Lincolnshire sessions rolls were later deposited with the Treasurer in London by one of the justices himself. See Elizabeth G Kimball, *Records of Some Sessions of the Peace in Lincolnshire, 1381–1396*, Lincoln Rec Soc, vol 65 (1971).

men of considerable local substance and standing, but collectively (unlike the borough magistrates) they had no court premises: in some counties they met in different places every quarter. Their clerks would have kept the quarter sessions records by them at home, and this did not necessarily ensure good record-keeping practice even in the post-medieval period.[20]

* * *

By contrast the English boroughs maintained and even extended their reputation for good record-keeping in the fourteenth and fifteenth centuries. Some, like the City of London, were already mature institutions by 1300.[21] They set great store by precedent and written evidence, and carefully preserved the documents that recorded their customs and traditions. At Southampton, the Oak Book, a custumal and guild merchant book begun about 1300, helped the town to maintain many of its ancient laws down to the early nineteenth century.[22] Along with the Oak Book, it preserved its charters (from 1199), a late fourteenth-century cartulary, port books and brokage books (records of tolls and customs) from the early fourteenth century, and a detailed survey or terrier of the town dating from 1454.[23]

That survey tells us that the burgesses of Southampton kept their archive in one of the gatehouses that formed part of the town's impressive defences.[24] The importance of designated repositories for borough records has already been referred to in Chapter 3. There are more frequent mentions of guildhalls from the later fourteenth century, and the early fifteenth saw a positive building boom.[25] At Sandwich, the first town books date from the 1430s, coinciding

[20] The counties palatine of Chester, Lancaster and Durham were exceptional cases.
[21] See Chapter 3.
[22] P Studer, ed, *The Oak Book of Southampton*, Southampton Rec Soc, vol 10 (1910), pxxxv.
[23] LA Burgess, ed, *The Southampton Terrier of 1454, ibid*, vol xv (1976).
[24] *Ibid*, pp38–9.
[25] RB Dobson, 'Urban Decline in Late Medieval England', in Richard Holt and Gervase Rosser, eds, *The English Medieval Town: a Reader in Urban History 1200–1540*, London and New York 1990, p272.

with the erection of a new town hall.[26] York acquired a town hall about 1450: before that the records had been stored in the chapel of St William on the Ouse Bridge.[27] Even small boroughs such as Bridgwater and Wallingford managed to preserve significant groups of medieval records, although it may have helped in both cases that the town lay in the protective shadow of a castle belonging to a powerful lord.[28]

As important as the existence of a muniment room was the role of the town clerk. At Southampton, there was a salaried common clerk by the early fourteenth century, and later the town benefited from a period of continuity when it had only three such clerks between 1488 and 1540.[29] The largest boroughs might also have chamberlains to act as chief financial officers. At Bristol, the chamberlain presided over an ever-increasing assemblage of non-current records.[30] At Ipswich, the appointment of a similar officer may explain the survival of financial records from the 1440s.[31] But of course not all municipal officers were models of archival rectitude. There are gaps even in the City of London's records, attributed to a clerk's having kept records at home rather than in the Guildhall.[32]

---

[26] Helen Clarke et al, *Sandwich, the 'Completest Medieval Town in England': a Study of the Town and Port from its Origins to 1600*, Oxford and Oakville, Ontario 2010, p87.

[27] David M Smith, 'The Foundation of Chantries in the Chapel of St William on Ouse Bridge', in David M Smith, ed, *The Church in Medieval York: Records Edited in Honour of Professor Barrie Dobson*, York (Borthwick Texts and Calendars no 24) 1999, pp51–68.

[28] HMC *First Report*, Appendix (1870), p99 and *Third Report*, Appendix (1872), pp310–20; TB Dilks, ed, *Bridgwater Borough Archives 1200–1377*, Somerset Rec Soc, vol xlviii (1933) and later vols to lxx (1971); HMC *Sixth Report*, Appendix (1876); Angela Green, 'Borough Records of Wallingford', *JSA*, vol 2 (1960–4), pp476–9; RH Hilton, 'Small Town Society in England before the Black Death', in Holt and Rosser, *op cit*, pp71–96.

[29] Cheryl Butler, ed, *The Book of Fines: the Annual Accounts of the Mayor of Southampton 1488–1540*, Southampton Rec Series xli (2008), pxiii.

[30] N Dermott Harding, 'The Archives of the Corporation of Bristol', *Trans Bristol and Gloucs Arch Soc*, vol xlviii (1926), pp227–49.

[31] David Allen, comp, *Ipswich Borough Archives 1255–1835, a Catalogue*, Suffolk Rec Soc, vol xlvii (2000), ppxxiv, 197.

[32] GH Martin, 'The English Borough in the Thirteenth Century', *TRHS*, 5th S vol 13 (1963), p136n.

In some boroughs, the late medieval archive overlapped with or was kept together with the archives of other local bodies – unsurprisingly when one considers that the merchants and others who ran them were usually members of the same small oligarchy. At York, for instance, the city's muniments shared the Ouse Bridge chapel with the records of four charities.[33] At some places, deeds for medieval hospitals or guilds can be found among the borough's records, possibly because the borough took them over at the Reformation. Stratford-upon-Avon was an unincorporated town in the Middle Ages, but when its leading guild was dissolved in 1547 its records were taken over by the new borough on its creation in 1553.[34]

In some of the larger urban centres guilds grew into bodies devoted to the interests of particular trades. Such were the livery companies, of which those of London are the prime example. Indeed their records from the fourteenth century onwards are unrivalled for their size and range not only in England but in Europe. Although integrated into the governance of the City, they also regulated their own trades, and sometimes acquired extensive charitable responsibilities. One of the largest, the Mercers, took four schools, two almshouses, a hospital and numerous smaller charities under its wing. The Goldsmiths, however, possess probably the earliest administrative document, the first minute book of its court of assistants starting in 1334. In it they recorded their 1370 ordinances, and a century later they started a separate book of ordinances. The richer companies had substantial halls in which to keep their archives, and salaried clerks make their appearance in the fifteenth century.[35] Outside London, the Merchant Adventurers of York are an outstanding example of such a company. Although in its present form a late sixteenth-century foundation, it boasts a continuous history going back to a fourteenth-century confraternity. Its hall, dating from that period, contains a fine evidence chest, and its copious surviving medieval records include deeds, accounts and admissions registers.[36]

---

[33] David M Smith, *The Church in Medieval York*.

[34] Mairi Macdonald, ed, *The Register of the Guild of the Holy Cross, St Mary and St John the Baptist, Stratford-upon-Avon*, Dugdale Soc, vol xlii (2007), pp1–2.

[35] CRH Cooper, 'The Archives of the City of London Livery Companies and Related Organisations', *Archives*, vol xvi no 72 (Oct 1984), pp323–53; Susan M Hare, 'The Records of the Goldsmiths' Company', *ibid*, pp376–84.

[36] David M Smith, *A Guide to the Archives of the Company of Merchant Adventurers of York*, York (Borthwick Texts and Calendars no 16) 1990.

The Cinque Ports were unique in that they were a confederation of boroughs. They combined to provide ships for the defence of England's south-eastern shores, and in return were granted extensive privileges. The five head ports and two other towns kept records from the thirteenth century, but the records of the Confederation and the Guestling Court (to regulate the fishing industry) date from the fifteenth and early sixteenth centuries respectively. These central records were kept at New Romney (Kent), where the town clerk could also act as recorder, and where there are references to a meeting place from 1444.[37]

* * *

After 1300 the survival rate for manorial court rolls increases. The records of the courts became more formal and elaborate as well as more bulky.[38] The fair-copy rolls continued to be written on parchment, but it became more common for drafts to be made on paper during the proceedings, and later fair-copied on to parchment.[39] As before 1300, some of the best runs of court records are those kept as part of the archives of large estates. Two outstanding examples come from the more northerly counties, those for the manors of Kirton-in-Lindsey (Lincolnshire) and Wakefield (Yorkshire). Both were lay estates of unusual extent and complexity. Kirton was part of the Duchy of Cornwall, while Wakefield belonged to the earls De Warenne and their successors. In both cases there were subsidiary courts, but the records were centralised. Kirton's were kept in the lord's hall at Kirton, and later in a court house on the town green. The principal courts at Wakefield were held in the moot hall, the jurisdiction there resembling that of a borough.[40]

---

[37] Felix Hull, *A Calendar of the White and Black Books of the Cinque Ports 1432–1955*, London (HMC and Kent Arch Rec Series) 1966, ppix–xix.

[38] For manorial accounts, see the section of this chapter on estate and personal archives.

[39] PDA Harvey, *Manorial Records*, rev edn 1999, p42.

[40] For Kirton, see Lincolnshire Archives Committee, *Archivists' Report 9* (1957–8), pp26–32. For Wakefield, see WP Baildon, ed, *Court Rolls of the Manor of Wakefield Vol 1: 1274–1297*, Yorks Arch Soc Rec Series, vol xxix (1901), and subsequent volumes in the series.

In the middle of the fourteenth century the depopulation resulting from the Black Death must have affected the creation of manorial records, but it was the popular rising of 1381, the Peasants' Revolt (see below), that caused a notable destruction of them, particularly where they were kept locally rather than in the central repositories of the great estates.[41]

The Church

Keeping bishops' registers was an established practice for the English dioceses from the fourteenth century. It became usual for registrars to keep the materials for these registers as files of documents, only later making them up into the bound volumes familiar to historians today.[42] But their survival depended on various factors, and it is not surprising that many dioceses have gaps in their series. Bishops continued to be peripatetic (as noted in Chapter 3), permanent registries were slow to evolve, and interregnums continued to present hazards. A register might remain in the hands of executors, as occurred at Bath and Wells in the early fourteenth century, or might be carried off by a bishop to his next see, as at Hereford in the sixteenth century.[43] Other records of diocesan administration were often not consistently preserved. Visitation records were regarded as of 'transitory importance', shown by the fact that in the fifteenth century they were more likely to be written on paper than on parchment.[44] Presentation deeds *were* prepared on parchment, but seem to have fared little better: Lincoln, a diocese that in general kept better records than most, has none earlier than 1485.[45] No wonder that Professor Cheney was led to remark on the

---

[41] RH Hilton and TH Aston, eds, *The English Rising of 1381*, Cambridge 1984, p13n. For Westminster Abbey losses, see Barbara Harvey, *Westminster Abbey and its Estates in the Middle Ages*, Oxford 1977, pp452–8.

[42] Nicholas Orme, 'William Elyot, a Fifteenth-Century Registrar and his Books', *Archives*, vol xxvi no 105 (Oct 2001), pp112–17.

[43] David M Smith, *Guide to Bishops' Registers of England and Wales: a Survey from the Middle Ages to the Abolition of Episcopacy in 1646*, London (RHS) 1981, pp30, 95.

[44] Ian Forrest, 'The Survival of Medieval Visitation Records', *Archives*, vol xxxvii no 125 (Apr 2012), p5.

[45] K Major, 'Fifteenth-Century Presentation Deeds in the Lincoln Diocesan

'extreme poverty of English diocesan registries today in records of any periods before the fifteenth century'.⁴⁶ It is a similar story with respect to the records of archdeacons and of the Church courts. At the provincial level, the Canterbury courts fared better than those of York. For other dioceses, even Exeter and Lincoln, the court records are decidedly patchy.⁴⁷

And what of the archives of the bishops as great landowners in the fourteenth and fifteenth centuries? The estate records for the extensive possessions of the bishops of Winchester were impressively well kept, and were preserved at their palace of Wolvesey, near their cathedral. Similarly, the Canterbury estate records were kept principally at the archbishop's palace there. For their muniments – their charters and other key documents – bishops continued to favour cathedral treasuries. But both legal and estate records might also be kept at the other palaces and manor houses that bishops visited in the course of their travels, or in the hands of local stewards. During the Peasants' Revolt there were losses of Canterbury records at Teynham and Thanet in Kent, at Croydon and Harrow, and at Lambeth Palace.⁴⁸ The difficulties encountered by the fourteenth-century compilers of a register of the bishop of Rochester's possessions were probably not untypical. They reported that

> many sheets of documents and charters were consumed by age and others lost through negligence, bad custody and fire in time of war. For there was never any safe place appointed as a

Record Office', in RW Hunt *et al*, eds, *Studies in Medieval History Presented to Frederick Maurice Powicke*, Oxford 1948, p462.

⁴⁶ CR Cheney, *Bishops' Chanceries 1100–1250*, Manchester 1950, p133.

⁴⁷ Brian L Woodcock, *Medieval Ecclesiastical Courts in the Diocese of Canterbury*, Oxford 1952; Dorothy Owen, 'Canterbury Archiepiscopal Archives in Lambeth Palace Library', *JSA*, vol 2 (1960–4), pp141–2; Audrey M Erskine, 'Ecclesiastical Courts and their Records in the Province of Canterbury', *Archives*, vol iii no 17 (Lady Day 1957), pp8–17; JS Purvis, 'The Ecclesiastical Courts of York', *ibid*, pp18–27.

⁴⁸ FRH Du Boulay, *The Lordship of Canterbury: an Essay on Medieval Society*, London 1966, pp13, 188–9; Jane E Sayers, 'The Medieval Care and Custody of the Archbishop of Canterbury's Archives', *BIHR*, vol xxxix (1966), p107. The lower stages of Chichele's Tower, later known as the Lollards' Tower, date from 1434–5. Tim Tatton-Brown, *Lambeth Palace: a History of the Archbishops of Canterbury and their Houses*, London 2000, pp49–50.

repository of muniments, but they were left about (*derelicta*), sometimes in the cathedral church or in the manor of Halling; and so, if this register be inadequate, let it not be accounted a sin to the compilers.[49]

At the secular cathedrals, consistent record-keeping seems to have got under way in the fourteenth century, but as archives increased in quantity and complexity they were not always kept together in one place. At Lincoln, administrative records were stored in a 'common chamber', a room between the chapter house and the north-west transept, not in the main muniment room. At Exeter, there was an Exchequer Chamber over the chapel of St Andrew on the north side of the choir.[50] As ever, survival rates vary. At Exeter, again, there are full medieval accounts but only one surviving pre-Reformation act book.

* * *

It is in the fourteenth century, and more particularly in the fifteenth, that parish records begin to make their mark in English archival history. The parish priest might keep the occasional note or set of memoranda, and by chance a very few of these have survived.[51] But the chief creators of records in every parish were the churchwardens. By the fourteenth century they had acquired a number of responsibilities – for the fabric of the church (apart from the chancel), for its ornaments, books and vestments, and for the church funds. By the early sixteenth century they were probably accumulating quite a wide range of documents during their terms of office, but what survive are usually the fair copies of the accounts that they had to present at the annual parish audit, often by the sixteenth century kept in a volume.

---

[49] Cheney, *op cit*, p134.

[50] Dorothy M Williamson, *The Muniments of the Dean and Chapter of Lincoln*, Lincoln 1956, pp4–5; HMC *Various Collections Vol 4* (1907), pp23ff. The bishop of Exeter had a muniment room over the chapel of St James on the south side of the choir of Exeter Cathedral (*ibid*, pp1–22).

[51] See eg Dorothy Owen, 'Two Medieval Parish Books from the Diocese of Ely: New College MS 98 and Wisbech Museum MS 1', in Malcolm Barber *et al*, eds, *East Anglian and Other Studies Presented to Barbara Dodwell*, Reading Medieval Studies vol xi (1985), pp121–31.

For the years before 1540 some two hundred and fifty sets of churchwardens' accounts exist. That figure may not seem high compared with the several thousand parishes of medieval England, but it represents a significantly higher survival rate than for elsewhere in Europe.[52] The largest number are early sixteenth-century, but there are around one hundred for the fifteenth century, and even a few for the fourteenth. Together with manorial records, they represent the most significant evidence for medieval record-keeping at the local level. They have survived better for the south of England than for the north, and in southern England the cities of London and Bristol are particularly well represented, along with the counties of Devon, Somerset, Kent and Suffolk. This suggests that it was by and large in the wealthier parishes that records were more regularly created and better preserved. Such parishes were more likely to have endowments in the form of land, houses and other property that had to be managed and accounted for;[53] and the wardens themselves were more likely to be men of substance, used to keeping business-like records. Such a man was Robert Reynes of Acle (Norfolk), warden of his parish and pillar of his community in the late fifteenth century.[54] Major church building projects, as at Ashburton (Devon), Yatton (Somerset) and Louth (Lincolnshire), might create a particular need for careful accounting.

The characteristic way of keeping these records was to place them in a chest, often called a common chest to distinguish it from chests containing vestments or money. It would normally have three locks, the keys of which would be held by the parson and the two wardens, and it would be placed somewhere in the parish church.[55] This could be near the high altar, but in the late Middle Ages, and in the larger churches, it became usual to designate a room for the storage of documents and other valuables – a vestry, perhaps, or a room over a porch. Mendlesham (Suffolk) has an example of

---

[52] See Ronald Hutton, *The Rise and Fall of Merry England: the Ritual Year 1400–1700*, Oxford 1994, pp263–93; Beat A Kumin, *The Shaping of a Community: the Rise and Reformation of the English Parish c1400–1560*, Aldershot and Brookfield VT 1996, pp265–9.

[53] See eg Henry Littlehales, ed, *The Medieval Records of a London City Church (St Mary-at-Hill)*, Early English Text Soc 1904–5; Kumin, *op cit*, p73.

[54] Cameron C Lewis, ed, *The Commonplace Book of Robert Reynes of Acle: an Edition of Tanner MS 407*, Garland Medieval Texts, New York and London 1980.

[55] For chests see also below, Chapter 5.

the latter arrangement. There the treasury or muniment room is approached through a fine iron-plated door with three locks, for which in 2008 the original keys were still in use.[56]

* * *

By 1300 many English monasteries held archives of which, and of whose care, they could be proud. But during the following two hundred years these archives became much more substantial, especially in the larger and wealthier houses. Charters accumulated, and finding aids became more sophisticated, sometimes linking them by symbols or numerical press marks to the documents themselves. Good fourteenth-century examples of cartularies cross-referenced to the physical arrangement of the record survive for Ely and the smaller house of Llanthony near Gloucester.[57]

At Durham, a great early fifteenth-century cartulary in four volumes was followed at the mid-century by the compilation of a comprehensive finding aid, the *Repertorium Magnum*. It was updated from time to time down to the early nineteenth century and stayed in use until the mid-twentieth. The records at Durham generally remain 'unsurpassed even by such other great monastic archives as those of Westminster Abbey, Norwich, Winchester and Christ Church Canterbury'.[58] Durham's muniments were a model of record-keeping in an otherwise poorly provided part of England, and its facilities were used by some of the local gentry as a safe place of deposit for their own documentary valuables – a practice, as we have seen, dating back to Anglo-Saxon times.[59]

It was not only deeds that swelled the contents of monastic muniment rooms. The late Middle Ages saw an increase in the

[56] David Sherlock, *Suffolk Church Chests*, Ipswich 2008, pp81–2.

[57] Dorothy Owen, 'The Muniments of Ely Cathedral Priory', in CNL Brooke et al, eds, *Church and Government in the Middle Ages: Essays Presented to C. R. Cheney on his Seventieth Birthday*, Cambridge 1976, p158; R Ian Jack, 'An Archival Case History: the Cartularies and Registers of Llanthony Priory in Gloucestershire', *JSA*, vol 4 (1970–3), pp375–6.

[58] RB Dobson, *Durham Priory 1400–1500*, Cambridge 1972, pp3–4.

[59] The depositors included Henry V (Dobson, *op cit*, pp175, 183). Durham was fortunate to escape major damage in disturbed times (see Richard Lomas, *North-East England in the Middle Ages*, Edinburgh 1992, p56).

production of court rolls, accounts and even correspondence and papers. Both Canterbury and Durham started to compile registers of correspondence, and Durham's use of paper was a feature of its late medieval archive.[60] As in earlier centuries, however, it is often difficult to discover precisely where these records were kept. At Ely in the fourteenth century and Peterborough in the late fifteenth, it is likely that deeds and related documents remained in the muniment room, but that financial and other records were to be found in a separate treasury or exchequer chamber.[61] Obedientiaries, moreover, kept their own archives. As for manorial records, the fact that so many were lost at St Albans and Westminster Abbey suggests that at neither place had they been lodged in the muniment room.

Reference has already been made to the dissolution of the Knights Templar in 1315. All its accounting records were lost at that point, but some charters passed to its successor body, the Knights Hospitallers, who must have held a substantial archive at their Clerkenwell (London) headquarters. Their large cartulary, begun in 1442, has been described as 'one of the most substantial and comprehensive of any medieval religious house in Britain', and it survived the dissolution of the Order in 1540.[62]

Institutional Archives

After 1300 there was a proliferation in the number of institutions founded to further charitable and religious objects. They were concerned, as they would be today, with the relief of poverty, the care of the sick and the education of the young, but their founders were mindful as much of the soul as of the body. Colleges of priests began to be favoured over monastic foundations by wealthy

---

[60] AJ Piper, 'Dr Thomas Swalwell, Monk of Durham, Archivist and Bibliophile (d1539)', in James P Corley and Colin GC Tite, eds, *Books and Collectors 1200–1700: Essays Presented to Andrew Watson*, London 1997, pp71–100; Michael Stansfield, 'The Archive', in David Brown, ed, *Durham Cathedral: History, Fabric and Culture*, New Haven CT and London 2015, pp423–33 and n60.

[61] Owen, *op cit*, p163; Janet D Martin, *The Cartularies and Registers of Peterborough Abbey*, Northants Rec Soc, vol xxviii (1978), pxiv.

[62] Evelyn Lord, *The Knights Templar in Britain*, London 2002; Michael Gevers, ed, *The Cartulary of the Knights of St John of Jerusalem in England, Secunda Camera Essex*, Oxford (British Academy) 1982.

patrons, and chantries, manned by single priests, were attached to parish churches. Hospitals were devoted as much to the care of the elderly and infirm as to the treatment of the sick, and they could range from small establishments to large and wealthy foundations.

The spread of such bodies over the country led to a considerable expansion in record-keeping. They were created by charter, or under the will of a founder, and in this resembled the monasteries. Importantly, however, their founding instruments gave them specific constitutions, in some cases including detailed instructions as to what documents should be kept and how. The duty of the chantry priest, for instance, was to say masses for the soul of the founder, but he was also responsible for keeping the deeds and accounts for the property that had endowed the charity, and for compiling inventories of the books and vestments in his charge. The mid-fourteenth-century founder of a chantry at Crich (Derbyshire) specified that a cartulary should be compiled for its evidences, since small deeds (*parvi libelli*) could so easily go astray; while in 1507 a Yorkshire donor decreed that a chantry chest should be provided, with one of its two compartments, carrying two locks, reserved for the evidences.[63]

This chest was no doubt placed near the side altar served by its priest, but for a larger foundation, staffed by a college of priests, more elaborate arrangements were in order. At the collegiate church of St Mary's, Warwick, a new chapel built for the tomb of the third Earl Beauchamp (d1439) incorporated a sanctuary or treasury for the valuables and evidences, with an outer room in which the sacristan employed to guard these treasures was to sleep.[64] Even grander was St George's Chapel, Windsor, founded by Edward III in 1348. This was a totally new church with its own collegiate buildings, including a treasury or aerary (from the Latin *aerarium*) that also acted as a muniment room. It lay above the vaulted entrance to the

---

[63] Avrom Saltman, ed, *The Cartularies of the Wadebridge Chantries at Crich*, Derbys Arch Soc Rec Series vol 6 (1976), pp30–2; William H Lewer and J Charles Wall, *The Church Chests of Essex*, London 1913, p43.

[64] Revd J Harvey Bloom, 'An Introduction to the Cartulary of St Mary's, Warwick', *Trans Bristol and Gloucs Arch Soc*, vol xxxvii (1914), pp79–91; James Willoughby, 'Inhabited Sacristies in Medieval England: the Case of St Mary's, Warwick', *Antiquaries Jnl*, no 92 (2012), pp331–45; Dorothy Styles, ed, *Ministers' Accounts of the Collegiate Church of St Mary, Warwick 1432–85*, Dugdale Soc, vol xvi (1969), ppxxiff.

college (a position later complicated by additional building around it), and had a tiled floor, one window, later strongly barred, and a stone-vaulted ceiling. The scheme was probably implemented by the king's Treasurer, Bishop Edington, and he may have been assisted by William Wykeham, soon to become in effect clerk of the king's works.[65]

The greatest corpus, however, of medieval collegiate records is that belonging to the older colleges of Oxford and Cambridge. Among them precedence must be given to the late thirteenth-century foundation of Merton College, Oxford, whose buildings included a structure near the chapel designed to house an exchequer with a treasury or muniment room above it.[66] Nearly a century later, in the early 1380s, William Wykeham, who had succeeded Edington as Chancellor and bishop of Winchester, not only provided a muniment tower for his Oxford foundation of New College, but specified the documents – title deeds, court rolls, bursars' accounts, admissions registers and so on – that were to be kept in it. For the sister foundation, Winchester College, a treasury was provided over the chapel vestry, with a second room for less important records above that.[67] Another century later, William Waynflete,

[65] Maurice F Bond, 'The Windsor Aerary', *Archives*, vol i no 4 (Mich 1950), pp2–6; Eleanor Cracknell, 'The Archives', in Nigel Saul and Tim Tatton-Brown, eds, *St George's Chapel, Windsor: History and Heritage*, Stanbridge 2010, pp212–20; Tim Tatton-Brown, 'The Constructional Sequence and Topography of the Chapel and College Buildings at St George's', in Colin Richmond and Eileen Scarff, eds, *St George's Chapel, Windsor, in the Later Middle Ages*, Windsor 2001, p30; John Steane, 'Medieval Muniment Rooms, their Furniture, Fittings and Information Retrieval Systems', *Trans Ancient Monuments Soc*, vol 54 (2010), p38. By the late fifteenth century the counting house had been moved to the Schorn Tower.

[66] JRL Highfield, ed, *The Early Rolls of Merton College, Oxford, with an Appendix of Thirteenth-Century Charters*, Oxford 1964, pp1–63. The *Liber Ruber* of 1288 is an early finding aid (Paul Delsalle, *A History of Archival Practice*, English edn, with Margaret Procter, London 2017, chap 5 and fig 5.2). As at Windsor, the original building was later surrounded by others.

[67] Francis W Steer, *The Archives of New College: a Catalogue*, London and Chichester 1974, ppxi–xiv; Jennifer Thorp, 'Archives', in Christopher Tyerman, ed, *New College*, London 2010, p99; John H Harvey, 'Winchester College Muniments', *Archives*, vol 5 no 28 (1962), pp201–9; Sheila Himsworth, *Winchester College Muniments: a Descriptive List*, 2 vols Chichester 1976, 1984. Security would have been a particular concern in the decade of the Peasants' Revolt. (I owe this point to Prof Christopher Currie.)

who had also succeeded to the chancellorship and the bishopric of Winchester, incorporated a three-storey muniment tower in his design for Magdalen College, Oxford. His statutes of 1480 decreed that the treasury should occupy the middle floor and the muniments the top floor, with original documents and copies being kept in separate chests.[68] In the smaller Oxford colleges it became customary to build gatehouse towers, with first-floor accommodation for the head of the house and a muniment room above.[69]

Cambridge colleges followed a little behind Oxford when it came to record-keeping. Henry VI's twin foundations of Eton and King's Colleges were planned on a magnificent scale, but not fully executed, and the projected muniment towers were never built. Nevertheless their archives were conscientiously curated from the start.[70] At both Oxford and Cambridge, the universities were constituted differently from the colleges, and their archives were less well kept than those of their constituent colleges, but in this respect Cambridge had the edge over Oxford.[71]

Among the major hospitals, that of St Leonard at York and two London foundations, St Bartholomew's and the Savoy, probably held the most impressive archives by 1530, dating respectively

---

[68] CM Woolgar, 'Two Oxford Archives in the Early Seventeenth Century', *Archives*, vol xvi no 71 (Apr 1984), pp258–72; Robin Darwall-Smith, 'The Muniment Room', in David Roberts, *Hidden Magdalen*, Oxford 2008, pp28–9; Robin Darwall-Smith and Michael Riordan, 'Archives for Administrators or Archives for Antiquarians? A History of Archive Cataloguing in Four Oxford Colleges', *JSA*, vol 30 no 1 (Apr 2009), p95. See also Chapter 5.

[69] John Newman, 'The Physical Setting: New Building and Adaptation', in James McConica, ed, *The History of the University of Oxford Vol 3: the Collegiate University*, Oxford 1986, pp624–5.

[70] Sir HC Maxwell Lyte, *A History of Eton College*, London 1899, pp43–7; information kindly supplied by successive archivists to the College; John Saltmarsh, 'The Muniments of King's College', *Proc Camb Ant Soc*, vol xxxiii (1931–2), pp83–97.

[71] Heather E Peek and Catherine P Hall, *The Archives of the University of Cambridge: an Historical Introduction*, Cambridge 1962, pp1–7; Dorothy Owen, *Cambridge University Archives: a Classified List*, Cambridge 1988; Reginald L Poole, *A Lecture on the History of the University Archives*, Oxford 1912; Trevor Aston, 'Muniment Rooms and their Fittings in Medieval and Early Modern England', in Ralph Evans, ed, *Lordship and Learning: Studies in Memory of Trevor Aston*, Woodbridge 2004, p237; information from Simon Bailey, Oxford University Archivist.

from the thirteenth, fourteenth and early sixteenth centuries. The well-appointed hospital of St Cross, just outside Winchester, was another foundation that benefited, archivally and otherwise, from the support of successive bishops of that exceptionally wealthy see. By the later medieval period, however, patrons were emerging from less traditional backgrounds. In London, the wealthy merchant Richard Whittington established both a college and almshouses, with the statutes for the latter giving instructions for the safe custody of its archive.[72] At Ewelme (Oxfordshire), the almshouses were endowed by its *nouveau riche* founders with properties whose muniments formed the basis of its institutional archive. Towards the end of the fifteenth century the local merchant and financier William Browne took similar trouble over the muniments of his almshouses at Stamford (Lincolnshire). The annual account rolls compiled by the Master were to be audited, entered in volumes, and kept in a large wooden chest that remains *in situ*.[73]

Of the numerous charities founded during the fourteenth and fifteenth centuries, many had short lives, and when, for various reasons, they failed, their archives were lost with them. Those that fared better were often those that benefited from the long-term support of powerful patrons. Thus Whittington's charity had the protection of the Mercers' Company; St George's, Windsor that of the sovereign himself. Sometimes a charity came under the aegis of a more permanent body: St George's acquired St Anthony's Hospital, London, and The Queen's College, Oxford took over God's House, Southampton, the archive in both cases being transferred to the new parent institution.[74]

Although most medieval non-governmental institutions were either primarily or partly religious in purpose, the latter part of the period saw the emergence of a few that were entirely secular. Two examples from London must suffice. In 1484 the Heralds were formed into a corporation or chapter, although their grant was

---

[72] Jean Imray, *The Charity of Richard Whittington: a History of the Trust Administered by the Mercers' Company, 1424–1966*, London 1968, pp117 *et passim*.

[73] Alan Rogers, 'William Browne's Title Deeds and Late Medieval Stamford', *Archives*, vol xxxiv no 120 (Apr 2009), pp1–7.

[74] Carole Rawcliffe, 'Passports to Paradise: How Medieval Hospitals and Almshouses Kept their Archives', *Archives*, vol xxvii no 106 (Apr 2002), pp2–22; JM Kaye, ed, *The Cartulary of God's House, Southampton Vol 1*, Southampton Rec Series, vol xix (1976).

revoked the following year, and for the remainder of the Middle Ages the College of Arms had a somewhat shadowy existence. The heralds kept rolls of arms and visitation books, but it was unclear whether they remained their own property or that of the College.[75] More substantial were those bodies of lawyers that became the Inns of Court. Although not corporations, they acquired property, and from the fifteenth century began to accumulate records. The council minutes of Lincoln's Inn begin in 1422.[76]

Estate and Personal Archives

Like the spiritual lords the secular magnates created ever larger archives during the late medieval period. The major components of those archives were of the kinds with which the reader will already have become familiar – deeds and other legal documents, manorial and other court records, estate accounts and household records. Where families acquired further estates by inheritance or marriage they also acquired the archives that went with them, and these were usually kept on the estates to which they related: thus in the early fourteenth century the earls of Lancaster kept muniments relating to their Ferrers estates at Tutbury (Staffordshire) and those relating to their Lacy estates at Pontefract (Yorkshire).[77] In the absence of the lord a constable would be left in charge of a castle and its muniments: thus the constable at Pleshey was responsible for the Essex records of Humphrey de Bohun, Earl of Hereford and Essex.[78]

Castles became more elaborate buildings at this period, increasing the number of places where archives might be stored. From the latter half of the fourteenth century the evolution of the courtyard plan provided one such – the entrance gateway tower and its adjacent buildings. The tower was defensible, and also strategically placed for monitoring movements in and out of the castle. Here was its business hub, where revenues were received and household expenditure

---

[75] AR Wagner, *The Records and Collections of the College of Arms*, London 1952, pp1–10 *et passim*.

[76] CM Rider, 'The Inns of Court and Inns of Chancery and their Records', *Archives*, vol xxiv no 101 (Oct 1999), pp27–36.

[77] Robert Somerville, *History of the Duchy of Lancaster Vol 1: 1265–1603*, London 1953, p74.

[78] GRC Davis, *Cartularies*, no 199.

supervised. At Wressle (Yorkshire), a well-designed late fourteenth-century castle belonging to the Percy earls of Northumberland, there was a counting house over the passage, and above it rooms for the steward, treasurer and comptroller. Accounting records would have been kept to hand in the counting house itself, but nearby there would be a secure place for storing money and other valuables. At Cockermouth (Cumberland), another Percy castle, a dungeon below the counting house served this purpose.[79]

Such a room, however, would not have been suitable for the long-term storage of muniments. A better place might be nearer to the lord's private apartments – in his keep, or later his lodging tower. In the early fourteenth century Edmund Mortimer, Earl of March, had a tower treasury at Wigmore Castle (Herefordshire), to judge from two inventories found when a vault in the long-ruined building was opened in 1795. At Tutbury, however, the chapel was the favoured repository.[80] Later the more up-to-date castles provided sets of privy lodgings, influenced by arrangements in the royal palaces, and these could include closets, studies and strong-rooms.[81] The fine brick tower of Tattershall Castle (Lincolnshire), built by Ralph, Lord Cromwell in the 1440s, is a good example, and in its day an influential one, of a building with private apartments on the lower floors and above them rooms for the storage of valuables and records.[82] The fifth earl of Northumberland had top-storey studies or libraries at Leconfield (Yorkshire), Wressle and Petworth (Sussex), where he could keep papers as well as books, and the first-named had an evidence room next to it.[83] Many late medieval nobles also had houses or inns in or near the City of London, but although convenient for lodging records on a temporary basis, for

---

[79] Maurice Howard, 'The Courtyard House, Medieval and After', in Malcolm Airs and PS Barnwell, eds, *The Medieval Great House*, Donington 2011, pp96–108; Peter Brears, 'The Administrative Role of Gatehouses in Fourteenth-Century North-Country Castles', *ibid*, pp200–13; Peter Brears, 'Wressle Castle', *Archaeological Jnl*, vol 167 (2010), p69.

[80] For Wigmore Castle, see GRC Davis, *Cartularies*, no 1294. For Tutbury, see GA Holmes, *The Estates of the Higher Nobility in Fourteenth-Century England*, Cambridge 1957, p134.

[81] KB McFarlane, *The Nobility of Later Medieval England: the Ford Lectures for 1953 and Related Studies*, Oxford 1973, pp93–4; Simon Thurley, *The Royal Palaces of Tudor England: Architecture and Court Life 1460–1547*, London 1993.

[82] Margaret Wood, *The English Medieval House*, new edn 1983, pp159, 173.

[83] Brears, 'Wressle Castle', pp83, 87, 97–8.

instance, when needed for a court case, they seem not to have been used for more permanent record storage.[84]

Very few of these large aristocratic archives have survived to the present day. The Duchy of Lancaster archive has done so thanks to the exceptional circumstances already described. The Berkeley family archive, kept at Berkeley Castle (Gloucestershire) since the late twelfth century, is another remarkable example of continuity. But other great lords, such as the earls of Warwick, have left only fragmentary remains. The principal reason for such losses appears to have been the vulnerability of the nobility to dynastic disasters. While some families rose through inheritance, others failed through lack of heirs or disputed successions. There were also not infrequent periods of rebellion or civil war. In the 1320s, and again in the 1450s and early 1480s, a number of heads of noble families were executed or killed in battle. Even the earls of Lancaster underwent vicissitudes in the fourteenth century, with consequent losses of records.[85] In the early sixteenth century the highly record-conscious third Stafford duke of Buckingham embarked on an ambitious plan to rebuild Thornbury Castle in Gloucestershire as his principal seat, complete with a record tower next to his private apartments. He was in the process of centralising his archive there and arranging it in iron-bound chests when he was attainted (losing his estates to the Crown) and subsequently executed.[86]

* * *

After 1300 there was also an increase in record-keeping among the lower ranks of landed society. The gentry were a more numerous

---

[84] John Schofield, *Medieval London Houses*, New Haven CT and London 1994. In 1376 there was a move to concentrate the Duchy of Lancaster archive at the Savoy, with unfortunate consequences five years later (Somerville, *op cit*, pp63–4).

[85] Somerville, *op cit*, pp29, 48 *et passim*. See also McFarlane, *op cit*, and Holmes, *op cit*.

[86] Carole Rawcliffe, 'A Tudor Nobleman as Archivist: the Papers of Edward, Third Duke of Buckingham', *JSA*, vol 5 (1974–7), pp294–5; Carole Rawcliffe, *The Staffords, Earls of Stafford and Dukes of Buckingham*, Cambridge 1978, pp148ff. A good proportion of the third duke's archive was taken into custody at the Tower of London, where much was subsequently lost, but some of the records at Caus Castle were salvaged by his son, who was created Baron Stafford.

body than the nobility, and by the fifteenth century they were probably producing a greater volume of archival material in total. They also tended to lead somewhat quieter lives than their superiors, and their families consequently had a higher chance of survival into the post-medieval period. Even today, estate records survive in reasonable numbers for five fifteenth-century Warwickshire families, with 'a certain amount of material' for a further five.[87] Among the late medieval gentry families whose archives would survive into modern times were the Arundells, Constables and Foljambes.[88]

One thing that distinguished the gentry archive from that of the magnate was that in the absence of a body of professional retainers the head of the family might take a more active personal part in the care of his legal and estate records; and this was more likely to be the case when the landowner had recently risen from the mercantile or professional classes. The late fourteenth-century gentleman Robert Hylle of Spaxton (Somerset) had inherited land but was the son of a judge and himself also a land agent. The cartulary that he compiled shows his familiarity with the intricacies of feudal incidents (financial and other obligations owed by a feudal tenant to his lord) and wardship and marriage arrangements.[89] John Pyel (d1382) and his mercantile partner Adam Frauncys (d1375) were Londoners who purchased estates and compiled or commissioned cartularies. The one created for Frauncys in 1362, on the completion of his landed portfolio, has been described as 'a document of social transition'.[90]

By 1400 many nobles were having to conduct a certain amount of business by correspondence, though no doubt mainly with the help of clerks or secretaries. By the mid-fifteenth century this habit had spread to the gentry, assisted by a greater availability of paper and the gradual standardisation of written English. The Pastons of Norfolk were nevertheless unusual, not only for the frequency with which they put pen to paper in letters or notes to family members and others but also for the care with which they preserved their

---

[87] Christine Carpenter, *Locality and Polity: a Study of Warwickshire Landed Society 1401–1499*, Cambridge 1992, p36.

[88] See HMC *Principal Family and Estate Collections*, Guides to Sources ... 10 and 11, 2 vols London 1996, 1999.

[89] Robert Dunning, ed, *The Hylle Cartulary*, Somerset Rec Soc, vol lxviii (1968).

[90] SJ O'Connor, ed, *A Calendar of the Cartularies of John Pyel and Adam Frauncys*, RHS Camden Soc 5th S, vol 2 (1993).

correspondence. John Paston I (d1466) set more store by his writings and evidences than by any other of his moveable goods. His widow Margaret, in a well-known letter to her son John II, advised him to look after his 'wrytyngs that ben of charge', and to take care that they did not fall into the wrong hands.[91] The Plumptons of Yorkshire and the Stonors of Oxfordshire were two other families whose correspondence has luckily come down to us, the latter via its passage through the legal system into the public records.[92]

Where did these gentry families keep their archives? A few, such as the Fastolfs and the Luttrells of Dunster (Somerset) were of sufficiently high status to have castles. In the manor houses that were the more typical gentry homes the most favoured place seems to have been somewhere in the family's private rooms. Robert Hylle refers to a 'treasury' for his evidences at Spaxton. Later there are occasional references to studies, as at Stonor and Raynham (Norfolk). But more often records were kept in an assortment of chests in different rooms, as with the Pastons.[93] The Pedwardines, however, possessed a cupboard in the late fourteenth century in which the deeds were stored at the top and various estate records below them.[94]

Some families were still using ecclesiastical institutions as places of safe deposit in the late Middle Ages. The Pastons, subject to periodic violence from their East Anglian neighbours, stored documents as well as other valuables in Norwich Cathedral Priory.[95] When the Fastolf properties were divided after the death of Sir John Fastolf in 1459, documents that related to the estates as a whole were lodged for the convenience of the heirs in the priory of St Mary Overie, Southwark.[96]

* * *

[91] See Norman Davis, ed, *Paston Letters of the Fifteenth Century Vol 1*, Oxford 1971.

[92] Thomas Stapleton, ed, *Plumpton Correspondence*, Camden Soc 1839; Christine Carpenter, ed, *Kingsford's Stonor Letters and Papers 1290–1483*, Cambridge 1986.

[93] Norman Davis, *op cit*, pp91, 96–8, 444–5, 568–9.

[94] Trevor Foulds, 'Medieval Cartularies', *Archives*, vol xviii no 77 (Apr 1987), p19; GRC Davis, *Cartularies*, no 1301.

[95] Norman Davis, *op cit*, pp46, 294.

[96] Colin Richmond, *The Paston Family in the Fifteenth Century: Fastolf's Will*, Cambridge 1996, pp270–1.

By the early sixteenth century there must have been many merchants, both in London and the major provincial centres, whose businesses could not have functioned without the documentation provided by ledgers, day books, bonds, bills of sale or correspondence. In general they have left not an archival wrack behind, but two rare exceptions should be mentioned. The Celys were wool merchants who purchased their wool from the Cotswold growers and shipped it from London to the Staple at Calais. A substantial part of their late fifteenth-century business archive has survived (like the Stonor correspondence) in the public records, as the result of a lawsuit.[97] On a much smaller scale is the account book of John Heritage, a wool merchant living in Moreton-in-Marsh (Gloucestershire). This volume, which he purchased on a visit to London in 1501, was inherited by his son, who appears to have deposited it with the muniments of Westminster Abbey, along with two further volumes of his own.[98]

The Peasants' Revolt

By the late fourteenth century the peasantry formed a numerous section of English society. Some were small landowners, and needed to keep a title deed or two, including perhaps a copy of an entry in a manorial court roll as proof of copyhold tenure. Some might even possess a simple seal.[99] Traces of their exiguous archives have survived only where they ended up as elements in more substantial higher-status archives, as a result of the absorption of small properties into much larger estates.[100]

---

[97] Alison Hanham, *The Celys and their World: an English Merchant Family of the Fifteenth Century*, Cambridge 2002.

[98] Christopher Dyer, *A Country Merchant, 1495–1520: Trading and Farming at the End of the Middle Ages*, Oxford 2012. Moreton-in-Marsh was a Westminster Abbey manor.

[99] Clanchy, *op cit*, pp51–3. Such seals – metal matrices incised with simple designs – have been found in their hundreds (Christopher Dyer, 'The Material World of English Peasants, 1200–1540: Archaeological Perspectives on Rural Economy and Welfare', *Agricultural Hist Rev*, vol 62 pt 1 (2014), p20).

[100] For the survival of tenants' copies of entries in seigneurial court rolls, some from the early fourteenth century, see CRJ Currie, 'Tenants' Copies of Court Rolls in England and Wales before 1400', *Archives*, vol lvi no 1 (Apr 2021), pp1–21.

Many of these small owners would not have been able to read the documents they owned, but that does not mean that they failed to appreciate their value and significance. The Peasants' Revolt of May and June 1381, already referred to more than once in these pages, revealed how much the commons of England knew about archives – not only what they contained but where they were stored and who was responsible for them. The fury of the rebels was directed particularly at the lawyers, already emerging as a profession closely connected with the production and deployment of records not only in the capital but elsewhere in the country. There was a widespread opinion that 'the land could not be free until all the lawyers had been killed'. 'This sentiment,' continued the chronicler, 'so excited the rustics that they went to further extremes and declared that all court rolls and old muniments should be burnt so that once the memory of ancient customs had been wiped out then their lords would be completely unable to vindicate their rights over them; and so it was done.'[101]

Their targets were wide-ranging. In London the archbishop of Canterbury and the prior of the Hospital of St John, both leading members of the government, had their houses ransacked and their archives pillaged. Outside London, records were used as weapons in tussles between local urban interests, while in the countryside, especially in East Anglia, manorial records were seized and destroyed. But perhaps the most notable disturbances were those that reflected anti-monastic sentiment. At St Albans, the insurgents got the monks of the abbey to surrender a number of royal charters and made a bonfire of them in the market place. At Bury St Edmunds, the rebels went further. They sought out John Lakenheath, the monk in charge of the abbey's archive, and chopped off his head, thus making him an early archival martyr.[102] Apart from manorial court rolls it seems that the documents most in danger of destruction were the charters of privileges that enabled religious houses, patrons of boroughs or great landed magnates to lord it over those who lived in their shadows. In more peaceful times a monastery such as Bury guarded its muniments

---

[101] RB Dobson, ed, *The Peasants' Revolt of 1381*, London 1970, pp133–4, quoting the chronicler Thomas Walsingham.

[102] *Ibid*, pp245–7. For Bury, see also MD Lobel, *The Borough of Bury St Edmunds: a Study in the Government and Development of a Monastic Town*, Oxford 1935, pp152–5.

successfully enough, but in 1381 its fortifications were well and truly breached.

A closer examination, however, reveals that popular attitudes to records were not straightforward. At Bury and St Albans, the rioters were not bent solely on destruction. At Bury, they demanded the return to them of 'charters of liberties of the town which Cnut, the founder of the monastery, had once granted'. At St Albans, a search was made for an even earlier document, a charter granted to the town by King Offa.[103] So not all charters were hostile weapons. And had these documents existed and been retrieved they could have formed the basis of lawsuits against the monks. In that case, however, the services of lawyers would have been required, always assuming that any were left to be found.

These incidents also reveal something about the continuing role of memory and its ambiguous relation to records and record-keeping. On the one hand the rebels thought that to destroy certain documents would be to destroy the memory that they represented, yet they relied on a potent collective memory when it came to royal charters that they believed had been issued in their favour in the distant past. By the fourteenth century the courts preferred to rely on written rather than oral evidence, but that did not mean that memory could be entirely dispensed with.[104] On the contrary, gaps in the written record had often to be filled by oral testimony. These memories were then incorporated in the written record, a process familiar to those attending a manorial court.

---

[103] Dobson, *op cit*, p276; RH Hilton and TH Aston, eds, *The English Rising of 1381*, Cambridge 1984, pp63–5; Stephen Justice, *Writing and Rebellion: England in 1381*, Berkeley and Los Angeles CA 1994, pp40–51, 148–91.
[104] Clanchy, *op cit*, pp262–8.

5

Archival Furniture in Medieval England

Today the standard container for archival material is a box made of acid-free cardboard. Available in various sizes, it can be used to store bundles of deeds or papers, bound volumes and rolls, although it is less suitable for very large items such as maps and plans. It is designed to rest on metal racking in the secure and controlled environment of a strongroom, often part of a larger repository. In the Middle Ages the situation was very different. Documents were stored in a variety of mainly wooden containers, of which the most common throughout the period was the chest or box. These containers might, as will be shown, have particular adaptations for record storage, but in their basic form they were not peculiar to record-keeping: they could be, and were, used for other purposes such as storing clothes, money or other valuables.

That said, it is still worthwhile to consider the subject of medieval archival furniture, in order to see whether any lines of historical development can be detected. The foundations of such a study were laid a few decades ago by the late Trevor Aston;[1] and more recently further progress has been made, especially through the application of dendrochronology, or tree-ring dating. But many obscurities remain. Little is known of where chests were made, although one recent piece of research points to a regional or local style.[2] The Latin and vernacular names used to describe containers in contemporary sources are various, and sometimes difficult to interpret when the objects to which they refer no longer survive. Above all, the thin

---

[1] Trevor Aston, 'Muniment Rooms and their Fittings in Medieval and Early Modern England', in Ralph Evans, ed, *Lordship and Learning: Studies in Memory of Trevor Aston*, Woodbridge 2004, pp235–47. For a more recent survey, see John Steane, 'Medieval Muniment Rooms, their Furniture, Fittings and Information Retrieval Systems', *Trans Ancient Monuments Soc*, vol 54 (2010), pp44–8.

[2] See David Sherlock, *Suffolk Church Chests*, Ipswich 2008, p3.

and scattered nature of the evidence makes it hard to establish a precise chronology; and this is the reason for treating the subject in a separate chapter, instead of trying to allocate developments to the shorter periods of Chapters 1–4. Some broad trends are tentatively postulated in the following paragraphs.

Much depended on the quantity of documentary material with which the medieval record-keeper had to deal, but also on the value and importance attached to the documents. As shown in Chapter 1, the early records of an institution such as a religious house could be very few in number, but they could also be of very high individual value, and therefore requiring storage conditions of the greatest security. In a monastery they were considered worthy of being placed on the high altar of the church, alongside or attached to sacred books.[3] An Anglo-Saxon king, however, might place his embryonic archive in his *haligdom* or treasury, with his money and jewels. There they might be laid with no further protection, but it is more likely that they were put inside a separate chest.

The word chest comes from the Latin *cista* and signifies a box for the keeping of valuables. In England early chests appear to have been of the 'dug-out' kind, hollowed from a single trunk.[4] But by 1200 the classic medieval chest may have emerged. It was constructed from wooden planks and uprights (or standards) and had a hinged lid. It also acquired various items of blacksmith's work in order to make it more secure: it was reinforced with iron bands, and fitted with locks, bolts and handles. A variant was the *hutch*, a chest with its end panels extended downwards, thus raising it off the floor and helping to protect it from damp.[5] For extra security, chests were fitted with more than one lock, either a plate lock or a padlock. The key to each lock was held by a different responsible person, and for the chest to be opened the presence of both or all the key-holders was necessary. Where documents were concerned it would be specified record-keepers who held the keys. The chest in which

---

[3] As late as c1217 the Salisbury diocesan statutes enjoined parish priests to record details of church property and furnishings in 'missals and other books'. MT Clanchy, *From Memory to Written Record: England 1066–1307*, 3rd edn Chichester 2013, p157.

[4] William H Lewer and J Charles Wall, *The Church Chests of Essex*, London 1913, pp41–2.

[5] FC Morgan, 'Church Chests of Herefordshire', *Trans Woolhope Naturalists' Field Club, Herefordshire*, vol xxxii (1949), p132.

Domesday Book was kept for many centuries had three locks, the keys to which were held by the two Deputy-Chamberlains of the Exchequer and the Treasurer's Clerk.[6] In the later Middle Ages the number of key-holders might increase: the common chests of the universities of Oxford and Cambridge had five or six locks.[7]

In the late eleventh century the archive of Worcester Cathedral Priory, a substantial one for that date, could be accommodated in a single chest.[8] The great thirteenth-century growth in the size of archives described in Chapter 3 demanded larger or more numerous receptacles. The largest chest in the muniment room of Westminster Abbey dates from the middle of that century and is so large that it must either have been constructed *in situ* or winched up from the floor of the abbey.[9] By the early fifteenth century even a parish church might need a chest too large to be carried up the narrow stairs to a first-floor muniment room or treasury. This seems to have been the case at Mendlesham (already cited in Chapter 4), where the chest is contemporary with the room in which it sits, and may have been winched into place there when the room was being built.[10]

As chests became more widely used for document storage, one disadvantage must have become apparent. As a chest filled with documents it became more tightly packed, impeding the circulation of air that helped to keep the records dry and making it harder to find the individual items or bundles that needed to be consulted. The act of rummaging through a chest, moreover, increased the risk of damage to the documents, particularly when they had fragile or unprotected wax seals.[11] The introduction of larger and heavier

---

[6] Elizabeth M Hallam, *Domesday Book through Nine Centuries*, London 1986, pp114–15, 127 (illustr).

[7] Aston, *op cit*, p239; Heather E Peek and Catherine P Hall, *The Archives of the University of Cambridge: an Historical Introduction*, Cambridge 1962, p1.

[8] Francesca Tinti, *Sustaining Belief: the Church of Worcester from c870 to c1100*, Farnham 2010, pp4–5.

[9] DWH Miles and MC Bridge, *Tree-Ring Dating of Chests and Fittings at Westminster Abbey*, English Heritage 2008. I am also indebted to the Abbey's Archivist, Matthew Payne. See also Matthew Payne and Richard Foster, 'The Medieval Sacristy of Westminster Abbey', *Antiquaries Jnl*, vol 100 (2020), p246.

[10] Sherlock, *op cit*, p4.

[11] Metal skippets or small containers to protect seals were a late medieval introduction. See Elizabeth New, *Seals and Sealing Practices*, London 2010, pp23–5.

chests lessened the risk that they might be stolen,[12] but it also made it even harder to locate individual documents inside them.

Two solutions were adopted. One was to modify the design of the chest itself, by fitting it with compartments, each with its own lid or lock. A variant was to fit the chest with a *till*, or small compartment within the main body, in which smaller or more valuable items such as seal matrices could be placed. The other solution was to pack the chest with small boxes, which could be labelled to identify their contents. Sometimes called *scrinie* or *pyxides*, these boxes became common in the late Middle Ages. They were not separately locked, but might have sliding lids with thumb holes, and could also be used singly and independent of any chest.[13] At Norwich, however, the monks eschewed boxes, preferring to fit a row of pegs inside a chest from which bags containing documents could be suspended.[14]

It seems to have been the larger institutions, particularly the monastic ones, that specialised in these comparatively sophisticated arrangements. For lesser but still growing archives, the most common response appears to have been simply to increase the number of chests. In some cases it might suffice to have two, perhaps one for the charters and deeds and the other for the accounts.[15] Elsewhere a common or principal chest might cater for the documents relating to the institution as a whole, with other chests for the records relating to particular properties or officials. It is occasionally possible to track the expansion of an archive by noting the number of chests in use at different periods. Fotheringhay College began in the early fifteenth century with one muniment chest, according to its founder's instructions, but by 1540 it had five.[16]

Around 1300, a new and quite different piece of archival furniture made its appearance – the *armariolum* or cupboard. Like the chest the

[12] For examples of a small chest chained to a wall or to the central pillar of a muniment room, see Lewer and Wall, *op cit*, p19; Aston, *op cit*, p239.

[13] For the boxes at Durham, there called *locelli*, see Alan J Piper, 'Dr Thomas Swalwell, Monk of Durham, Archivist and Bibliophile (d1539)', in James P Carley and Colin GC Tite, eds, *Books and Collectors 1200–1700: Essays Presented to Andrew Watson*, London 1997, p77 (illustr).

[14] Barbara Dodwell, 'The Muniments and the Library', in Ian Atherton *et al*, eds, *Norwich Cathedral: Church, City and Diocese 1096–1996*, London and Rio Grande OH 1996, p330; Steane, *op cit*, p45 (illustr).

[15] Eg, at least to start with, at Merton College, Oxford. JRL Highfield, ed, *The Early Rolls of Merton College, Oxford*, Oxford 1964, pp62–3.

[16] VCH *Northants*, vol 11 (1970), p173.

cupboard was a multi-purpose container, as it still is, but its adaptation for the accommodation of substantial quantities of documents was an important development in record-keeping. In the late thirteenth century the archbishop of Canterbury had such a cupboard, in the priory of St Gregory, Canterbury, where he kept his estate records.[17] In the early 1320s, as described in Chapter 4, Bishop Stapledon had a cupboard built in the Tower of London in connection with the reorganisation of the records there. Neither of these still exists, but from the few later examples that survive it seems that record cupboards belonged to two main types. The first, exemplified by the cupboard still in the former muniment room at Salisbury Cathedral, consisted of a large wooden structure divided into a number of smaller cupboards each with a lockable door.[18] The second type, of which the Windsor Aerary has an example, was a wooden framework creating a number of pigeon holes, without doors.[19]

Armariola of either type could house the same amount of documents as several chests, and could do so more tidily and economically. Instead of chests lying haphazardly around the floor of a muniment room, the cupboard was a more permanent structure, attached firmly to a wall. As long as it was not attached too closely to a *damp* wall it was likely to provide a better atmospheric environment than a chest, as well as an opportunity to arrange records in a more easily accessible way. This in turn could lead to the compilation of more accurate and detailed finding aids, with cross-references to particular divisions of a cupboard or nest of drawers.[20]

Significant as it was, however, the cupboard did not lead to a revolution in record-keeping practice. In many or most cases it did not supersede the chest but co-existed with it. An early

---

[17] Jane E Sayers, 'The Medieval Care and Custody of the Archbishop of Canterbury's Archives', *BIHR*, vol xxxix (1966), pp97, 103.

[18] Tim Tatton-Brown and John Crook, *Salisbury Cathedral: the Making of a Medieval Masterpiece*, rev edn London 2014, pp69–74. The divisions or compartments of a cupboard were sometimes known as *vasa*.

[19] Eleanor Cracknell, 'The Archives', in Nigel Saul and Tim Tatton-Brown, eds, *St George's Chapel, Windsor: History and Heritage*, Stanbridge 2010, pp213–14; Steane, *op cit*, pp38, 46 (illustr).

[20] See eg Sir Francis Palgrave, *The Antient Kalendars and Inventories of the Treasury of His Majesty's Exchequer*, 3 vols London 1836, i.1–155; Clanchy, *op cit*, pp174–9.

nineteenth-century view of the Salisbury muniment room shows chests on the floor as well as the *armariolum*.[21] New statutes promulgated for the collegiate church of St Mary's, Warwick in 1441 refer to a 'nyewe hie almerie', but the 'great old ark' as well as 'certain old cupboards' were to continue in use.[22] Nor was there any consistency in the type of document consigned to the cupboard rather than the chest. In the early fifteenth century the nuns of Syon Abbey (Middlesex) installed a cupboard for their deeds, but retained a large chest for their rolls.[23] A century or so later the cupboards in the muniment room at Magdalen College, Oxford held *pyxides* with evidences for individual properties.[24] The fine cupboard of c1395 in the Westminster Abbey muniment room on the other hand was probably intended for rolls and other documents rather than deed boxes.[25] The introduction of the cupboard coincided with a period when volumes such as registers and act books were beginning to supersede rolls. It was certainly the case that cupboards could be shelved, and that volumes would be happier sitting on shelves than squeezed into chests. But evidence for any significant connection between the two developments appears to be lacking, and the use of open shelves for storing series of minute books and similar volumes was to be a characteristic of the early modern rather than the medieval period.

In the late Middle Ages lay owners of archives seem generally not to have gone in for muniment cupboards. The Pastons relied on a number of coffers and other containers for keeping their evidences, and had periodic difficulties in retrieving the documents that they were looking for.[26] Even a grandee like the Third Duke of Buckingham, when concentrating his archive at Thornbury in the

[21] Tatton-Brown and Crook, *op cit*; Thomas Cocke and Peter Kidson, *Salisbury Cathedral: Perspectives on the Architectural History*, London 1993, p7 and Plate 15. The chests are now displayed in the body of the cathedral.

[22] James Willoughby, 'Inhabited Sacristies', *Antiquaries Jnl*, vol 92 (2012), pp337–8.

[23] R Dunning, 'The Muniments of Syon Abbey', *BIHR*, vol xxxvii (1964), pp103–11.

[24] For Magdalen College, see Robin Darwall-Smith, 'The Muniment Room', in David Roberts, *Hidden Magdalen*, Oxford 2008, pp28–9; Steane, *op cit*, pp47–8 (illustr).

[25] Aston, *op cit*, p242.

[26] For the Pastons, see also Chapter 4, and Norman Davis, ed, *Paston Letters of the Fifteenth Century Vol 1*, Oxford 1971, *passim*. The words coffer and coffin

early sixteenth century, housed it in the traditional manner in six iron-bound chests secured with plate locks, padlocks and strong bolts.[27] Parishes were especially attached to the chest in the late medieval period, and they retain a significant number of examples today. Among them are some that started their existence in private houses. One, at Theydon Garnon (Essex), reached the parish church with family papers still inside it.[28] For the most modest lay archives the equivalent of the chest was the small box, suitable for keeping a few deeds, bonds or wills.[29]

At the other end of the archival scale were the records of central government. Long before the end of the Middle Ages they outgrew the usual chests and cupboards, and *ad hoc* measures were devised to cope in particular with bulky runs of subsidiary records. In the case of Chancery, as described in Chapter 3, this process was already under way in the thirteenth century. The favoured receptacles included skippets (little skips) of turned wood, and hanapers (or hampers), normally a form of woven basket; but the great resource of the record-keeper was the bag or pouch made of canvas or leather. Suitable for documents such as returned writs, or later for paper documents of various sorts, it was labelled with a brief description of its contents and sometimes sealed for greater security. Bundles of documents, bagged or not, were often put away in attics or basements where they could become a prey to damp and neglect. The 'limbo' repository, not to mention the *oubliette,* was to become one of the less attractive features of early modern and modern record-keeping.

(from the Latin *cophina*) were commonly used in the late Middle Ages instead of chest. Coffers were often round-topped.

[27] Carole Rawcliffe, 'A Tudor Nobleman as Archivist: the Papers of Edward, Third Duke of Buckingham', *JSA*, vol 5 (1974–7), p295.

[28] Lewer and Wall, *op cit*, pp20, 208.

[29] In the mid-sixteenth century the deeds for a small Norfolk property were kept in boxes or *pyxides* each holding about twenty-four small deeds. *Ex inf* Dr Anthony Smith.

II

The Age of the Antiquary 1530–1830

Record-keeping is a conservative craft and thrives best in times of peace and stability. In some ways the early modern period was not conducive to good archival practice. It began with the disruption and destruction of the Reformation and the dissolution of the monasteries. They were followed in the next century by the upheavals of the Civil War and Commonwealth. In the period 1700–1830 the country saw the major economic changes of the Industrial Revolution and the emergence of Great Britain as a leading commercial and global power. All three had archival consequences. The machinery of government was reformed; new societies and organisations came into being; business and industry began to create significant quantities of records; and the habit of preserving personal and family archives spread among the prospering middle classes. The influence of the Church diminished, but piety was privatised, with the personal as well as commercial record-keeping habits of many businessmen influenced by their nonconformist allegiances.

Changes in the types of document used for different purposes reflected these developments. Parchment rolls were gradually superseded by paper volumes, and cartularies by deed registers and abstracts of title. Antiquated forms of accounting gave way to double-entry book-keeping; and minute books, entry books and index books became the favoured tools in managing the accumulating papers of large institutional archives.

Nevertheless, the forces of conservatism were not vanquished. The post-medieval Exchequer was outflanked by the Treasury, but it was not abolished, and preserved its time-honoured archival habits into the early nineteenth century. Outside London, diocesan bishops and registrars, cathedral chapters and their clerks, municipal corporations, universities and colleges all continued to follow precedents that in some cases antedated the Reformation. Institutional resistance to change was paralleled by a reluctance on the part of government to interfere with vested interests, both at Westminster and in the country at large.

In one respect, however, the culture of individualism brought some benefit to archives. Interest grew in the study of England's history, and in the absence of official action individual scholars took the initiative in preserving the material and manuscript evidence of the past. Their methods have been criticised, but through their efforts much archival material was preserved that would otherwise have been lost.

The period 1730–1800 can be said to have seen the apogee of archival laissez-faire. In the first three decades of the nineteenth century, however, there was a movement for reform, beginning with the records of the government itself, although its full impact was not felt until after 1830.

6

Dissolution and Reformation 1530–1560

The mid-sixteenth century saw the emergence of patterns of record-keeping that owed little to medieval precedents. Those precedents had been to a considerable degree of monastic origin, but, as shown in Part I, the archival influence of the religious houses had been waning in the late Middle Ages. Nevertheless, the dissolution of the monasteries in the late 1530s was a uniquely catastrophic period in English archival history. It is with that episode that this chapter must begin.

The catastrophe was not intended or planned by the government of the day. Its architect, Thomas Cromwell, understood the value of records, and indeed carefully preserved his own papers.[1] Commissioners were appointed to travel the country in order to close down the monasteries, but also to make provision for their muniments. Local custodians took charge of the archival material that was left on site, presumably what was needed for the continuing administration of the estates that had fallen into the King's hands, but important evidences of title were intended to be sent mainly to London. There a new department of State, the Court of Augmentations, was set up to receive them, and to supervise the exploitation of the confiscated properties until they could be transferred, together with the relevant documents, to their purchasers.

In practice things were not so tidy. The commissioners had to work quickly, increasingly so in the closing months of 1539, and

---

[1] From 1533 he kept his papers in his chamber and in a 'new cowberd'. Dockets on his letters suggest that he stored his correspondence in alphabetical bundles. Michael Everett, *The Rise of Thomas Cromwell: Power and Politics in the Reign of Henry VIII*, New Haven CT and London 2015, p183. For the State Papers, see further below.

the records left *in situ* were not always adequately secured.² At Ulverscroft (Leicestershire), the muniment room was broken into.³ The last abbot of Abingdon is thought to have taken records to his manor of Cumnor.⁴ At Newstead (Nottinghamshire), the monks were said to have consigned their muniments to the bottom of their lake rather than see them fall into sacrilegious hands.⁵

Where documents were left unattended they might be taken away by local people or left to decay in derelict buildings. At Malmesbury (Wiltshire), the monastic site was purchased by a weaver called William Stump who put some of the documents that he found there to mundane practical use in his business, but many years later his great-grandson still had in his possession 'severall old deedes granted to the Lord Abbots with their seals attached'.⁶ Elsewhere, parchments were recycled as book covers, and loose papers used by householders to 'serve their jakes'.⁷ In 1566 Archbishop Parker complained to William Cecil that cartularies and other documents were being exported by 'couetouse statyoners, or spoyled in the potyicarye shopis'.⁸ Later, John Aubrey famously recalled that in his grandfather's day manuscripts had flown about like butterflies.

Not all the records gathered up for preservation were sent to the capital. Some for the Yorkshire houses were transported to

---

² Joyce Youings, *The Dissolution of the Monasteries*, London 1971, *passim*. Particularly heavy losses of documents may reflect the haste with which they were dealt with in late 1539. NR Ker, ed, *Medieval Libraries of Great Britain: a List of Surviving Books*, London (RHS) 1941, pxii.

³ Trevor Foulds, 'Medieval Cartularies', *Archives*, vol xviii (Apr 1987), p10.

⁴ The abbey's steward, who had retained the key to the exchequer house, also helped himself to 'a coffer full of evidences'. Ironically, some documents from these two sources have survived, whereas much else from the abbey muniments has been lost. SE Kelly, ed, *Anglo-Saxon Charters Vol 7: Charters of Abingdon Abbey, Part 1*, London and Oxford (British Academy) 2000, ppxlv–li.

⁵ Foulds, *op cit*, p10. The antiquary Thomas Hearne thought that archival volumes had a better chance of survival than illuminated manuscripts because they were plainer and looked less popish. Theodore Harmsen, *Antiquarianism in the Augustan Age: Thomas Hearne 1678–1735*, Oxford 2000, p196.

⁶ SE Kelly, ed, *Anglo-Saxon Charters Vol 11: Charters of Malmesbury Abbey*, London and Oxford (British Academy) 2006, pp34–41.

⁷ Harmsen, *op cit*, p172; Kelly, *op cit*, p41.

⁸ Quoted in May McKisack, *Medieval History in the Tudor Age*, Oxford 1971, p27.

St Mary's Tower, York, where they were to remain until the tower was blown up during the Civil War.[9] The muniments that did reach Westminster do not appear to have been very systematically looked after. Some archives were dismembered when the estates to which they related were resold. A cellarer's register for Bury St Edmunds, for instance, was broken up so that each purchaser could carry away the relevant quire.[10] What remained in central custody gradually deteriorated into mess and muddle.

Nevertheless, a proportion of these records, albeit a small one, has survived into modern times. Individual documents such as cartularies were rescued by collectors at different periods and eventually found their way into repositories such as the British Library. Archbishop Parker's own collection went to Corpus Christi College, Cambridge. In three areas there are more substantial remains. In the first place eight monastic cathedral priories were replaced by secular cathedral chapters, and in some cases significant quantities of monastic records passed to and remained with the new authorities. Continuity was strongest where the last prior became the first dean, as at Durham. There even the obedientiaries' records survived, although papal privileges were no doubt discarded.[11] It was a similar story at Norwich.[12] At Ely, more was lost, and what was kept was transferred to a 'distinctly insecure vestry',[13] while at Carlisle the entire medieval archive was at some point lost. In five cases the church of the dissolved house became the cathedral church of a new diocese, but in only two, Gloucester and Peterborough, did this ensure the survival of a substantial portion of the muniments. Even at Peterborough there were major losses. Only two of its cartularies passed directly to the new dean

[9] BA English and CBL Barr, 'The Records Formerly in St Mary's Tower, York', *Yorks Arch Jnl*, vol xlii (1967–70), pp198–235, 359–86, 465–518.

[10] Youings, *op cit*, p119; Rodney M Thomson, *The Archives of the Abbey of Bury St Edmunds*, Suffolk Rec Soc, vol xxi (1980), p3.

[11] Michael Stansfield, 'The Archive', in David Brown, ed, *Durham Cathedral: History, Fabric and Culture*, New Haven CT and London 2015, pp423–33; WA Pantin, *Report on the Muniments of the Dean and Chapter of Durham*, pr 1939, p7.

[12] Barbara Dodwell, 'The Muniments and the Library', in Ian Atherton *et al*, eds, *Norwich Cathedral: Church, City and Diocese 1096–1996*, London and Rio Grande OH 1996, pp325–38.

[13] Peter Meadows and Nigel Ramsay, eds, *A History of Ely Cathedral*, Woodbridge 2003, pp261–4.

and chapter. Of another seventeen cartularies or registers still in existence in 1700, eleven had passed into the hands of local families that had acquired abbey estates, and the other six had been widely scattered.[14] Westminster Abbey was a unique case among the ecclesiastical survivals. Although it lost some of its estates and eventually became a collegiate church it retained its royal patronage, and its medieval archive was little disturbed.

Secondly, a number of laymen who purchased or were granted ex-monastic estates also obtained sections of the relevant muniments, either directly or more usually through the Court of Augmentations. Some of the early alienations were to courtiers and senior civil servants, several of whom had themselves been involved in the dissolution process.[15] Not a few of these men founded families and accumulated large estates that survived, together with their archives, down to modern times. The Burton Abbey muniments acquired by William Paget now form part of the Anglesey papers, while the Tavistock Abbey records passed to John Russell and now survive in the Duke of Bedford's family archive.[16] Along with deeds and related material could come substantial runs of manorial documents. William Petre obtained the manor of Ingatestone (Essex), formerly a possession of Barking Abbey: its records from 1279 to 1937 now form part of the Petre papers in Essex Record Office. Court records for several Glastonbury manors were among the abbey muniments carted off by Sir John Thynne to his new house at Longleat.[17] Not all monastic records to be found in present-day family and estate collections, however, arrived there soon after the Dissolution. Some came with later purchases, or as the resulting of collecting activity by a member of the family.

---

[14] Janet D Martin, *The Cartularies and Registers of Peterborough Abbey*, Northants Rec Soc, vol xxviii (1978). Today, of those seventeen volumes, four have been repatriated to Peterborough, nine are in the British Library and two are with the Society of Antiquaries. Two are lost (or were in 1978).

[15] Youings, *op cit*, p130.

[16] HMC, *Principal Family and Estate Collections*, Guides to Sources ... 10 and 11, 2 vols London 1996, 1999, esp nos 18, 79 and 90.

[17] Kate Harris and William Smith, *Glastonbury Abbey Records at Longleat House: a Summary List*, Somerset Rec Soc, vol 81 (1991), pvii. Since the last abbot was attainted the records may have gone to the Surveyor of Land Values rather than the Augmentations Office. Later, Thynne resisted or ignored a demand for their return from Lord Treasurer Winchester. Walter C Richardson, *History of the Court of Augmentations 1536–1554*, Baton Rouge LA 1961, pp134–5.

Thirdly, a significant quantity of monastic documents remains in The National Archives, though scattered through a number of departmental archives or collections.[18] As with those in private possession, however, not all these documents derive directly from the original deposits in the Court of Augmentations. Of the three most substantial groups, those for Syon Abbey and Lewes Priory reached public custody following the attainders of their first lay owners, while those for Llanthony Priory arrived as the result of an early nineteenth-century lawsuit.[19] A few items were handed in by public-spirited people – for instance, the Chertsey Abbey cartulary that Sir Henry Spiller retrieved from Mrs Coggs of Egham in 1653.[20]

* * *

The Reformation's abolition of Purgatory resulted in a second wave of archival destruction in the late 1540s. The Chantries Act of 1547 brought to an end all those colleges and chantries that had been set up to pray for their founders' souls, affecting not only large and wealthy foundations but also smaller ones at local and parish level. But St George's Chapel, Windsor survived, since, like Westminster Abbey, it enjoyed royal patronage, and the major collegiate churches of Manchester and Ripon were also spared. (Southwell was dissolved but re-founded in 1585.) Elsewhere, exceptions were made when the chief purpose of the institution was philanthropic or educational. Thus the Oxford and Cambridge colleges largely avoided drastic change, as did Eton and Winchester. Among the major hospitals, St Leonard's, York was lost, together with its archive, but in London St Bartholomew's was given a new constitution under the Corporation of London, and in Norwich the great hospital of St Giles acquired a further lease of life under the

---

[18] Vanessa Harding, 'Monastic Records and the Dissolution: a Tudor Revolution in the Archives?' *European History Quarterly*, vol 46 (2016), pp482–92; Maureen Jurkowski, 'Monastic Archives in the National Archives', *Archives*, vol xxxii no 116 (Apr 2007), pp1–18.

[19] Jurkowski, *op cit*; R Ian Jack, 'An Archival Case History: the Cartularies and Registers of Llanthony Priory in Gloucestershire', *JSA*, vol 4 (1970–3), pp370–83.

[20] GRC Davis, *Medieval Cartularies of Great Britain: a Short Catalogue*, 2nd edn, ed Claire Breay *et al*, London (BL) 2010, no 753.

auspices of the civic authorities. St Cross Hospital, Winchester and the Ewelme almshouses maintained their independence in the new era. In some cases boroughs took over the properties of chantries and guilds, together with their records.

Even among these fortunate exceptions there were discontinuities in record-keeping. Bart's retained its medieval deeds but not, it seems, its older estate records, while at Norwich St Giles's lost its more recent day books and annual accounts.[21] At Bart's, the new era was marked by the start of new series of minutes and accounts in the late 1540s. In the City some of the livery companies lost properties left for religious uses, but were otherwise able to survive.[22] Whittington's college was abolished, but his charity continued under the Mercers' Company. At Rochester, the charity founded in the late fourteenth century to maintain the Medway bridge continued to fulfil that purpose, but it lost its chapel. In consequence it had to find a new home for its archive, which may account for the gap in its accounts between 1480 and the 1540s.[23]

For the Church, the Reformation meant a period of rapid adaptation to new duties and ways of working, with significant archival implications. The archbishop of Canterbury had new matters to adjudicate, such as faculties (permissions or dispensations), that had previously been referred to Rome. New courts were established, and the trend for the provincial courts (ie those for the province rather than the diocese) to be concentrated at Lambeth rather than at Canterbury was accelerated. Similar though more limited changes affected the province of York. Diocesan bishops were also given more responsibilities to do with licensing and the grant of faculties, and the work of the Church courts increased. As already mentioned, five new dioceses were created, entailing the

---

[21] Nellie JM Kerling, 'Archives', in VC Medvei and John L Thornton, eds, *The Royal Hospital of St Bartholomew 1123–1973*, London 1974, pp299–307; Carole Rawcliffe, *Medicine for the Soul: the Life, Death and Resurrection of an English Hospital, St Giles's, Norwich c1249–1550*, Stroud 1999, pp67–8, 202–7.

[22] CRH Cooper, 'The Archives of the City of London Livery Companies and Related Organisations', *Archives*, vol xvi no 72 (Oct 1984), p351.

[23] Janet M Becker, *Rochester Bridge 1387–1856: a History of its Early Years Compiled from the Warden's Accounts*, London 1930; Nigel Yates and James M Gibson, eds, *Traffic and Politics: the Construction and Management of Rochester Bridge, AD 43–1993*, Woodbridge 1994, p311. The charity received a new Act in 1576, after which its accounts were more regularly kept.

redrawing of boundaries at diocesan and archidiaconal level. The disruption was less when a whole archdeaconry was transferred from one diocese to another, but more when an archdeaconry was divided: a notable case was that of the archdeaconry of Richmond, which was divided between York and the new diocese of Chester.[24] The temporalities of the bishops (their estates and jurisdictions) were also disturbed. Some bishoprics received accessions of ex-monastic property, but Lincoln and Bath and Wells in particular lost estates to the Crown.[25] In the period 1535–60 there were frequent changes of personnel at episcopal level, adding to the difficulties of maintaining good record-keeping.

For many people, however, the Reformation had its greatest impact on the parishes. The parish priest and his chief officers, the churchwardens, survived, and endowments for the church fabric and the maintenance of the poor were in many cases preserved, but the chantries came to an end, together with many parochial guilds. Only very rarely did their archives, or parts of them, remain among the parish records. The changes and uncertainties of the period are reflected in churchwardens' accounts. One authority has commented on the small number that have survived for these years, and 'their often sorry state'.[26] Some parishes achieved a surprising degree of continuity, but they were a small minority.[27]

* * *

At Westminster, the Reformation had an immediate effect on government. The newly created Court of Augmentations was given

---

[24] Pilgrim Trust, Survey of Ecclesiastical Archives, unpublished TS 1951.

[25] Kathleen Major, *A Handlist of the Records of the Bishop of Lincoln and of the Archdeacons of Lincoln and Stow*, Oxford 1953, p106; Phyllis M Hembry, *The Bishops of Bath and Wells 1540–1640: Social and Economic Problems*, London 1967, pp3, 106, 132.

[26] Beat A Kumin, *The Shaping of a Community: the Rise and Reformation of the English Parish c1400–1560*, Aldershot and Brookfield VT 1996, p204; Ronald Hutton, *The Rise and Fall of Merry England: the Ritual Year 1400–1700*, Oxford 1994, pp263–93.

[27] At Morebath (Somerset) the incumbent from 1520 to 1574 carefully preserved the loose churchwardens' accounts, copying them into books. Eamon Duffy, *The Voices of Morebath: Reformation and Rebellion in an English Village*, New Haven CT and London 2001, pp17–19.

its own premises within the Palace in 1537, and twelve presses reinforced with iron, along with bags and strong boxes, were provided for its rapidly accumulating records. The office developed into a fully fledged court of record, and in 1547 acquired a keeper of the records.[28] Other changes were part of a wider process of governmental reform. New offices, with their attendant courts, included a general surveyorship of Crown lands (merged with Augmentations in 1547), an Office of First Fruits and Tenths, to handle sources of ecclesiastical revenue that had previously accrued to the papacy, and a court of Wards and Liveries, to ensure the exploitation of revenues deriving from the feudal rights of the Crown. There was nothing particularly revolutionary, however, about the record-keeping practices of these bodies, derived as they largely were from older precedents.[29] They existed, moreover, alongside the Exchequer, which as ever was resistant to change. William Paulet, appointed Lord Treasurer in 1550, was largely unsuccessful in his efforts to reform it, although he did bring the Court (now Office) of Augmentations under Exchequer control in 1554.[30]

Of greater significance for the development of the royal archive was the extension of conciliar government. The Privy Council took on a more formal role following the fall of Cromwell in 1540, and the registers of its court, which met in the Star Chamber in the palace of Westminster, date from that year.[31] Of even more importance was the development under Henry VIII of functions connected with the royal prerogative. They ranged from the conduct of foreign affairs and the defence of the realm to petitions from individual subjects, and by 1400 had already generated a flow of correspondence large enough to warrant the help of a private secretary. Under Henry VIII, the secretarial role was expanded by Thomas Cromwell, and would eventually develop into a leading department of State. Its correspondence and papers would not be kept at Westminster, however, but at the palace of Whitehall, the former residence of

---

[28] WC Richardson, *Court of Augmentations*, pp91, 153.

[29] WC Richardson, *Tudor Chamber Administration*, Baton Rouge LA 1952, pp396, 407.

[30] David Loades, *The Life and Career of William Paulet (c1475–1572), Lord Treasurer and First Marquess of Winchester*, Aldershot 2008, pp124–9.

[31] JA Guy, *The Court of Star Chamber and its Records to the Reign of Elizabeth I*, London (PRO Handbooks no 21) 1985.

Cardinal Wolsey as archbishop of York that the king had taken over in 1529. One of the founding elements of this archival accumulation, which came to be known as the State Papers, was the personal archive of Cromwell himself, taken into official custody after his fall. Three other large archive-creating bureaucracies that dated their origins from this period were the Council of Marine and the Board of Ordnance, both serving the navy, and the General Post Office.

* * *

It was not only in Westminster and Whitehall that reformation in religion was accompanied by reformation in government. For the counties on England's northern border a new body had already been set up, the Council of the North. It had a council and a court but was not simply an offshoot of central administration: it grew out of the old marcher lordships, and derived some of its powers from the sheriffs and the commissions of the peace. From the archival point of view it is noteworthy that its key series of documents were its registers, indicating a commitment to up-to-date record-keeping.[32]

At county level, an interesting innovation was the passage of an Act in 1536 for the enrolment of deeds (bargains and sales). A few survivals – Somerset has a series that runs from 1536 to 1655 – are among the earliest records in English county council custody today.[33] Of more lasting significance, however, was the introduction of parochial registration, an early use of a primarily religious institution for secular purposes. In 1538 an Act was passed to require the keeping of registers of baptisms, marriages and funerals in every parish. They were to be preserved in the parish church, in a coffer with two locks and keys, one for the priest and the other for the wardens. Their maintenance became the parson's chief record-keeping duty, and he would sometimes add comments to the factual entries. The 1539 Act was followed by a second, and seemingly more effective, one twenty years later. Of 160 parish registers begun in the sixteenth century and on deposit in the

---

[32] See RR Reid, *The King's Council in the North*, London 1921.
[33] Thomas G Barnes, *Somerset 1620–40: a County's Government during the 'Personal Rule'*, London 1961, pp66, 340.

Lincolnshire Archives Office in the early 1970s, only twenty-one started between 1538 and 1557.[34]

* * *

Both the Dissolution and the Reformation had consequences for the way in which country people thought about records and record-keeping. Many would have been aware that a nearby religious house had been replaced by a secular landowner, and that the documents recording their relations with their landlords were no longer kept in a monastic muniment room but in a secular house or office. Not only that: the Reformation demystified documents that had formerly been accorded semi-sacred status. In 1642 a squad of Parliamentary soldiers began to destroy documents in the archive of Peterborough Cathedral under the impression that they were papal bulls, and as such symbols of superstition, although they desisted when told that they were not popish relics but 'the evidences of several Mens estates', in other words deeds affecting property rights.[35] Old beliefs on the other hand could die hard. When in 1626 the men of Haxey, in a somewhat remote corner of Lincolnshire, were trying to defend their common rights against the encroachments of a major drainage project, they remembered that they could produce a relevant charter of 1360 from their parish chest.[36]

---

[34] Lincolnshire Archives Committee, *Archivists' Report no 25* (1973–5), pp94–100.

[35] Janet D Martin, *op cit*, ppxvi–xvii, quoting Simon Gunton's *History of the Church of Peterborough* (1686).

[36] Clive Holmes, *Seventeenth-Century Lincolnshire*, Lincoln 1980, p124; and see also Adam Fox, 'Remembering the Past in Early Modern England: Oral and Written Tradition', *TRHS*, 6th S vol ix (1999), pp233–56.

7

Early Modern Archives 1560–1640

Central Government

If the period 1530–60 had been one of administrative innovation, the succeeding decades of relative stability saw the more consistent adoption of 'modern' methods of record creation, and greater attention to matters of storage and retrieval. Nowhere was this more evident than in Whitehall, and most conspicuously in the arrangements made for keeping those letters and documents that related to matters of State.

By 1600 there was a Principal Secretary of State, but as yet no formal office to support him. As early as 1578, however, it had been thought necessary to appoint a Keeper of the State Papers. In 1592 a 'Discourse touching the Office of Principal Secretary of State' recommended that papers should be made up into bundles on a daily basis and placed in a chest before being consigned to more permanent storage in coffers or cabinets.[1] In 1610 a regular State Paper Office was created, occupying the Holbein Gate and some adjacent rooms at the southern entrance to Whitehall. The immediate impetus was the deposit of part of Lord Salisbury's papers as Secretary, which Sir Thomas Wilson as Keeper spent the next eight years putting into order. The new repository was referred to as a 'library', indicating an intention to get at least some of the papers out of their chests and into bound volumes. It was also intended to retain documents such as treaties that had previously been sent to the Exchequer Treasury, and even to winkle out of the Treasury similar documents for the reign of Henry VIII and transfer them to Whitehall.[2]

---

[1] James Daybell, *The Material Letter in Early Modern England: Manuscript Letters and the Culture and Practice of Letter-Writing 1512–1635*, Plymouth 2012, p8.

[2] *Thirtieth Annual Report of the Deputy Keeper of the Public Records*,

As at Westminster, however, Whitehall was slow to provide purpose-built archival accommodation. The Holbein Gate was not an ideal repository, and the records there were lucky to escape the serious fire that swept through Whitehall in 1619. (They were, however, thrown into confusion when they were 'cast into blankets' during the rescue operation.)[3] Another problem was highlighted by the precedent of the Salisbury papers – the habit of Secretaries of State to keep current papers by them in their private quarters, and to take them home with them when they left office. Wilson and his successors tried on occasion to retrieve them from executors or relatives, but with very mixed success. By 1639, when Sir John Coke ceased to be Secretary, his chamber was full of trunks, baskets and presses of documents. He declared the following year that that he had handed over the greater part of them, but a sizeable residue remained in his hands and later passed to his descendants.[4]

The Court of Star Chamber was another organ of post-Reformation government that had to deal with a burgeoning archive. Its proceedings, like those of Chancery and the Church courts, were based on written pleadings and proofs. By 1608 these had become so bulky that the court itself was fitted with presses to hold them, the documents themselves being placed in buckram or canvas bags tied together with Hungary leather straps. This did not solve the problem of office space, and the clerk of the court had already been obliged to set up an office in Gray's Inn at his own expense.[5]

Chancery had already established itself in premises on the legal fringe of London by 1540, as described in Chapter 4. The proceedings of its court were handled by the Six Clerks, who by 1600 had their

---

Appendix 7: Calendar of Documents Relating to the State Paper Office, London 1869, pp212–93.

[3] SC Lomas, 'The State Papers of the Early Stuarts and the Interregnum', *TRHS*, New S vol xvi (1902), p99.

[4] *Ibid*, pp100, 122; Florence M Greir Evans (CSS Higham), *The Principal Secretary of State: a Survey of the Office from 1558 to 1680*, Manchester 1923, p186n.

[5] Thomas G Barnes, 'The Archives and Archival Problems of the Elizabethan and Early Stuart Star Chamber', *JSA*, vol 2 (1960–4), pp358–9; JA Guy, *The Court of Star Chamber and its Records to the Reign of Elizabeth I*, London (PRO Handbooks no 21) 1985.

Early Modern Archives 1560–1640   103

own office near the Rolls Chapel in Chancery Lane, only to suffer a serious fire there in 1621.[6] The rolls of Chancery meanwhile were piling up in the Chapel itself, and periodic attempts to transfer them to more permanent storage in the Tower of London were not always successful.[7] King's Bench and Common Pleas were able to find overflow accommodation for their court records within the purlieus of Westminster itself. The Abbey's fine Chapter House had become available for other uses at the Dissolution, and after a short period as a meeting place for the Commons it became a record repository in 1547.[8] The House of Lords also found a local home for its archive, in the Jewel Tower that had been erected in the private part of the Palace in the mid-fourteenth century. In the late sixteenth century a room on its middle floor was fitted with a press and a case for the Lords' journals and other records, and in 1621 it was given a brick-vaulted ceiling and a stout iron door that is still *in situ*.[9]

By the late sixteenth century the Exchequer had been accumulating records for over four hundred years. The National Archives are estimated to hold about five thousand linear feet of its records dating from before 1600, and that must represent only a fraction of what once existed.[10] During the latter part of the sixteenth century some improvements were made in its accommodation. In 1565–70 the Court itself on the west side of Westminster Hall and its adjacent offices were rebuilt, the new premises including a record house whose foundation stone was laid by the Queen herself.[11]

---

[6] Henry Horwitz, *Chancery Equity Records and Proceedings 1600–1800: a Guide to Documents in the Public Record Office*, London 1995, p45.

[7] FS Thomas, *Notes of Materials for the History of Public Departments*, printed London 1846, p149.

[8] Elizabeth Hallam Smith, 'The Chapter House as a Record Office', in Warwick Rodwell and Richard Mortimer, eds, *Westminster Abbey Chapter House: the History, Art and Architecture of 'a Chapter House Beyond Compare'*, London (Society of Antiquaries) 2010, pp124–38; Alasdair Hawkyard, 'From Painted Chamber to St Stephen's Chapel: the Meeting Places of the House of Commons at Westminster until 1603', *Parliamentary History*, vol 21 (2001), pp68–9, 77.

[9] Andrew Thrush, 'The House of Lords' Record Repository and the Clerk of the Parliaments' House: a Tudor Achievement', *Parl Hist*, vol 21 pt 3 (2002), pp367–73. I owe this reference to Sir John Sainty.

[10] Edwin Green, 'The Management of Exchequer Records in the 1560s', *JSA*, vol 5 (1974–7), p25.

[11] Mark Collins, 'The Topography of the Old Palace of Westminster 1510–1834', in Warwick Rodwell and Tim Tatton-Brown, eds, *The Art, Architecture and*

But the various departments of which the Exchequer was comprised continued to keep their own records. Two, those of the King's and Lord Treasurer's Remembrancers, migrated to the City, but the rest had to make do with a motley assortment of premises in Westminster itself. Around 1600, the Exchequer of Receipt kept documents of Treasury status near the Exchequer Court, but also in a room next to the Tally Court on the other side of the Hall, in the gatehouse over the way from New Palace Yard to St Margaret's Lane and in the old Chapel of the Pyx.[12]

These important records were not, however, just left to moulder away.[13] In the early seventeenth century an Exchequer official, Arthur Agard (1535/6–1615), undertook some particularly useful archival work. He spent one summer in the Chapter House, bringing the King's Bench writs into order in a series of labelled chests, but his efforts were concentrated in the gatehouse, where he listed a wide variety of documents in the presses and cupboards, distinguishing those receptacles with symbols in chalk.[14] In 1610 he published a *Compendium*, or inventory, in which he drew the essential distinction between the Court and other records in which the king's subjects had a legitimate interest and the *Arcana Imperii*, or documents concerning the royal prerogative and revenues, in which the king had an exclusive interest. It was a distinction especially relevant at a time when the State Paper Office was being established.

Agard's *Compendium* was built on by a later Deputy-Chamberlain of the Exchequer, Scipio Le Squyer (1579–1659), and long remained an influential manual. One section discussed the hazards to which archives were often exposed, and put fire at the top of the list, whereas a medieval archivist would probably have

---

Archaeology of the Royal Abbey and Palace of Westminster, 2 vols Leeds 2015, ii.216, 228.

[12] Thomas, *op cit*, p155. Of these the least used by 1600 was the Chapel of the Pyx: the last treaty deposited there was in 1624. PRO *Lists and Indexes*, vol xlix (1923).

[13] I owe this point to Dr Hallam Smith.

[14] Hallam Smith, 'The Chapter House as a Record Office'; Sir Francis Palgrave, *The Antient Kalendars and Inventories of the Treasury of His Majesty's Exchequer*, 3 vols London 1836, ii.311–35; F Taylor, ed, 'An Early Seventeenth-Century Calendar of Records Preserved in Westminster Palace Treasury', *Bulletin of the John Rylands Library*, vol 23 no 1 (Apr 1939).

put water. He advocated fireproof vaults for repositories, and the careful observance of rules regarding naked candle flames. But it was also important to check record stores for any ingress of water after heavy falls of snow or rain, and to dry out any damaged documents slowly rather than put them too close to a fire. Chests and presses should be regularly checked for rodent infestation. Finally, he reminded his readers of the losses incurred when documents were misplaced, or lent out and not returned.

Local Government

During this period the work that local officials were asked to do on behalf of the central government greatly increased. In the late sixteenth century a new officer appeared, the lord lieutenant, with responsibility for the defence of his county. He had a clerk to assist him, but little or no trace of his activities survives locally in official custody. Occasionally, however, evidence may survive in a family archive. The Duke of Northumberland's, for instance, contains an entry book for the Earl of Hertford's lieutenancy of Wiltshire and Somerset for 1603–8.[15]

For matters of civil administration, the government relied for the most part on the existing local machinery. The office of sheriff, and the hundredal structure that underpinned it, were in decline, but the royal government made increasing use of the justices of the peace, particularly in Poor Law and vagrancy matters. The justices were unpaid, but they had the services of a salaried clerk, although he was appointed not by them but by the Custos Rotulorum of the county.[16] The principal duty of the clerk of the peace, or clerk of the county, was to keep the records of the court of quarter sessions, but he also had registration or enrolment responsibilities under specific pieces of legislation. In fact some of the earliest surviving county records relate to that function. The enrolments of deeds in Somerset has already been mentioned. Slightly later is the first minute book or notebook of the clerk of the peace for Wiltshire, covering the

---

[15] WPD Murphy, ed, *The Earl of Hertford's Lieutenancy Papers*, Wilts Rec Soc, vol xxxii (1969).

[16] HC Johnson, 'The Origin and Office of Clerk of the Peace', in Sir Edgar Stephens, *The Clerks of the Counties 1360–1960*, 1961, pp29–47. Later it was customary to hold the office of Custos with the lord lieutenancy.

years 1563 and 1574–92, which is partly a register of badgers, or corn dealers, under an Act of 1562/3.[17]

County record-keeping seems to have improved from the 1590s, possibly encouraged by directives from the Privy Council. For Somerset, there are indictment rolls from 1602 and order books from 1613, while for Staffordshire the first entry (or minute) book begins in 1619.[18] But in general the survival rate for pre-1640 records is poor.[19] The county magistrates were usually peripatetic, and the ratepayers were reluctant to spend money on sessions houses. Much therefore depended on the attitudes of individual clerks of the peace. William Lambarde (1536–1601), lawyer, archivist and historian of Kent, published in 1581 a manual for country justices entitled *Eirenarcha*, in which he recommended that the clerk should keep his records in 'some special and proper roome under safe custodie, and not without an Inventorie (or Register)'.[20] He was aware, nevertheless, how easily county records could go astray. Clerks often kept them at home, and when they died their widows, servants or executors might 'embezzle, conceal or misuse what they will'.[21]

At parish level, the magistrates had to rely on another group of unpaid officers. Surveyors of highways were appointed from 1555, and overseers of the poor from 1597. Their accounts and papers have survived for very few parishes for the years before 1640, although their work may occasionally be documented in churchwardens' accounts.[22] More substantial are the records of those local drainage authorities the Commissions of Sewers, established under an Act of 1531 and owing something in their procedures and

---

[17] HC Johnson, ed, *Minutes of Proceedings in Sessions 1563 and 1574–92*, Wilts Arch and Nat Hist Soc Records Branch, vol iv (1948), ppxv–xvi.

[18] Thomas G Barnes, *Somerset 1625–40: a County's Government during the 'Personal Rule'*, London 1961, pp66, 340; SC Newton, 'Staffordshire Quarter Sessions: Archives and Procedure in the Earlier 17th Century', in NW Greenslade, ed, *Essays in Staffordshire History Presented to SAH Burne*, Staffs Rec Soc Collections, 4th S vol vi (1970), pp66–85.

[19] See FG Emmison and Irvine Gray, *County Records*, London (Historical Assoc) 1948, pp28–32.

[20] Quoted in G Herbert Fowler, *The Care of County Muniments*, London 1923.

[21] Quoted in HC Johnson, *Minutes*, pxiv.

[22] See, for instance, Lincs Archives Committee, *Archivists' Report 1957–8*, pp55–6.

documentary forms to both parochial and manorial practice. The East Lindsey courts of sewers preserved their laws and dikereeves' accounts from soon after 1560 and their minutes from 1626.[23]

* * *

For many towns the early modern period was one of expansion, and this is reflected in the growing quantity of documentation that they produced. Some boroughs were of course of medieval origin, but others were created after 1540, and had to start their archival traditions from scratch. As described in Chapter 6, some boroughs took over hospitals and educational charities, and those corporations that had commissions of the peace found their responsibilities increasing like those of their counterparts in the shires. In the City of London the seventeenth century saw the minutes of Common Council and its committees become the Corporation's key series of documents.[24] At Bristol, rentals for the city's properties were started in 1561, and the minutes of its Common Council were preserved from 1598.[25] Smaller places were less forward-looking, but their very conservatism fostered habits of record-keeping. Warwick began its Black Book, or general register, in the reign of Elizabeth, and was still referring to it in the eighteenth century.[26]

Unlike the counties, some at least of the boroughs were prepared to adapt old premises for record storage or even provide new ones. At Bristol, the former chapel in the guildhall was converted to a repository for deeds and papers under the care of the Chamberlain.[27] At Sandwich, the town's new premises, built in 1577, incorporated

---

[23] AEB Owen, 'Land Drainage Authorities and their Records', *JSA*, vol 2 (1960–4), pp417–23. The records were kept in chests in the church porches of Louth, Alford and Spilsby.

[24] See Philip E Jones and Raymond Smith, *A Guide to the Records in the Corporation of London Record Office and the Guildhall Library Muniment Room*, London 1951.

[25] N Dermott Harding, 'The Archives of the Corporation of Bristol', *Trans Bristol and Gloucs Arch Soc*, vol lxviii (1926), pp238, 227–49, *passim*.

[26] EG Tibbits, *Ancient Records of Warwick*, Dugdale Soc Occasional Papers no 5 (1938), p3.

[27] Dermott Harding, *op cit*, pp234, 239.

an inner room behind the council chamber, probably used as a treasury, with further accommodation for records in the attics.[28] Exeter acquired a new council house in 1593.[29] Smaller boroughs, however, managed with less extensive accommodation. In the mid-sixteenth century the principal repository for Great Yarmouth's municipal archive was a hutch in the parish church, and the same was true at Grantham a hundred years later.[30]

By the late sixteenth century the need for finding aids, together with growing antiquarian interest in the older records, was resulting in useful archival work in some boroughs. At Exeter, the historian John Hooker, or Vowell, who was also the City's Chamberlain, arranged and listed its records, provided lockable presses for them and made rules for their protection.[31] In the City of London the Town Clerk employed an official, Robert Smith, to compile an impressive series of transcripts, calendars and indexes over a period of thirty years from 1580.[32] At Yarmouth, the archive was muddled, and some of the documents removed, by the antiquary Thomas Damet in the 1590s; but order was restored by a fellow antiquary, Henry Manship, in 1612–13, and the muniments were moved to a room under the guildhall in 1638.[33]

---

[28] Helen Clarke *et al*, *Sandwich, the 'Completest Medieval Town in England': a Study of the Town and Port from its Origins to 1600*, Oxford and Oakville, Ontario 2010, p244.

[29] See Peter Clark and Paul Slack, *English Towns in Transition 1500–1700*, London 1976.

[30] Paul Rutledge, 'Archive Management at Great Yarmouth since 1540', *JSA*, vol 3 (1965–9), pp89–91; Andy Wood, 'Tales from the Yarmouth Hutch: Civic Identities and Hidden Histories in an Urban Archive', in Liesbeth Corens *et al*, eds, *The Social History of the Archive: Record-Keeping in Early Modern Europe*, Oxford (*Past and Present* Supplement 11) 2016, p217 (illustr); John B Manterfield, ed, *Borough Government in Newton's Grantham: the Hall Book of Grantham 1649–1662*, Lincoln Rec Soc, vol 106 (2016), px.

[31] May McKisack, *Medieval History in the Tudor Age*, Oxford 1971, p93; WJ Harte *et al*, eds, *[Hooker's] Description of the Citie of Excester*, Trans Devon and Cornwall Rec Soc, 2 vols Exeter 1919, ii.2.

[32] Piers Cain, 'Robert Smith and the Reform of the Records of the City of London 1586–1623', *JSA*, vol 13 no 1 (1987–8), pp13–16.

[33] Rutledge, *op cit*.

The Church of England

After 1560 a number of English diocesan archives began to acquire a range and solidity that had previously been lacking. The trend was perhaps most notable in the area of court and visitation records. In the diocese of Lincoln, for instance, parish register transcripts are preserved from 1561, churchwardens' presentments mainly from 1570 and glebe terriers (surveys of the property belonging to the living) from 1577.[34] It is a similar story in the diocese of Ely.[35] Good practice in records management was encouraged through archiepiscopal and diocesan injunctions, notably those of Matthew Parker as archbishop of Canterbury from 1559 until his death in 1575.[36] Nor should the contemporary interest in Church history be ignored as a factor, with the foundation of Lambeth Palace Library by Archbishop Bancroft in 1610 an important landmark.

Some dioceses on the other hand have serious gaps in their archives for this period. Bishops continued to travel round their dioceses with their registers, sometimes losing them on the way.[37] Lincoln, otherwise so well provided with post-Reformation records, has gaps in its series of bishops' registers for Elizabeth's reign, though perhaps through the fault of negligent registrars rather than that of the bishops themselves. *Lacunae* for the early seventeenth century for Bath and Wells, however, may reflect not only the failings of registrars but also the effects of the upheavals of the 1640s and 50s, of which more in the next chapter.[38]

By 1560 the older secular cathedrals had very well-established patterns of record-keeping, and the new cathedrals and those previously administered by priories followed along the same archival lines. They were given statutes specifying among other things that they should create 'common treasuries', with two

---

[34] See Kathleen Major, *A Handlist of the Records of the Bishop of Lincoln and of the Archdeacons of Lincoln and Stow*, Oxford 1953.

[35] Dorothy Owen, *Ely Records: a Handlist of the Records of the Bishop and Archdeacon of Ely*, [1971].

[36] For the Canons of 1603, see Dorothy Owen, *The Records of the Established Church in England, excluding Parochial Records*, London (BRA Archives and the User no 1) 1970, p20.

[37] *Ibid*, p13.

[38] Phyllis M Hembry, *The Bishops of Bath and Wells 1540–1640: Social and Economic Problems*, London 1967, pp3, 106, 132.

110 *English Archives*

rooms, an outer one for current records and an inner one in which to keep a chest with three locks for the charters and muniments of title. Norwich acquired such a treasury in 1567, with a minor canon to act as archivist.[39] As with the dioceses, deans and chapters were reminded from time to time to be vigilant in archival matters, ensuring that their lease registers were properly maintained or that temporary withdrawals of documents were recorded in a loans book. It cannot, of course, be assumed that such guidelines were consistently followed: in fact injunctions may sometimes have been issued in response to cases of neglect.

Charitable Foundations

From the mid-sixteenth century many charities were founded in order to fill gaps left by the Dissolution. Some were small parochial ones, such as a bequest to provide an annual distribution of loaves to poor widows, and these generated few records. Others were substantial organisations, involving the management of large estates or sums of money. They were created by will or by a deed of gift and were run by a body of trustees or governors, whose powers and duties might be confirmed by letters patent, a Chancery decree or even an Act of parliament. As with a medieval foundation charter, these documents might prescribe not only how the charity should be run but what records it should keep. The archive of the London Charterhouse, founded by Thomas Sutton in 1613, includes numerous deeds and papers for its estates in London and elsewhere and a set of governors' minutes from 1613.[40] On a smaller scale was Whitgift's almshouse and school at Croydon, whose archive includes governors' minutes and accounts from 1599, statutes of 1600 and deeds and legal papers for its properties in and around Croydon.[41]

Those medieval colleges concerned with education that had survived the Reformation remained attached to old record-keeping practices well into the early modern era. At St John's College, Cambridge the muniments were governed by statutes promulgated

---

[39] Barbara Dodwell, 'The Muniments and the Library', in Ian Atherton *et al*, eds, *Norwich Cathedral: Church, City and Diocese 1096–1996*, London and Rio Grande OH 1996, p331.

[40] Oxford, Bodleian Library Tanner MS 161; NRA 1104, 7252.

[41] FHG Percy, *Whitgift School, a History*, Croydon 1991, pp23–44; NRA 13902.

Early Modern Archives 1560–1640 111

in the late Middle Ages, and its bursar's rolls were kept up alongside the more accessible volumes of accounts until 1770.⁴² At Winchester College, the annual accounts and the court rolls were changed to volume form in 1556, but the main headings of the accounts did not change between 1394 and 1865.⁴³

As elsewhere, however, the early seventeenth century saw some marked improvements in the care and cataloguing of college archives. At Magdalen, Oxford, where the muniments had got into some disorder by 1600, a new catalogue was prepared around 1611, listing some thirteen thousand deeds.⁴⁴ At Corpus Christi, Oxford, Brian Twyne arranged the deeds in the muniment room by place and county, built a nest of drawers in which to store them and provided a thirty-volume 'cartulary' or calendar and location guide.⁴⁵ He went on to reorganise the Oxford University archive, arranging the muniments in specially designed drawers and pigeon holes, and producing an admirable finding aid.⁴⁶ His twentieth-century successor at both Corpus and the University Archives, Trevor Aston, has described him as 'perhaps the greatest archivist England has ever produced'.⁴⁷ Nevertheless, he was building on much previous practice. Gone were the old chests, but the new presses, although they had lockable doors, were not that different from, say, the furniture installed in the Magdalen College muniment room more than a century before. The university muniment room itself followed the traditional practice, in being placed in the tower of the new Schools Quadrangle. At Cambridge at the same period the registrar of the university was presiding over a growing mass of recent records, reflecting an increase in university business and its

---

⁴² Malcolm Underwood, 'The Defences of a College: the Law's Demands and Early Record Keeping in St John's College, Cambridge', in Ralph Evans, ed, *Lordship and Learning: Studies in Memory of Trevor Aston*, Woodbridge 2004, pp225–34.

⁴³ John H Harvey, 'Winchester College Muniments', *Archives*, vol v no 28 (Mich 1962), pp201–9.

⁴⁴ CM Woolgar, 'Two Oxford Archives in the Early Seventeenth Century', *Archives*, vol xvi no 71 (Apr 1984), pp258–72.

⁴⁵ Trevor Aston, 'Muniment Rooms and their Fittings in Medieval and Early Modern England', in Evans, *op cit*, p243.

⁴⁶ *Ibid*, p246; Reginald L Poole, *A Lecture on the History of the University Archives*, Oxford 1912, pp20, 30–100; information from Simon Bailey and Anna Petre of the University Archives.

⁴⁷ Aston, *op cit*, p245.

secularisation, but the older muniments, under the control of the vice-chancellor and proctors, remained in chests in the chapel near the Divinity School.[48]

The Archives of Landed Society

During the early modern era the great landowners retained their dominant position, under the Crown, in English society, and their archives continued to form a major element in lay record-keeping. But as they evolved from feudal magnates into more business-like landlords they ceased to be served by officials such as receivers, bailiffs and manorial reeves, and instead retained solicitors, agents, accountants and surveyors. These new men produced new kinds of document. Instead of charters and cartularies, muniment rooms filled with conveyances such as bargains and sales, and with deed registers, schedules and abstracts of title.[49] Wills and marriage settlements grew ever longer and more elaborate.[50] Estate archives began to feature more detailed surveys and maps, and bulkier series of rentals and accounts, counterpart leases, tenancy agreements and bundles of correspondence.

By 1640, however, the transformation had not proceeded very far. From the late sixteenth century estate surveys were sometimes accompanied by handsome maps, drawn to scale by professional surveyors such as John Norden. But in the 1620s the ninth earl of Northumberland was still presiding over a decidedly old-fashioned estate. He employed a 'solicitor' to keep track of his expenses, and retained lawyers in the courts, but he also kept a close personal eye on his affairs. He had been a prisoner in the Tower for some years, and while there had spent much time reducing his surveys, 'plotts of manors' and other records to order.[51] Nor was he unusual

---

[48] Heather E Peek and Catherine P Hall, *The Archives of the University of Cambridge: an Historical Introduction*, Cambridge 1962, pp6–20.

[49] There are few secular cartularies later than 1540. See GRC Davis, *Medieval Cartularies of Great Britain: a Short Catalogue*, 2nd edn, ed Claire Breay *et al*, London (BL) 2010.

[50] See John Habakkuk, *Marriage, Debt and the Estate System: English Landownership 1650–1950*, Oxford 1994.

[51] ME James, ed, *Estate Accounts of the Earls of Northumberland 1562–1637*, Surtees Soc, vol clxiii (1948).

in this attention to detail. Sir Edward Coke at Gostwick (Norfolk) and Thomas Brudenell at Deene (Northamptonshire) were both assiduous copyists and arrangers of their estate papers.[52] Brudenell was an antiquary as well as a man of business and saw his record-keeping as part of a family tradition of caring, in his brother Edward's words, 'for the advancement of their house and the continuing of their manors, lands and possessions in their name'.[53]

Great landowners could also take pride in the proper housing of their archives. Writing probably in the 1630s, Richard Braithwaite, in his *Rules and Orders for the Government of the House of an Earl*, considered that a nobleman should have 'more care of the safe-keeping of his evidences than either of his plate or jewels'. His strong-room should be constructed of brick or stone, with an iron-plated door, and be furnished with a cupboard of labelled drawers for the deeds, 'standards' (chests) for the surveys, accounts and court rolls, and a table at which to work.[54] Between 1604 and 1609 the ninth earl of Northumberland had built a free-standing evidence room at Syon House, his seat near London. At his death three decades later it contained 'two great boxes [presses or chests of drawers?] to put writings in; one table; a carpett; two stools; [and] three ould chests'.[55]

When, back in the mid-sixteenth century, Sir William Sharington acquired Lacock Abbey in Wiltshire, and with it a tranche of its monastic archive, he built a muniment tower in a corner of the old cloister: the unusual stone fittings of its muniment room can still be seen today. Elsewhere, however, it is not always easy to tell where in the grander newly built Elizabethan houses the muniment room was situated, especially where, as at Longleat, subsequent alterations have obscured the original interior arrangements. Perhaps the

---

[52] Robert FW Smith, 'Sir Edward Coke's Collection of Knowledge: the Inception of the Holkham Archive', *Archives*, vol li nos 132–3 (Apr–Oct 2016), pp1–7; Mary E Finch, *The Wealth of Five Northamptonshire Families 1540–1640*, Northants Rec Soc, vol xix (1956), p208.

[53] Quoted in Joan Wake, *The Brudenells of Deene*, London 1953, p90.

[54] Richard Braithwaite, *Rules and Orders for the Government of the House of an Earl*, pr 1821.

[55] GR Batho, ed, *The Household Papers of Henry Percy, Ninth Earl of Northumberland (1564–1632)*, Camden 3rd S , vol xciii (1962), ppl–li; information kindly supplied by Christopher Hunwick, Archivist to the Duke of Northumberland.

most likely position was near the private family apartments, as in the well-preserved example at Hardwick Hall (Derbyshire).[56] Some great landowners made their London houses their archival headquarters. In the mid-sixteenth century Protector Somerset would no doubt have had a muniment room at Somerset House, possibly in the gatehouse that fronted the Strand. At various dates Salisbury, Dorset and Essex (formerly Leicester) Houses all had muniment rooms. The gentry did not normally have town houses, and on small country estates the arrangements for record-keeping would have been much more modest, if not sometimes inadequate. In the 1620s one Warwickshire squire kept his evidences in a large trunk, where visiting antiquaries found them 'utterly rotted with wett and rayne'.[57]

Business Archives

Early modern England was full of small businessmen – merchants, tradesmen, craftsmen, farmers and shopkeepers – who must have kept records of some kind, perhaps a volume of miscellaneous accounts and memoranda, but unsurprisingly these have mostly failed to survive. At a more sophisticated level merchants might keep volumes of a more specific type – ledgers containing accounts with individual customers and day books or journals recording transactions as they occurred. For John Smythe, a successful Bristol merchant, we have a ledger, for Sir Thomas Gresham, the eminent London financier, a day book. For the merchant adventurer Thomas Lawrence we have both a ledger and part of a journal.[58] Especially where a mercantile business became a family concern it would have been necessary to keep correspondence and related documents, but I know of no example for the period 1560–1640 to compare with the Cely papers described in Chapter 4.

---

[56] The muniment room at Hardwick Hall is no longer in use but retains its furniture of more than 400 drawers.

[57] Philip Styles, *Sir Simon Archer 1581–1662*, Dugdale Soc Occasional Papers no 6 (1946), p48.

[58] Jean Vanes, ed, *The Ledger of John Smythe 1538–1550*, Bristol Rec Soc, vol xxviii (1975); AC Littleton and BS Yamey, *Studies in the History of Accounting*, London 1956, pp197–8. Gresham's volume is preserved among the records of the Mercers' Company.

Merchants had their counting houses in which to keep their accounts and business papers. One such was Robert Lee's office in Leadenhall Street in the City of London, which in 1607 had a door with a double plate lock with three keys, and inside the room a set of six shelves, a nest of three boxes at the window and a square table covered with buckram with five more boxes underneath it.[59] But stray documents from such places are likely to have survived only if they ended up among the records of a court of law, or if they happened to pass down in the family of the creator. In the case of John Smythe, he built a country house outside Bristol, where his ledger was placed in the muniment room and became part of the family archive.

By 1607 Leadenhall Street also housed a nascent business archive on a totally different scale. The East India Company was destined to expand, along with its archive, until it was eventually transformed into a government department. Its principal series of records were the minutes of its Court of Directors, its accounts and correspondence, and copies of the papers generated by its branches in India. As the Company's interests and responsibilities grew, its archive was bulked out by papers transmitted from India to East India House, sent in duplicate or triplicate in case they were lost in transit, and, at the London end, by growing heaps of financial, staff and shipping records.[60]

The Personal Archive

In the Middle Ages writing had been a predominantly clerical occupation. Letters might be signed and sealed by high-status individuals, but they normally had others to write or fair-copy them. In the period 1560–1640 a number of magnates continued to employ secretaries. It has been estimated that over one-third of the letters sent by Elizabeth Hardwick, Countess of Shrewsbury, were written by a secretary or 'bear the signs of collaborative

---

[59] John Schofield, *Medieval London Houses*, New Haven CT and London 1994, pp233–5. Buckram, a coarse and stiffened cloth, had long been used for bags to contain documents.

[60] Antonia Moon, 'Destroying Records, Keeping Records: Some Practices at the East India Company and the India Office', *Archives*, vol xxxiii no 119 (Oct 2008), pp114–25.

authorship'.⁶¹ But by the early seventeenth century more people were writing their own letters. Literacy was more common among both men and women, and letter-writing became a literary occupation as well as a business necessity. One study has identified well over three thousand manuscript letters by more than 650 women writers between 1540 and 1603.⁶² Even that seemingly driest of documents, the account book, could take on a more personal character. Joyce Jeffreys, an elderly gentlewoman living in Hereford, kept an account book covering the years 1638 to 1648. It has elements of an estate book, a business record and a household account, but it also tells us something of her character, and how she wished to be remembered.⁶³

Letter-writing was a serious matter, and the paper that it used was still expensive, so it is not surprising that letters were valued and carefully kept. Aristocratic men and women had writing desks in their chambers, and for those with extensive political, business and personal correspondence Richard Braithwaite recommended a closet where a secretary could keep the papers in order.⁶⁴ The ninth earl of Northumberland had such a closet at Petworth, where he kept 'a wainscot box with mappes and other writings in it'.⁶⁵ In the long run, however, the survival of such papers depended on the formation of a family archive and its transmission from generation to generation. Some families, such as the Cecils at Hatfield, established a record-keeping tradition that has continued to the present day. In that case the habits established by William, Lord Burghley and Robert, Lord Salisbury were the formative influence, but matriarchs could also influence succeeding generations, as did Lady Shrewsbury (Bess of Hardwick) and Lady Ann Clifford. At a more modest level of society, Joyce Jeffreys's account book passed with her house in Hereford to her nephew and then to her great-nephew, who at the end of the seventeenth century was keeping it in a drawer under his 'scrittore' or writing desk in his lower study. Later it descended to the Winnington family of Stanford Court

---

⁶¹ James Daybell, *Women Letter-Writers in Tudor England*, Oxford 2006, p2.

⁶² *Ibid*, p5.

⁶³ Judith M Spicksley, ed, *The Business and Household Accounts of Joyce Jeffreys, Spinster of Hereford 1638–48*, Oxford (British Academy) 2012.

⁶⁴ Arnold Hunt, 'The Early Modern Secretary and the Early Modern Archive', in Liesbeth Corens *et al*, *Archives and Information in the Early Modern World*, Oxford 2018, pp116–17.

⁶⁵ Daybell, *The Material Letter*, p220.

(Worcestershire), from whom it was acquired by the British Museum in 1932.[66] Occasionally a family diary or genealogical record would be started by one member of the family and maintained by his successors. A volume of this kind initiated by William Lambarde remained in use in his family until 1868.[67]

The Antiquaries

The years 1560 to 1640 saw a burgeoning of interest in English history, topography and archaeology. It was an interest, moreover, concerned not with the perpetuation of myth or legend but with the careful examination and recording of evidence from the past. The great jurist and antiquary John Selden (1584–1654) praised the herald and archivist Augustine Vincent (c1584–1626) for his illumination of 'the more abstruse parts of history which lie hid, either in private manuscripts, or in the publick records of the kingdom'.[68] This more rigorous approach was contrasted by Lambarde with the efforts of the medieval chroniclers – 'the fond dreames of doting Monkes and fabling Frears'.[69] Among the consequences of the Dissolution and Reformation was a concern among Church historians to justify the Elizabethan settlement, but also an awareness that the Dissolution had damaged or destroyed an enormous quantity of medieval documents. A further consequence, already touched on in this chapter, was a growing interest among landed families in their ancestry and in the counties and neighbourhoods where they lived and owned estates. It was an interest sedulously fostered by the College of Arms, which was refounded on a more secure footing in the mid-1550s, with permanent premises (that it still occupies) in the former Derby House near St Paul's Cathedral.

The Elizabethan and Jacobean antiquaries explored and exploited a wide range of archival sources, from the records in the Exchequer, Tower and State Paper Office to collections in the hands of boroughs, colleges and private owners. In the mid-1580s a

---

[66] Spicksley, *op cit*.

[67] See William Matthews, *British Diaries: an Annotated Bibliography of British Diaries Written between 1442 and 1942*, Berkeley CA and London 1950.

[68] Quoted in Daniel Woolf, *The Social Circulation of the Past: English Historical Culture 1530–1730*, Oxford 2003, p366.

[69] Quoted in McKisack, *op cit*, p136.

118   *English Archives*

number of scholars and others came together to form a Society of Antiquaries that remained in existence until 1608. It was supported by William Cecil, and its membership included men such as Arthur Agard and Sir Robert Cotton (for whom see below). The influence of antiquarian studies was destined to exert an influence on English archival history that lasted throughout the early modern period.

One way in which this influence was exercised has already been noted in this chapter – the work of antiquaries as official custodians of archives. The activities of Agard and Le Squyer at the Exchequer was paralleled at the Tower by that of William and Robert Bowyer and Henry Elsynge. But antiquaries also kept their own papers, including their correspondence with fellow scholars and notes and transcripts relating to their own publications. Perhaps of equal or greater value in the longer term were the original manuscripts that they garnered from archival sources during their work. They were not always scrupulous in their borrowings or meticulous in recording details of provenance, but through their activities much was preserved for posterity that would otherwise have been lost.[70]

This material included cartularies and charters from monastic sources, as already noted, but also 'strays' from the public records. The greatest collector of the age was Sir Robert Cotton (1571–1631), who managed to acquire not only a large number of cartularies but many important documents such as the charter with which this book begins and two of the four known exemplifications of Magna Carta. He alarmed Sir Thomas Wilson of the State Paper Office and others by his acquisitiveness, yet he was careful to provide for the future survival of his collection and to make it available to other scholars.[71] Another important bequest, already noted, was that of Archbishop Parker's collection of over four hundred manuscripts to his Cambridge college, Corpus Christi. Other antiquaries passed documents to each other, or to their own descendants, and many items appeared in the salerooms at some point in their life cycles,

---

[70] For the surviving papers of antiquaries generally, see HMC Guides to Sources for British History 12: *Papers of British Antiquaries and Historians*, London 2003.

[71] For Cotton and his library, see eg Colin GC Tite, *Catalogue of the Manuscripts in the Cottonian Library 1696*, Cambridge 1984; Colin GC Tite, *The Panizzi Lectures 1993: the Manuscript Library of Sir Robert Cotton*, London 1994; CJ Wright, ed, *Sir Robert Cotton as Collector: Essays on an Early Stuart Courtier and his Legacy*, London 1997.

Early Modern Archives 1560–1640 119

but a large number eventually found homes in repositories such as the Bodleian Library, Lambeth Palace Library, the College of Arms or the library of one of the Inns of Court, while many more, including Sir Robert Cotton's manuscripts, came to rest in the British Museum.

8

Civil War, Commonwealth and Protectorate 1641–1660

The period 1641–60 was unsurprisingly one of change, uncertainty and disruption in English record-keeping, not to mention archival loss and destruction. At the same time it was one of innovation and creativity, and this was particularly true of the records of government. The early part of the Civil War (1642–3) was certainly disruptive, with rival governments set up in London and Oxford, but from 1644 Parliament established a new system, headed by a Committee of Both Kingdoms that met at Derby House until 1648 to direct the conduct of the war, while various parliamentary committees dealt with specific financial and other matters.

Fortunately, Parliament believed in the importance of good record-keeping: indeed Sir John Coke had claimed for it the status of a court of record. Documentary evidence was crucial in its constitutional battles with the king, but Parliament also emphasised the right of access to the public records by individual subjects for legal purposes.[1] Although some of the older departments of State such as the Exchequer were sidelined, they were not (with the exceptions shortly to be noted) abolished, and their records, though not accorded much attention, were not badly neglected.[2] Parliament set up a Committee for the Safe-keeping of the Records, and in October 1643 appointed Selden to look after the records in the Tower. In 1647 there was even a proposal to create a general

---

[1] Kate Peters, '"Friction in the Archives": Access and the Politics of Record-Keeping in Revolutionary England', in Liesbeth Corens *et al*, *Archives and Information in the Early Modern World*, Oxford 2018, pp169–72.

[2] Cromwell revived the Exchequer in 1654. Henry Roseveare, *The Treasury: the Evolution of a British Institution*, London 1969, pp169–72.

repository for governmental archives, anticipating by two hundred years the creation of the Public Record Office.[3]

Unsurprisingly, however, given wartime exigencies, there were losses and failures. The Court of Star Chamber was abolished in 1641, and the subsequent history of its records is a good illustration of the dangers to which an archive is exposed when the body that created it has no heir or successor. The court papers kept in the Chamber itself were transferred to the Westminster Chapter House, but those kept by the clerk of the court in his Gray's Inn office, including the main series of bound volumes, were moved to a house in St Bartholomew's Close, perhaps in the late 1640s, and subsequently lost sight of.[4] The archive of the Council of the North, abolished in the same year, had almost completely vanished by 1700.[5] The Court of Wards and Liveries came to an end in 1645, and for some decades its records languished in a leaky attic near Westminster Hall before being moved to the Chapter House in 1732.[6]

Outside London and Westminster it was the records of the Church of England that were most affected by the rule of Parliament. Episcopacy was abolished in 1646, and committees were appointed to deal with the appointment, supervision and payment of parochial ministers.[7] There were breaks in the continuity of parish record-keeping, especially where there were changes of incumbent. At diocesan level, the bishops' estates passed into parliamentary hands, and episcopal muniments were transferred to London. There a 'register' or registrar was appointed to keep them in order, but they were stored in unsatisfactory conditions and became increasingly muddled. They were joined by muniments from the cathedrals when deans and chapters too were abolished, in 1649.[8]

---

[3] FS Thomas, *Notes of Materials for the History of Public Departments*, printed London 1846, pp124, 141.

[4] Thomas G Barnes, 'The Archives and Archival Problems of the Elizabethan and Early Stuart Star Chamber', *JSA*, vol 2 (1960–4), p360.

[5] RR Reid, *The King's Council in the North*, London 1921, p469.

[6] Thomas, *op cit*, p134.

[7] Jane Houston, *Catalogue of Ecclesiastical Records of the Commonwealth 1643–1660, in the Lambeth Palace Library*, Farnborough 1968.

[8] Thomas, *op cit*, p142; Dorothy Owen, 'Bringing Home the Records: the Recovery of the Ely Chapter Muniments at the Restoration', *Archives*, vol viii no 39 (Apr 1968), pp1, 23–9.

Civil War, Commonwealth and Protectorate 1641–1660   123

There was also widespread disruption in the record-keeping of secular estates. Some of those on the losing side had their lands confiscated and sold, and many others had theirs sequestrated, that is, taken into administration by Parliament through a system of county committees. A separate committee, which included Selden and the antiquary Sir Simonds D'Ewes, endeavoured to prevent the sale or dispersal of the estate papers needed to manage these properties, but inevitably there were losses.[9] Locally, current records of both ecclesiastical and lay estates were left with their stewards, but some of these fell into different hands or were otherwise lost sight of during the following years.

It is difficult to estimate the extent of the archival losses due directly to the wars of the 1640s. Some were blamed on the conflict when they were probably due to administrative breakdown. It was claimed in 1655, for instance, that some of the recent records of the manor of Cobham (Surrey) had been 'lost in the late troubles', but it is more likely that the court had been unable to meet between October 1642 and January 1646.[10] Nevertheless, it is certain that much damage was inflicted, particularly in the south, south-west and Midlands, and more especially in the first phase of the conflict, when military discipline was weak. The case of Peterborough Cathedral in the spring of 1643 has already been mentioned.[11] A little earlier, Winchester Cathedral had been despoiled, and at Chichester the Chapter House was broken into and some 'ancient city records' destroyed there.[12]

Although the troops had no time for popish documentary relics it is likely that these repositories were raided in the hope of finding other and more valuable objects, and that in many places the destruction of records was merely collateral damage. When castles or fortified houses were looted the muniments could suffer

---

[9] Peters, *op cit*, p171.

[10] John Gurney, *Brave Community: the Digger Movement in the English Revolution*, Manchester 2007, p49.

[11] See Chapter 7. The soldiers also discovered a precious cartulary hidden above the ceiling of the choir, but on being told that it was an old Latin bible they surrendered it on payment of ten shillings. Janet D Martin, *The Cartularies and Registers of Peterborough Abbey*, Northants Rec Soc vol xxviii (1978), pxvi.

[12] Revd GN Godwin, *The Civil War in Hampshire (1642–45) and the Story of Basing House*, new edn Southampton and London 1904, pp49, 60.

along with their other contents. A well-documented case is that of Berkeley Castle, which changed hands five times during the conflict, and where nearly seven hundred documents were stolen from the evidence house, with others damaged and disordered.[13] Wardour Castle (Wiltshire) appears to have suffered similar depredations, and perhaps also Basing House (Hampshire) when it fell in October 1645.[14] Where towns as well as castles were besieged, other buildings, such as the parish church, could find themselves in the line of fire, as at Bridgnorth.[15] When Leicester was captured by the royalists in 1645 the corporation lost some records from its muniment room, and had to buy back its borough seal and charters.[16] Duchy of Cornwall records were lost at Lostwithiel; and the destruction of St Mary's Tower, York, with the loss of many monastic muniments, has already been mentioned.[17] Even where country houses were not the scene of fighting they could be occupied, looted and then slighted if considered of potential value to the enemy. And in the country districts it was not only the gentry that suffered. The village of Boarstall (Buckinghamshire) was burnt by the royalist garrison of the big house in 1645, leaving the villagers unable to document a claim for compensation 'by reason our houses with writings have been consumed with fyer [and] we dispersed soe that we are altogether in confusion'.[18]

Sometimes, however, disasters were averted, or the actual losses, as distinct from the chaos and confusion, were less than initially feared or reported. This seems to have been true of country house archives. The Earl of Lindsey's deeds at Grimsthorpe (Lincolnshire)

---

[13] David Smith, 'The Berkeley Castle Muniments', *Trans Bristol and Gloucs Arch Soc*, vol 125 (2008), p18.

[14] Godwin, *op cit*, pp357–61. A leiger book of Shaftesbury Abbey was thought to have been among the losses at Wardour Castle, but it was referred to in a legal dispute in 1721. John Bettey, '"Ancient Custom Time out of Mind": Copyhold Tenure in the West Country in the Sixteenth and Seventeenth Centuries', *Antiquaries Jnl*, vol 89 (2009), p311. Similarly, some of the records of St Mary's Tower, York survived the explosion, but were later lost. BA English and CBL Barr, 'The Records Formerly in St Mary's Tower, York', *Yorks Arch Jnl*, c1970, pp213–16.

[15] Stephen Porter, *Destruction in the English Civil Wars*, Stroud 1994, p98.

[16] AKB Evans, 'The Custody of Leicester's Archives from 1273 to 1947', *Leics Arch and Hist Soc Trans*, vol lxvi (1992), p113.

[17] See Chapter 6; but also above, n14.

[18] Quoted in Porter, *op cit*, p1.

Civil War, Commonwealth and Protectorate 1641–1660   125

were 'confusedly mixt and scattered' by Parliamentary soldiers in 1643, but later partially restored to order by that great antiquary William Dugdale.[19] Lady Anne Clifford managed to avoid serious damage to her archive at Skipton Castle (Yorkshire). After the fall of Hull and its surrender by Sir John Hotham his wife was allowed to remove evidences from the family seat at Scorborough (Yorkshire) and take them to London with her.[20] It was long thought that the Dudley papers were destroyed when Kenilworth Castle was slighted in 1649, but in fact some of them had left the castle many years previously, and were to survive in archivally related collections.[21] Dugdale also helped to save the archive of St Paul's Cathedral, and he was not the only friend of manuscripts to exert himself during the troubles. Selden used his influence with Parliament to protect the Cotton Library, and he took some of the contents of the archbishop's study at Lambeth into his protective custody.[22] Altogether, London seems to have emerged from the Civil War comparatively unscathed in archival terms, and it was a similar story at Oxford, where General Fairfax is thought to have protected the Bodleian Library from spoliation following the fall of the city to Parliament in 1646.[23]

In one instance documents of national importance were recovered from the battlefield. When in 1645 the king was forced to flee from the field at Naseby he left behind all his baggage, including 'his own cabinet, where his most secret papers were, and letters between the Queen and him'. These documents were captured, taken to London, deciphered and partially published in order to embarrass

---

[19] Andrew G Watson, *The Library of Sir Simonds D'Ewes*, London 1966, pp34–5. At Deene Thomas Brudenell's closet was broken into by Parliamentary soldiers in March 1643 and its contents ransacked, but he was able to recover the greater part of them in 1660. Joan Wake, *The Brudenells of Deene*, London 1953, pp129, 165.

[20] Barbara English, 'Sir John Hotham and the English Civil War', *Archives*, vol xx no 88 (Oct 1992), p222.

[21] Simon Adams, 'The Papers of Robert Dudley, Earl of Leicester: 1. The Browne-Evelyn Collection', *Archives*, vol xx no 87 (Apr 1992), pp63–4.

[22] After his death they remained in private hands until reacquired by Lambeth in 1963. EGW Bill, 'Records of the Church of England Recently Recovered by Lambeth Palace Library', *JSA*, vol 3 (1965–9), pp24–6.

[23] Jan Broadway, *'No Historie So Meete': Gentry Culture and the Development of Local History in Elizabethan and Early Stuart England*, Manchester 2006, p46.

the royalists, and then lodged in the parliamentary archive, where they remain to this day.[24]

* * *

The execution of the King in 1649 marked the start of a new phase in government administration and record-keeping. A Council of State was created that continued to sit, and to keep its entry books, until 1659, and the start of the Protectorate in 1653 saw a revival of the role of Secretary of State. The post was filled by John Thurloe (1616–68), who had been appointed to the secretaryship of the Council the previous year. Assisted by an office in Whitehall, he built up an intelligence system unrivalled since the days of William Cecil, and accumulated a large archive of letters and papers.[25] The Protectorate also saw the creation of new bodies or boards to supervise the Navy, the Admiralty, the Ordnance and the Post Office, organisations that anticipated and influenced the shape of government after the Restoration.[26]

The somewhat more settled times of the 1650s also enabled archival work to be resumed on the older records of government, most notably the accumulations in the Tower. In the late 1650s William Prynne (1600–69), controversialist and no mean archivist, tackled a pile of documents ' buried in one confused chaos under corroding, putrefying cobwebs, dust and filth in the darkest corner of Caesar's [ie St John's] Chapel'. The old clerks did not want to get themselves dirty, and an *ad hoc* band of 'soldiers and women' engaged for the job soon gave up, so he and his own clerk had to roll up their sleeves and conduct a sorting and cleaning operation. They were rewarded by the emergence of 'many rare antient pearls and golden records' from the 'dust heap'.[27]

---

[24] Edward Hyde, Earl of Clarendon, *The History of the Great Rebellion*, ed Roger Lockyer, Oxford 1967, p272; HMC *First Report*, 1870. Later in 1645 Lord Digby lost his 'cabinet of papers' and other baggage at Sherburn-in-Elmet. Hyde, *op cit*, p297.

[25] Florence M Greir Evans (CSS Higham), *The Principal Secretary of State: a Survey of the Office from 1550 to 1680*, Manchester 1923, pp108–19.

[26] See eg Howard Robinson, *The British Post Office: a History*, Princeton NJ 1948, pp37–48.

[27] Quoted in Thomas, *op cit*, p122. In 1657 Prynne compiled a list of records in the Tower based on earlier work by Cotton.

Civil War, Commonwealth and Protectorate 1641–1660

The records of the House of Lords survived the abolition of that House in 1649, no doubt because they were seen by the Commons as an integral and indeed essential part of the parliamentary archive. The Clerk of the Parliaments, John Browne, was ordered to hand over his records to Henry Scobell, Clerk of the Commons, but they remained in safety during the following decade.[28] In ecclesiastical matters a Central Court of Probate replaced the Prerogative Court of Canterbury in 1653. (The Prerogative Court was where the archbishop dealt with matters reserved to himself, for instance, where a will related to property in more than one diocese.) Registration was secularised, but parochial affairs, and the preservation of the records relating them, continued to be closely supervised until the Restoration.[29]

* * *

In some areas of the national life the restoration of the monarchy in 1660 was a smooth operation in archival terms. Record-keepers simply picked up where they had left off in the early 1640s. The Clerk of the Parliaments got his job back, and his records with it. The Prerogative Court of Canterbury was restored, along with the central probate records, and in 1661 Parliament directed that the parliamentary records relating to ecclesiastical administration should be lodged with Lambeth Palace Library. Bishops went back to their dioceses (or were promoted to different ones); their registrars returned to their offices; and in the parishes the newly restored incumbents resumed the maintenance of their registers. At Salisbury Cathedral, the chapter act book, put away in November 1642, was brought back into use in September 1660.[30]

Elsewhere, however, the transition was not effected so easily. The central government in Whitehall made efforts to impound

---

[28] *Ex inf* Sir John Sainty; Maurice F Bond, 'The Clerks of the Parliaments', *EHR*, 1958, p84.

[29] CJ Kitching, 'Probate during the Civil War and Interregnum', *JSA*, vol 5 (1974–7), pp283–93, 346–56. There are gaps, however, for the period 1643–53. Similarly, some parish registers re-start in 1653, with the appointment of civilian 'registers', after gaps from the mid-1640s.

[30] Kathleen Edwards, *Salisbury Cathedral, an Ecclesiastical History*, Oxford 1986, p192.

records left in the hands of Protectorate officials, but with varying success. Thurloe delivered up some of his papers, but 'burnt what would have hanged many', and hid others in the false ceiling of his chambers in Lincoln's Inn, where they were discovered by a later tenant.[31] The papers of the royal government in exile were a complicated story. Sir Edward Nicholas (1593–1669) is said to have destroyed Charles I's papers from 1641 to 1646,[32] when he was acting as his Principal Secretary, but he kept his own papers relating to his service to Charles II in exile in the 1650s and was then restored briefly to the Principal Secretaryship after the Restoration. After his death his private papers remained in family possession until sold in the nineteenth and twentieth centuries. Many of them reached the British Museum, but other collections, including those of Clarendon and Thurloe, ended up in the Bodleian Library.

Those official papers from the Interregnum that remained in Whitehall survived to give archival headaches to generations of custodians of the public records. They presented problems of classification and arrangement that appear to have defeated the Victorian Public Record Office, and today the historian has to search for them both among the State Papers and in various other classes.[33] The worst muddles, however, had been created among the records of the episcopal and capitular estates that had been taken to London. After the Restoration they were sorted and where possible returned to their former muniment rooms, but many went astray, and the medieval estate archive of the archbishops of York appears to have been altogether lost.[34]

---

[31] SC Lomas, 'The State Papers of the Early Stuarts and the Interregnum', *TRHS*, New S vol xvi (1902), pp100, 124.

[32] PRO *Thirtieth Report*, 1869, pp216, 244.

[33] NAM Rodger, 'Drowning in a Sea of Paper: British Archives of Naval Warfare', *Archives*, vol xxxii no 117 (Oct 2007), pp104–14.

[34] IJ Gentles and WJ Sheils, *Confiscation and Restoration: the Archbishop's Estates and the Civil War*, Borthwick Papers no 59 (1981), p22. Stray Ely records were still turning up as late as 1678. Owen, *op cit*.

9

The Later Seventeenth Century 1660–1700

The Archives of Government

In terms of governmental record-keeping the most significant development of the Restoration period was the rise of the Treasury. The ancient office of Lord Treasurer was in commission, and the principal commissioner, the First Lord of the Treasury, became increasingly powerful as his department extended its control over many aspects of the nation's finances. By 1702 it was 'by far the largest departmental empire yet seen in English government', with a burgeoning archive to match.[1] The Exchequer continued its ancient course, with its tallies, chests and Roman numerals, but after 1660 it failed to recover the position that it had held before the Civil War, and its somewhat neglected archives around the Palace of Westminster contrasted increasingly with the accumulations of the Treasury in Whitehall.[2]

It was Sir George Downing, Treasury Secretary from 1667 to 1671, who had most influence on departmental record-keeping. He ensured that incoming papers were properly filed, and that the work of the department was systematically recorded in series of minute books and entry (or memorandum) books. The 'bold No 1s upon the covers of the 1667 volumes', we are told by the Treasury's historian, 'still testify to this novel initiative'.[3] Unfortunately Downing's successor in the 1680s, Henry Guy, was not so archivally minded.

---

[1] Henry Roseveare, *The Treasury: the Evolution of a British Institution*, London 1969, p71.

[2] See Stephen B Baxter, *The Development of the Treasury 1660–1702*, London 1957.

[3] Roseveare, *op cit*, p62.

He took minute books away with him when he left office, and they subsequently disappeared.[4] In 1686 the Treasury acquired new chambers. Although they were destroyed in the fire that swept through Whitehall in 1698, no papers were lost, and new premises were subsequently provided on the west side of Whitehall, on or near the site of the old Cockpit.

In the years after 1660 various bodies were set up that were either linked to the Treasury or were influenced by Treasury practice. They were run by boards or commissions, and although some had sixteenth-century predecessors they followed up-to-date record-keeping practice, using minute books, entry books, letter books, bill books, establishment books and so on. Excise Commissioners were appointed (independently of the Exchequer) in 1660, followed by Commissioners of Customs in 1671. The year 1660 also saw the reorganisation of the General Post Office and the creation of a new post of Secretary-at-War, while various aspects of naval administration were placed under new boards. Not all these bodies were based in Whitehall – the Board of Ordnance continued at the Tower, and the Customs Office and the GPO in the City – but all established long-lasting archival traditions. The Navy and Admiralty in particular created records on a very large scale.[5]

The years 1660–1700 saw the continued growth of another bureaucracy, the department headed by the two Principal Secretaries of State.[6] Perhaps the key period was 1662–74, when Henry Bennet, first earl of Arlington, was Secretary for the South (the senior office) and Sir Joseph Williamson was his chief clerk as well as acting as Clerk to the Privy Council (from 1666) and (until he retired from the post in 1702) Keeper of the State Papers. By 1700 the Secretary's clerks who kept the regular correspondence and papers were headed by an official coming to be known as the Under-Secretary,[7] but at the same time the Secretaries of State kept papers by them in their own offices, or in their private London houses. Despite Williamson's efforts these papers were not consistently handed in to the State

[4] Baxter, *op cit*, p180.

[5] For naval and Admiralty records, see especially Randolph Cock and NAM Rodger, *A Guide to the Naval Records in the National Archives of the UK*, London 2008.

[6] See Florence M Greir Evans (CSS Higham), *The Principal Secretary of State: a Survey of the Office from 1558 to 1680*, Manchester 1923.

[7] *Ibid*, pp149, 164.

Paper Office when Secretaries of State left office but were handed to their successors or taken home with them, just as they had been earlier in the century. Arlington's own papers have not survived, and when his successor Henry Coventry left office in 1680 he took papers home with him despite being served with a warrant to deliver them up.[8] They are now among the collections of the Marquess of Bath at Longleat. To add to the archival complications, Secretaries of State employed private secretaries to keep their unofficial papers in order, docketing or endorsing letters, putting them into bundles, maintaining registers of them and compiling formularies or precedent books for their own guidance. Some of these too could remain in the hands of secretaries and eventually pass to their descendants.[9]

The restored Clerk of the Parliaments, John Browne, continued in office until he died in 1691, maintaining the principal series of journals and committee minutes. Less commendably he lent papers to the historian John Nalson that were never returned, and at Browne's death other papers then in his possession passed into the hands of his family.[10] At this period the records of the House of Commons were no better safeguarded. After 1695 its journals were indeed systematically preserved, but for many years it lacked a secure repository comparable to the Jewel House used by the Lords.[11]

Religious Archives

Although the bishops were soon back in their palaces in 1660, and the deans in their deaneries, it was not always easy to revive their administrative machinery. The cathedrals, with their less wide-ranging responsibilities, were quicker off the mark, but both cathedral chapters and bishops had suffered the confiscation of

---

[8] *Ibid*, p186n.

[9] See also Arnold Hunt, 'The Early Modern Secretary and the Early Modern Archive', in Liesbeth Corens *et al*, *Archives and Information in the Early Modern World*, Oxford 2018, pp105–30.

[10] Maurice F Bond, 'The Formation of the Archives of Parliament 1497–1691', *JSA*, vol 1 (1955–9), p157. The Nalson papers passed into the Portland collection, and thence to the Bodleian Library. Browne's remaining papers passed to the Cave family, Barons Braye, and more recently were purchased in part by the House of Lords Record Office.

[11] Bond, *op cit*, p155.

their estates, as described in Chapter 8, and local officials had to be re-appointed or replaced.[12] It was almost inevitable in these circumstances that the care of the older and non-current records would be neglected, unless they received the attentions of bishops, deans or registrars motivated by historical interest as well as a desire for tidiness and order. There were a few such – Dean Honeywood at Lincoln, Chancellor Drake at Salisbury, an assistant registrar at Ely. At Lincoln, the evidence chamber acquired a 'great press' in 1664, and in 1670 Honeywood reclaimed some records from a Lincoln attorney who had been concerned with the management of the chapter estates during the Interregnum.[13]

At St Paul's Cathedral, London the difficulties of the early 1660s were compounded by the Great Fire of 1666 (for which see also the last section of this chapter). The current muniment (or act) book, begun in 1660, survived, but earlier volumes appear to have been lost. The rest of the older muniments, however, were evacuated to Fulham Palace, in an operation supervised by the Clerk of the Works. When they returned to London, accompanied by some papers that a former dean had sequestered in his house in Chiswick, they were accommodated in temporary quarters near the cathedral pending its rebuilding. The records of the College of Minor Canons had been saved by an official who had given them shelter in his own house.[14]

* * *

While the Church of England was busy restoring its archival routines a far more radical development in religious record-keeping was taking place elsewhere. The archival history of Protestant nonconformity can be traced back well before the Civil War, but it had been the period of the Commonwealth and Protectorate that had seen a great burgeoning of sectarian activity, and it was the early 1660s, especially after the passage of the Act of Uniformity

---

[12] See IM Green, *The Re-Establishment of the Church of England 1660–1663*, Oxford 1978.

[13] Dorothy M Williamson, *The Muniments of the Dean and Chapter of Lincoln*, Lincoln 1956, p8.

[14] William M Atkins, 'The Preservation of the Records of St Paul's Cathedral in the Seventeenth Century', *JSA*, vol 1 (1955–9), p50; Geoffrey Yeo, 'Record-Keeping at St Paul's Cathedral', *JSA*, vol 8 no 1 (1986), p34.

The Later Seventeenth Century 1660–1700

in 1662, that saw the formal separation of many dissenting groups from the Established Church. By 1700 a number of major denominations can be identified – Presbyterian, General and Particular Baptist, Independent (later Congregationalist) and the Society of Friends – all with their characteristic modes of record-keeping.[15]

Prima facie one would not expect the nonconformists to be good record-keepers. The early period was one of enthusiasm rather than bureaucracy, and if one believed in the imminence of the Second Coming the preservation of one's papers for future reference might seem a low priority. The succeeding years were quieter, but denominations waxed and waned, and overall numbers were not large: in 1715–18 there were probably no more than 1,845 dissenting congregations, embracing perhaps no more than 6 per cent of the total population of England and Wales.[16] It is all the more remarkable, therefore, that so many nonconformist records have survived for the late seventeenth and early eighteenth centuries, at both national and local level.

Not every denomination set up an overarching national body. The Independents did not choose to be organised in that way. But the General Baptist Assembly preserved its minutes from its foundation in 1654, while the Society of Friends (the Quakers) adopted its permanent structure in the late 1660s, although its central records can be said to have started in the mid-1650s.[17] The General Body of Protestant Dissenting Ministers of the Three Denominations (Presbyterian, Independent and General Baptist) did not begin its series of minutes until 1727, but it had a precedent in the Westminster Assembly of Divines of 1643–52.[18]

---

[15] Michael Mullett, *Sources for the History of English Nonconformity 1660–1830*, BRA Archives and the User no 8, 1991; Clive D Field, 'Preserving Zion: the Anatomy of Protestant Nonconformist Archives in Great Britain and Ireland', *Archives*, vol xxxiii no 118 (Apr 2008), pp14–51.

[16] Michael R Watts, *The Dissenters: Vol 1: From the Reformation to the French Revolution*, Oxford 1978, pp3, 269.

[17] For the Baptists, see WT Whiteley, ed, *The Minutes of the General Assembly of General Baptist Churches*, 1909. The large number of published editions of connexional records is another indication of the importance attached to them. For the archive of the Muggletonians, complete from 1652 to the death of the last adherent in 1979, and now BL Add MSS 60207–30, see William Lamont, 'The Muggletonian Archive', in Christopher Hill *et al*, eds, *The World of the Muggletonians*, London 1983, pp1–5; Mullett, *op cit*, pp112–13.

[18] Mullett, *op cit*, pp9–10.

In the case of the Quakers, as with the Methodists a century later, the influence of the founder was crucial in putting the careful creation and preservation of records at the heart of their organisation. George Fox was a man of outstanding energy and administrative ability, and an indefatigable writer of letters and keeper of journals.[19] He believed it to be essential not only to communicate regularly with his followers but also to compile for posterity a spiritual record of his ministry. In his testamentary directions he desired his papers in London and those at his and his wife's Lancashire base at Swarthmoor Hall to be 'joined ... to make a history of passages of the spreading of Truth' and to be preserved as a 'library'.[20] In the more formal organisation of the late 1660s there was a hierarchy of local, district, county and national meetings, forming an administrative ladder down which passed injunctions and questionnaires and up which passed the responses. As one historian has put it, 'the sinews that held the society together were of ink and paper'.[21]

Denominations with national organisations established headquarters in London, where archives could be stored and where libraries could serve as collecting points for manuscript and printed material. The Quakers set up such a library in 1673, the Presbyterians (at Dr Williams's Library) in 1729.[22] At a local level dissenting congregations kept church books or minute books, registers of births, deaths and marriages, and records relating to the fabric of their meeting houses and (where they had a salaried minister) the maintenance of their pastor. Like Fox's journals these records had a spiritual as well as an administrative function: they documented the way in which each congregation preserved its cohesion as a community of believers. They were usually compiled not by the minister but by leading members of his congregation, in all likelihood members of the middling sort.[23] As with Anglican churchwardens, archival material could be retained in family hands, but the chances of long-term preservation increased

---

[19] So were Richard Baxter and later Philip Doddridge.

[20] William C Braithwaite, *The Beginnings of Quakerism*, London 1912, p359. The papers at Swarthmoor Hall were sold with the estate in 1759, but later reacquired by the Society.

[21] Mullett, *op cit*, p95.

[22] *Ibid*, pp103, 109–10.

[23] Richard T Vann, *The Social Development of English Quakerism 1655–1755*, Cambridge MA 1969, p101. The Quakers had no salaried ministry.

when congregations acquired permanent meeting places. Chapels were erected during the times of persecution, but many more followed the Toleration Act of 1689. The Quakers were also in the van in creating more than purely local record centres. Thus in 1708 the Lancaster meeting house was enlarged to accommodate the quarterly as well as the 'particular' meeting, and its safe became the repository of an important accumulation of records.[24]

Institutions and Organisations

In the universities, as in the Church, the 1660s saw efforts to repair the ravages and counter the neglect of the previous couple of decades. At Cambridge, the university archive, which had probably been removed for safety to private houses, was given new premises in the Old Schools.[25] At Oxford, the university's muniments were provided by their keeper, John Wallis, with a repertory based on Twyne's earlier work that was to serve as a catalogue into the twentieth century.[26] At University College, William Smith acted as both the college's historian and its archivist, while at New College its capable warden Michael Woodward found time to work on the archive.[27]

In London a different group of scholars was making its own contribution to archival history. The Royal Society, founded in 1660 'for the promotion of experimental learning', was the first institution of its kind in England, and was to be followed in the early eighteenth century by the Society of Antiquaries.[28] From its inception, and no doubt conscious of losses of scientific papers during the troubles, the Royal Society laid emphasis on the careful preservation of its journals (or minute books), fellowship records, correspondence and letter books, despite a lack of permanent

---

[24] Mullett, *op cit*, p103.

[25] Heather E Peek and Catherine P Hall, *The Archives of the University of Cambridge: an Historical Introduction*, Cambridge 1962, p19.

[26] Reginald L Poole, *A Lecture on the History of the University Archives*, Oxford 1912, p26.

[27] Robin Darwall-Smith, *A History of University College, Oxford*, Oxford 2008, pp224–6; Francis W Steer, *The Archives of New College, Oxford: a Catalogue*, London and Chichester 1974, pxiv.

[28] See Marie Boas Hall, *The Library and Archives of the Royal Society 1660–1990*, London 1992.

premises in its early decades.²⁹ Its Secretaries kept in touch by letter with the fellowship, and kept the papers sent in as contributions to the Society's proceedings or transactions. This led to an accumulation of manuscripts and objects that formed a kind of library-cum-museum that was closely connected to the Society's archive. (Significantly, the early Secretaries tended also to act as Librarians.) In its record-consciousness the Society had affinities with the dissenting bodies, but also with the historians and antiquaries whose work is discussed below. There was in fact a considerable overlap between the membership of the Royal Society and that of the Society of Antiquaries in its early years.³⁰

Estate and Business Archives

The nobility and gentry of England had already begun to modernise their methods of estate management before 1640, as noted in Chapter 7. Like the large institutional owners, they had in many cases to reclaim their properties at the Restoration and reconstruct their administrations. They seem by and large to have done so successfully, and they were joined by new landed proprietors such as the Osborne dukes of Leeds and the Bentinck earls of Portland that rose to wealth and prominence both before and after the Revolution of 1688.³¹ In a new and more commercial age – feudalism had been all but abolished in 1660 – there was a greater emphasis on efficiency. More accurate surveys were made, more carefully drawn leases granted; and to oversee the work, especially on the larger and more scattered estates, a more professional cadre of lawyers and agents emerged. The fifth earl of Bedford, for instance, retained a lawyer from the late 1650s, and from 1682 to 1697 the post was

---

[29] Its royal charter of 1662 specified the keeping of a minute book. Hall, *op cit*, p1. On a more archaic note, the Society's first treasurer presented it with a muniment chest. See Michael Hunter, ed, *Archives of the Scientific Revolution: the Formation and Exchange of Ideas in Seventeenth-Century Europe*, Woodbridge 1998, frontispiece. See also Mordechai Feingold, 'Of Records and Grandeur: the Archive of the Royal Society', *ibid*, pp171–84.

[30] Joan Evans, *A History of the Society of Antiquaries*, Oxford 1956, pp26ff.

[31] See HMC, *Principal Family and Estate Collections*, Guides to Sources ... 10 and 11, 2 vols London 1996, 1999, *sub* Osborne (ii.46) and Cavendish-Bentinck (i.27).

combined with that of receiver-general or head agent.³² By 1700 the archives of great magnates such as the dukes of Devonshire and Somerset were already very considerable, although they were due to expand further and more rapidly during the eighteenth century.³³

For more dramatic advances in record-keeping, however, it is necessary to turn again to London, this time to the rapidly expanding world of commerce and finance. By 1700 the great trading companies were holding substantial archives. (The Russia, Levant and East India Companies had been joined in 1670 by the Hudson's Bay Company.) The late seventeenth century also saw the rise of private banks. They were not companies established by charter but private partnerships: nevertheless, they kept detailed and meticulous records, including partnership deeds, profit and loss accounts, customer ledgers and papers relating to premises and other jointly owned assets. Accurate accounting went hand in hand with a culture of solidity and reliability, and it is no coincidence that the firms of Messrs Child, Coutts and Hoare have preserved their archives from the late seventeenth century to the present day.³⁴

These banks grew out of the tradition of the goldsmiths, but another group of businesses had their origin in the work of the scriveners. These men – their name literally means writers – had, like the notaries, specialised in drawing up legal documents, and had formed their own City company in 1617. A leading firm from the mid-seventeenth century was that of Clayton and Morris, formerly Abbott. Its journals have not survived, but its series of great ledgers runs, with gaps, from 1646 to 1686, and is supplemented by a mass of legal and financial papers, including documents that prefigure the cheque and the promissory note of a later banking age, and a variety of documents relating to their activities as mortgage brokers. From 1672 the firm's office was in Sir Robert Clayton's mansion in Old Jewry, where valuables were kept in iron chests in the great hall. The scriveners were in decline by 1700, but in terms of records creation their heirs included the accountancy and land agency professions.³⁵

---

[32] Gladys Scott Thomson, *Life in a Noble Household*, London 1937, pp115–16.

[33] See *Principal Family and Estate Collections*, *sub* Cavendish (i.24) and Percy (ii.59). See also Chapter 10.

[34] John Orbell and Alison Turton, *British Banking: a Guide to Historical Records*, Aldershot 2001.

[35] Frank T Melton, 'The Clayton Papers', *BIHR*, vol lii (1979), pp91–9; Melton, *Sir Robert Clayton and the Origins of English Deposit Banking*, Cambridge 1986.

The Personal Archive

By 1660 the manuscript letter had become part of the common currency of the political and social elite. After 1660 it also became increasingly prominent in the lives of the middling sort. Correspondence, and the keeping of letters, was an important aspect of business activity, and of the conduct of religious and secular institutions, but it also took on a more social and personal function, as men and women wrote more frequently to spouses, family members and friends.[36] The preservation of incoming letters came to form the basis of the personal archive, as their recipients filed them or folded them into bundles and stowed them away in desk drawers or cabinets. Samuel Pepys filed his letters not on a piece of string but on a metal spike, a device still used for bills or vouchers in much more recent times, before weeding them every few years and discarding those not 'worth keeping'.[37] The scientist Robert Boyle preferred the use of pasteboard 'cases' in which to keep his letters, some of them pinned together for greater security.[38] Samuel Hartlib, another prominent scientist, is thought to have kept his correspondence in alphabetical bundles.[39]

Another element in the personal archive was the document designed for the personal use of its creator. One way of keeping track of the information flowing across one's desk was to keep a commonplace book in which notes and extracts or quotations were entered, in other words a kind of filing system within hard covers.[40] And from maintaining a commonplace book it was but a short step to keeping a diary or journal, recording the writer's doings, thoughts and observations on a daily basis.[41] The

---

[36] Susan E Whyman, *The Pen and the People: English Letter-Writers 1660–1800*, Oxford 2009, p6.

[37] Heather Wolfe and Peter Stallybrass, 'The Material Culture of Record-Keeping in Early Modern England', in Liesbeth Corens *et al*, *op cit*, pp189–91.

[38] Michael Hunter, 'Mapping the Mind of Robert Boyle: the Evidence of the Boyle Papers', in Hunter, *op cit*, pp127–8.

[39] Mark Greengrass, 'Archive Refractions: Hartlib's Papers and the Workings of an Intelligencer', *ibid*, p43.

[40] *Ibid*, p13. Pepys kept a copy of John Locke's 1686 article on commonplace books among his own papers. For commonplace books, see also Ann M Blair, *Too Much to Know: Managing Scholarly Information before the Modern Age*, New Haven CT and London 2010, pp72 *et passim*.

[41] Hartlib believed in keeping a diary, but what survives for him is more like a series of commonplace books. Greengrass in Hunter, *op cit*, p44.

diary is seldom found before 1600, but it blossomed during the seventeenth century, and particularly after 1660.⁴² It appealed to the middle-class instinct for keeping accounts, and provided a way of monitoring the writer's financial position. (The word journal, of course, had book-keeping connotations.) But it could also be used to reflect on one's spiritual life, and to chasten oneself after episodes of backsliding. A good example of the diary of a seventeenth-century cleric is that of Ralph Josselin.⁴³ The life of Samuel Pepys, the period's best-known diarist, was very different from that of a country clergyman, but it nevertheless reveals a self-conscious and introspective side to his character: in the narrative he constructs he is both the observer and the observed. He was also a meticulous man – he was not an Exchequer-trained civil servant for nothing – and 'one to whom the keeping of records was necessary to the act of living'. He was aware, too, that his public life might have an interest for posterity, and it was his (unfulfilled) intention to write a major work of naval history.⁴⁴

In the late seventeenth century there were few opportunities for middle-class creators of personal archives to pass their papers to a library or similar repository, either during their lifetimes or by leaving instructions to their executors.⁴⁵ It was generally left to the family to determine whether such papers survived or not. Josselin's diary was luckier than most. It passed to a daughter and then into the hands of a landed family through which it descended until the twentieth century, albeit with a hitch at one point when it strayed from custody and was rescued from a London bookstall, on payment of sixpence, by the Victorian novelist Mrs Oliphant.⁴⁶ John Evelyn's autobiographical writings, intended for posterity, also remained with his descendants for many generations. Some diaries, however, were written with no intention that anyone but their

---

⁴² See William Matthews, *British Diaries: an Annotated Bibliography of British Diaries written between 1442 and 1942*, Berkeley CA and London 1950.

⁴³ Alan Macfarlane, ed, *The Diary of Ralph Josselin 1616–1683*, London 1976.

⁴⁴ Robert Latham and William Matthews, eds, *The Diary of Samuel Pepys Vol 1: 1660*, London 1970, ppxxviii, cii, cvii, cix.

⁴⁵ It seems that eminent scientists of the period did not leave their papers to the Royal Society. For the vicissitudes of Sir William Petty's papers after his death, see Frances Harris, 'Ireland as a Laboratory: the Archive of Sir William Petty', in Hunter, *op cit*, pp73–90.

⁴⁶ Macfarlane, *op cit*, pxix.

creators would read them, and some carried instructions that they were to be destroyed unread. In other cases there was an element of ambiguity. Pepys used shorthand to protect the privacy of his diary during his lifetime, but it appears to be a fair copy, and at his death it formed part of the library that he bequeathed to Magdalene College, Cambridge. Helpfully for posterity he also included in the bequest the code book that he had used for the shorthand passages.

Historians and Antiquaries

The new culture of empirical enquiry extended beyond the fellowship of the Royal Society. In historical and antiquarian studies it showed itself in an emphasis on the examination and evaluation of written, particularly archival, evidence.[47] Among the antiquaries the great exemplar was Sir William Dugdale. 'Here for the first time,' wrote one scholar of his *Baronage of England* (1675–6), 'is a vast and solid work of scholarship, almost every statement of which is directly referred to an original source.'[48] In 1681 the French archivist and scholar Jean Mabillon published *De re diplomatica*, a pioneering work on the forms and conventions (the diplomatic) of charters. Among his friends in England was the Oxford scholar Edward Bernard (1638–1697), who masterminded the compilation of a survey of English manuscript collections. This important work, published in 1697 under the title *Catalogi librorum manuscriptorum Angliae et Hiberniae*, began with the Bodleian Library and went on to list collections in numerous public and private libraries and archives, including the Tower of London (based on a list compiled by William Petyt) and the Cottonian Library (contributed by its unpaid librarian Thomas Smith, a friend of Bernard's).[49]

Dugdale was no stranger to the records at the Tower and at Westminster, and for their part the keepers there such as Petyt and Peter Le Neve were well-connected in the antiquarian world. One interesting aspect of their professional work was its contribution

---

[47] Randolph C Head, 'Documents, Archives and Proof around 1700', *Historical Jnl*, vol 56 (2013), pp909–30.

[48] Michael Maclagan, 'Genealogy and Heraldry in the Sixteenth and Seventeenth Centuries', in Levi Fox, ed, *English Historical Scholarship in the Seventeenth and Eighteenth Centuries*, Oxford 1956, p46.

[49] David C Douglas, *English Scholars 1660–1730*, 2nd edn London 1951, p111.

to the study of archival history. In examining series of medieval records they became aware of gaps and speculated on the reasons for them. Prynne, for instance, came to believe that periods of civil war were peculiarly disruptive of the processes of records creation, a belief informed by his own personal experience. There was also much interest in the origins of Parliament, and the question of whether it anteceded the earliest surviving records. Such questions were part of a wider historical concern with tracing the Anglo-Saxon origins of English liberties, for which Domesday Book was regarded as a key source.[50]

That such studies made only limited progress at this period may be attributed partly to the practical difficulties of working on the records themselves. The record office at the Tower was not always open for research, and access to Domesday Book in the Tally Court was limited, uncomfortable and expensive.[51] William Rymer, as Historiographer Royal under William III, had privileged access to treaties held in the Chapel of the Pyx for his *Foedera*, but he had to complain about the conditions there, and later they were transferred to the Chapter House.[52] Elsewhere at Westminster many of the older records were, in modern parlance, unfit for production, and lacked even the most rudimentary finding aids.

The Great Fire of London

Urban fires have been a recurrent feature of English archival history, from Viking raids to the efforts of the *Luftwaffe*, but perhaps the best known is the one that consumed three-quarters of the City of London in 1666. As with other disasters, the extent of the damage is almost impossible to quantify, but the losses of parish records, business records and personal papers must have been considerable. Documents do not burn as well as rotten sticks, but the fire spread

---

[50] Elizabeth M Hallam, *Domesday Book through Nine Centuries*, London 1986, pp124–6; Douglas, *op cit*, pp135–7.

[51] By 1700 two seats were reserved for readers at the record table there. Hallam, *op cit*, p115. For the Tower record office in the late seventeenth century, see Elizabeth M Hallam, 'The Tower of London as a Record Office', *Archives*, vol xiv no 61 (1979), pp6–7.

[52] FS Thomas, *Notes of Materials for the History of Public Departments*, printed London 1846, p160.

rapidly, and when fleeing the flames the rescue of archives was not always uppermost in people's minds. Some documents were certainly rescued, and, like Pepys's diary, taken to places of greater safety. Others may have been buried in back gardens (not generally speaking a good idea).

The records of government at Westminster and in the Tower were out of reach of the Fire, but there were casualties in the City itself, notably at the Customs House, the General Post Office and the Lord Treasurer's Remembrancer's Office in Ivy Lane.[53] The contents of the City Corporation's Book House were moved into requisitioned accommodation nearby: they survived, but languished in disorder for several years.[54] The most conspicuous casualty of the Fire, architecturally speaking, was St Paul's Cathedral, but again, as already noted, there were only limited archival losses. More significant in terms of ecclesiastical records was the destruction at Doctors' Commons of much of the pre-1660 archive of the Court of Arches, and of the probate inventories and administration accounts that that were part of the archive of the Prerogative Court of Canterbury. There must have been losses among the records of some of the smaller livery companies, but the Mercers, Stationers and Goldsmiths were not badly affected, although the Goldsmiths' records suffered in a later blaze in 1681. On the western edge of the City the Fire reached the Temple, where some records of the inns of court may have been lost.[55] Some of the Heralds lost their personal records, but their College library was evacuated (tardily, according to Pepys) by water to Whitehall.[56]

---

[53] *Ibid*, p155.

[54] Philip E Jones and Raymond Smith, *A Guide to the Records in the Corporation of London Record Office and the Guildhall Library Muniment Room*, London 1951, p13.

[55] The bench table orders of the Inner Temple start in 1668. CM Rider, 'The Inns of Court and Inns of Chancery and their Records', *Archives*, vol xxiv no 101 (Oct 1999), p30.

[56] AR Wagner, *The Records and Collections of the College of Arms*, London 1952, p20.

10

The Long Eighteenth Century 1700–1830

Central Government

The late seventeenth century had seen a growing divergence in archival terms between the ancient institutions of the country and those of more recent creation. In the period 1700–1830 this divergence became ever more marked as England became less of an agricultural and rural country and more of an industrial and commercial one. In the context of governmental record-keeping the trend is exemplified by the differing histories of the Treasury, the Secretaryships of State and the Exchequer.

During the eighteenth century the Treasury continued to extend its oversight in many areas of the public finances; and as it grew so did its archive. In the 1720s and 30s it took four years to fill a minute book: in the nineteenth century it took only a month.[1] In 1728 a post of Treasury record-keeper was created, and in the mid-1730s the department acquired handsome new premises in Whitehall, with a room for the records over the Board Room where the Lords of the Treasury met. Between 1763 and 1789 'Methodizers' were employed to restore order to the archive,[2] but by 1793 a further archival post became necessary, and in 1807 a complete reclassification of the papers was undertaken, involving the introduction of that classic nineteenth-century archival feature, the subject file.[3]

---

[1] Henry Roseveare, *The Treasury: the Evolution of a British Institution*, London 1969, p157.

[2] *Ex inf* Sir John Sainty. The term 'methodizing', meaning reducing to order, was in fairly general usage by this date.

[3] Roseveare, *op cit*, pp100–1, 159. The Admiralty followed suit in the 1830s. RB Pugh, 'The Early History of the Admiralty Record Office', in J Conway Davies, ed, *Studies Presented to Sir Hilary Jenkinson*, London 1957, p330.

These administrative changes reflected important political ones. The post of First Lord, or Commissioner, of the Treasury developed into that of Prime Minister, the minister who headed a political party in Parliament and acted as chief channel of communication between the Sovereign and his ministers. The kinds of document generated by this office, notably royal and ministerial correspondence and papers relating to patronage and parliamentary management, were different in nature from those relating to the oversight of budgets and revenues, and less formal than those created by the business of the Secretaries of State. Unlike those officers the prime minister had no department of his own, and no record was kept of the proceedings of the committee of the Privy Council – the Cabinet – over which he presided.[4] In these circumstances it was inevitable that he should accumulate his own archive, and that, as with the private papers of Secretaries of State, it should remain in private hands after he retired from office. The first archive of this kind was that of Sir Robert Walpole, but perhaps the best example from the eighteenth century is that of the Duke of Newcastle, Prime Minister from 1754 to 1756 and again from 1757 to 1762. The papers of Lord Liverpool, Prime Minister 1812–27, are the most substantial early nineteenth-century collection.[5]

The rise of the Prime Minister had the effect of diminishing the status of the Secretaries of State, and this is reflected in the history of the State Paper Office. In the early eighteenth century its energetic Keeper, John Tucker, secured additional accommodation over the Treasury Chambers, but the principal repository remained the Holbein Gate, which became increasingly unsatisfactory. It was demolished in 1759–60, but the premises to which its contents were removed were no more suitable, and it was not until the early 1830s that the State Papers were given adequate accommodation. Meanwhile, as at the Treasury, Methodizers were appointed in the mid-1760s to sort and calendar them, but they succeeded only in muddling them, and the system had to be overhauled in the 1790s.[6]

[4] No formal record was kept of Cabinet meetings until 1916.

[5] For the Liverpool papers, see HMC *Guide to Papers of British Cabinet Ministers 1782–1900*, London 1982, p34.

[6] Elizabeth M Hallam, 'Problems with Record-Keeping in Early Eighteenth-Century London: Some Pictorial Representations of the State Paper Office 1705–6', *JSA*, vol 6 (1978–81), pp219–26; FS Thomas, *Notes of Materials for the History of Public Departments*, printed London 1846, p171.

The Long Eighteenth Century 1700–1830   145

The 1780s saw a major structural reform. In 1782 the two Principal Secretaries, one for the North and one for the South, were replaced by a Home Secretary and a Foreign Secretary, each heading his own department, and they were joined by a third Secretary, for the Colonies, in 1794. Of the new departments the Foreign Office provides a particularly good example of the development of the governmental machine and its associated records, during a period in which the Napoleonic Wars had a significant impact on the workings of Whitehall. Despatches (the Foreign Secretary's formal correspondence with diplomats abroad) were copied by hand by a small body of clerks, but the Office also began to make more use of printed and lithographed circulars, and from 1829 it embraced confidential print. Another milestone was the creation of a registry in 1810. It was the responsibility of Lewis Hertslett as Foreign Office Librarian to bind up the despatches and consign them to permanent storage, although for many years they could not be accommodated in the cramped quarters of the Foreign Office itself and were instead deposited with the State Paper Office.[7]

At the same period the much larger bureaucracy of the Admiralty was also having to deal with its mounting archives. In 1809 it established a Paper Office (or registry) where records were digested and indexed.[8] Yet more prolific were the records of the government of India. In 1784 a new department, the Board of Control, was brought into being to oversee the East India Company, thus creating an additional tier of record-keeping.[9]

Meanwhile, a variety of archives, current and non-current, continued to be stored in and around the Palace of Westminster. The situation regarding the Exchequer records was little different from that obtaining in the seventeenth century (for which see above, Chapter 7). Next in order of magnitude and importance were the court records of the King's Bench and Common Pleas, some of which were now lodged in the Chapter House. Then there were a number of orphaned archives, including relics of courts or departments that had been abolished: such were the Courts of

---

[7] Michael Roper, *The Records of the Foreign Office 1782–1968*, PRO 2002, pp4ff.

[8] Pugh, *op cit*, pp327–30. Digest books were similar to précis books.

[9] Antonia Moon, 'Destroying Records, Keeping Records: Some Practices at the East India Company and the India Office', *Archives*, vol xxxiii no 119 (Oct 2008), pp114–25.

Requests; Wards and Liveries; First Fruits and Tenths; and Star Chamber. Unlike the older Exchequer records and the records of the Court of Augmentations, which were still under the eye of responsible officials, these orphaned records were in a distinctly parlous state, occupying holes and corners in badly maintained or makeshift premises. The records of the Court of Wards and Liveries were a case in point. Languishing in an attic once belonging to the Royal Fishmonger, they were said in 1709 to be 'in a very good condition, except where the rain came in', although 'the loose records that lie about and are trodden under foot will be a work of time to sort'.[10] Court papers from Star Chamber had reached the Chapter House by 1719, but remained there 'in a very great heap, undigested, without any covering from dust, or security from rats and mice'.[11] Throughout Westminster officials worked in rooms heated by open fires and divided by flimsy partitions. At one period the vault under the Chapter House was used for storing spiritous liquors, and adjacent buildings included a wash-house and brewhouse.[12] The whole palace was a gigantic fire risk.

These conditions did not go entirely unnoticed. In the early eighteenth century they were the subject of detailed investigation by a committee of the House of Lords. Its report in 1719 identified the need for the better covering and protection of documents, more sorting and listing (or methodizing) and better accommodation for staff and readers as well as for the records themselves. Crucial factors were a lack of dedicated archival posts and sources of funds; and the committee also deplored the fact that where finding aids did exist they could be removed as the private property of their compilers. But few improvements followed, apart from the creation of an archival post within the Exchequer in 1724.[13]

In the late 1720s, however, events prompted more progress. In 1728 it was decided to demolish the St Margaret's gatehouse; and

---

[10] Thomas, *op cit*, p134.

[11] JA Guy, *The Court of Star Chamber and its Records to the Reign of Elizabeth I*, PRO 1985, p19.

[12] Elizabeth Hallam Smith, 'The Chapter House as a Record Office', in Warwick Rodwell and Richard Mortimer, eds, *Westminster Abbey Chapter House: the History, Art and Architecture of 'a Chapter House Beyond Compare'*, London (Society of Antiquaries) 2010, pp124–38.

[13] Elizabeth M Hallam, *Domesday Book through Nine Centuries*, London 1986, pp129–30.

in 1731 Ashburnham House, a building near the Abbey to which the Cottonian Library had recently been moved, caught fire, with disastrous results for a considerable part of that immensely valuable collection.[14] A select committee of the House of Commons in 1732 was more productive than its Lords' predecessor. The Chapter House, identified as having the potential to hold more records, was repaired and provided with additional chests. It took in displaced muniments from the St Margaret's gatehouse, together with the records of the Courts of Requests and Wards and Liveries. And more deposits followed in the succeeding decades, including Domesday Book and other documents from the Exchequer repository near the Tally Court.[15]

The mid-eighteenth and early nineteenth centuries saw periodic efforts to improve the fabric of the Palace of Westminster. Between 1755 and 1770 new stone buildings were erected on the west side of the Hall, and they included a store for some of the King's Bench records. In the early 1790s the ancient buildings housing the Court of Augmentations were demolished and its records transferred to the stone buildings. But in 1800 a Commons committee, the first to deal with the subject since 1732, undertook a wide-ranging enquiry into the state of the public records. It revealed, depressingly enough, that the building operations of the second half of the eighteenth century had done little to solve Westminster's archival problems. In fact some of the records displaced by that activity had been moved into yet more unsatisfactory quarters, including the damp and insecure vaults of the only recently completed Somerset House.[16]

Nor can much further progress be recorded, as far as record storage at Westminster is concerned, during the first three decades of the nineteenth century. One observer was to remark in 1832 that 'every passage' of the 1800 Report exhibited 'evils to which

---

[14] The Library had only recently been moved to Ashburnham House from Essex House because the latter was considered a fire risk.

[15] Thomas, *op cit*, p134; Hallam, *op cit*.

[16] One researcher was laid up with rheumatism for a week after spending an hour and a half transcribing a document in one of the vaults. *Papers and Documents Relating to the Evidence of Certain Witnesses Examined before the Select Committee of the House of Commons Appointed 'to Inquire into the Management and Affairs of the Record Commission'*, 1837, p209. For building projects at Westminster, see HM Colvin, gen ed, *The History of the King's Works Vol 5: 1660–1782*, London 1975.

the lapse of thirty years has only served to give a more luxurious and more vigorous growth'.[17] More building work was undertaken in the 1820s, under the direction of Sir John Soane, and in 1822 the courts in Westminster Hall were rearranged, causing records stored there to be moved to a 'dark, damp and almost pestilential' wooden shed.[18] The shed had to be demolished in connection with preparations for the coronation of William IV, and the records were moved again, to the old Royal Mews at Charing Cross, where a dog was employed to chase away the rats that set up home among the documents. The Chapter House deteriorated in the early nineteenth century, and that period has been described as the least secure in the custodial history of Domesday Book.[19]

The records of Parliament were not, as already stated, public records, but it is appropriate to mention them here before leaving the Palace of Westminster. By the early nineteenth century the Jewel Tower, the main repository for the records of the House of Lords, had become overcrowded, but in 1827 a fireproof strongroom underneath Soane's new Royal Gallery was taken into use as an overflow store. The position regarding the records of the Commons remained less tidy. The journals were presumably kept in the Journal Office, but a quantity of subsidiary records dating from the early seventeenth century onwards was still, around 1830, housed in a number of places near the Commons chamber (the former St Stephen's Chapel).[20]

* * *

Between 1700 and 1830 the White Tower in the Tower of London remained one of only two repositories for the public records that maintained a search room for readers, the other being the Westminster Chapter House. Like the Chapter House, the Tower

---

[17] CP Cooper, *An Account of the Most Important Public Records of Great Britain, and the Publications of the Record Commissioners*, London 1832, pv. For the more general conclusions of the 1800 select committee, see below in this chapter.

[18] *Papers and Documents*, pp112–13.

[19] Hallam, *op cit*, p152.

[20] Previously use had been made of the capacious roof space above St Stephen's Chapel. *Ex inf* Dr Hallam Smith.

received some attention in the 1730s. The building was repaired, and its capacity for housing records increased by fitting presses into every available space in the Chapel of St John and the large room to the north of it.[21] But one serious drawback to the security of the repository remained – the presence in a vault below it of an enormous powder magazine belonging to the Board of Ordnance. Had it exploded it would have destroyed not only the Tower and its contents but much of the surrounding neighbourhood. Nevertheless, requests for its removal were resisted.[22]

The headquarters of Chancery were still at this period in the area of Chancery Lane. The office of the Six Clerks moved to Lincoln's Inn in the late 1770s, but the Rolls estate remained the centre of the Court's administration. To relieve pressure on storage space reliance had customarily been placed on periodic transfers to the Tower. These were suspended in the early eighteenth century but resumed after the Tower expanded its capacity in the 1730s, and continued after that into the early nineteenth century. Even so conditions in the Rolls Chapel became increasingly congested. In 1772 some relief was obtained by exercising 'the extremist economy of space', which involved cramming documents not only into more presses but also into the spaces below the seats in the chapel.[23]

* * *

The Exchequer and Chancery records were only part of a wider tranche of public records to come under the scrutiny of the select committee in 1800. It also concerned itself with matters of conservation as well as custody and showed both an appreciation of the historical value of the records and of the need to improve public access to them. But its specific recommendations were disappointing. It condemned the State Paper Office and the old Exchequer buildings, proposed a scheme to ventilate the basements of Somerset House and advocated better conditions for staff and readers at the Chapter

---

[21] See the plan of 1754 (TNA, WORK 31/98) in Elizabeth M Hallam and Michael Roper, 'The Capital and the Records of the Nation: Seven Centuries of Housing the Public Records in London', *London Jnl*, vol 4 no 1 (May 1978), p82.

[22] Elizabeth M Hallam, 'The Tower of London as a Record Office', *Archives*, vol xiv no 61 (1979), p8.

[23] Thomas, *op cit*, p150.

House. But, despite having before it the model of the General Register House in Edinburgh, it failed to produce a scheme for a central repository for the public records. Instead it concentrated on the need for more and better catalogues, indexes and publications, building on the labours of the eighteenth-century Methodizers. It saw the appointment of a royal commission as the best way to forward this work, a course adopted by the government the following year. The Record Commission, as it came to be known, lasted for thirty-six years, being renewed on the accession of a new Sovereign in 1820 and again in 1830. It produced a number of publications, some of permanent historical value, but also acquired a reputation for poor management, extravagance and internal dissension.[24]

Local Government

During the eighteenth century the counties continued to be governed by those unpaid gentlemen, the justices of the peace, and they were still served by part-time officials, generally attorneys who also had private practices. The work of both magistrates and clerks, however, steadily increased during the century. (It should be noted here that some of the remarks in this section also apply to the years 1660–1700, not separately covered in Chapter 9.) The judicial business conducted in quarter sessions grew, especially in those counties where industries developed and the population increased, and outside the courts the responsibilities of the magistrates were widened by legislation, for instance to provide prisons or houses of correction. From 1780 to 1830 the pace of change quickened, reflecting in particular the demands of the Napoleonic War period. The county expenditure of Warwickshire rose from £1,800 in 1782 to £20,393 in 1837.[25]

County records grew proportionately. Sessions books and files expanded; financial and rating records proliferated, prompted, for instance, by the County Rates Act of 1739; and there was an increase

---

[24] *Papers and Documents*; Peter Walne, 'The Record Commissions 1800–1837', *JSA*, vol 2 (1960–4), pp8–16.

[25] Philip Styles, *The Development of County Administration in the Late XVIIIth and Early XIXth Centuries, Illustrated by the Records of the Warwickshire Court of Quarter Sessions 1773–1837*, Dugdale Soc Occasional Papers no 4 (1934), p6. (The figures for the county reflect the presence within it of much of Birmingham.)

in the number of documents required to be deposited with the clerk of the peace, such as copies of parliamentary enclosure awards and land tax duplicates. Especially after 1780 the clerks found themselves involved in a growing amount of correspondence, with chairmen of quarter sessions and other active magistrates but also sometimes with the Home Secretary in London. The clerk of the peace might also double as clerk of lieutenancy, involving letters to and from the lord lieutenant and the deputy-lieutenants in each division of the county.

The preservation of these records, however, remained haphazard. After 1660 there appears to have been an endeavour in some counties to adopt more systematic record-keeping habits.[26] In the eighteenth century there was an increase in county consciousness, encouraged by antiquarian work on county histories, and this may have inspired some county leaders to take an interest in the records. In 1751 the Surrey magistrates were concerned to discover that the 'publick Records of this county' were in a bad state, and the 'Ancient Records' lost altogether, although their recommendations for the future custody of the surviving ones appear to have had little effect.[27] In Gloucestershire it was the clerk of the peace who in the 1730s took the initiative by providing accommodation for the records, largely at his own expense.[28] But elsewhere the clerk might take a more limited view of his responsibilities, and might receive little encouragement from the Custos Rotulorum to do otherwise.

As always, secure permanent accommodation for the records was crucial, but even by 1800 not every county had a shire hall where a record room could be provided. The Cambridgeshire clerk reported to the select committee of that year that when he had taken on the office in 1793 he had received records jumbled up in sacks from the representatives of his predecessor, records that he had had to accommodate in premises he provided himself. The magistrates of the Parts of Holland in Lincolnshire took the view that they could not spend the ratepayers' money on sorting and arranging their muniments, although they did allow the clerk eight pounds a

---

[26] The Gloucestershire order books, for instance, begin in 1672.
[27] Dorothy L Powell, *Guide to Archives ... Relating to Surrey: Quarter Sessions Records, with Other Records of the Justices of the Peace for the County of Surrey*, Surrey Rec Soc vol xxxii (1931), p31 (introduction by Hilary Jenkinson).
[28] IE Gray, *Gloucestershire Quarter Sessions Archives 1660–1889 and other Official Records*, Gloucester 1958, pxi.

year for keeping them safe and dry in his own office.[29] The building of shire halls could be delayed by a reluctance to spend money but also by rivalries among the towns where quarter sessions were customarily held.[30]

* * *

Like the county, the parish found its responsibilities increasing during the eighteenth century, particularly as regarded highways and the Poor Laws. Some parishes kept the relevant documents carefully, and even purchased new chests, generally plain wooden boxes, for them, as the churchwardens of Thaxted (Essex) did in 1789.[31] Elsewhere record-keeping might be more casual. It was said of one overseer of the poor, a farmer, that he 'kept his accounts in a pair of boots, putting into one the money he had received, and into the other the acknowledgments for the sums which he expended'.[32] Even so, the records accumulated in England's ten thousand or so parishes by 1800 must have amounted in total to a formidable quantity; but in fact only a few parishes now hold a significant quantity of vestry minute books (recording the proceedings of the annual parish meetings), poor law papers or churchwardens', overseers' or highways accounts dating from before the early nineteenth century.[33] Much must have been considered unworthy of longer-term preservation, or have passed into private hands. The most notable archival event of the early nineteenth century in parochial terms was the introduction under an Act of 1812 of iron safes or chests for parish registers. They may have been more secure than the old wooden

[29] *House of Commons Select Committee Report on the Public Records*, pp263, 277. Only twenty out of fifty-two English and Welsh counties had offices 'constructed at the public expense'. See *ibid*, pp10, 162ff.

[30] For early nineteenth-century problems in Lincolnshire, see RJ Olney, *Rural Society and County Government in Nineteenth-Century Lincolnshire*, Lincoln 1979, pp104ff.

[31] WE Tate, *The Parish Chest: a Study of the Records of Parochial Administration in England*, 3rd edn Cambridge 1969, p41.

[32] Sidney Webb and Beatrice Webb, *English Local Government from the Revolution to the Municipal Corporations Act, 1: the Parish and the County*, London 1906, p67.

[33] Tate, *op cit*, p71, quoting the evidence of the Webbs to the 1912–19 Record Commission.

ones, but in damp churches they could lead to serious problems. One authority describes them as 'register death traps'.[34]

The foregoing remarks apply in particular to England's rural parishes, which in 1830 still made up the great majority. By the early nineteenth century urban expansion was putting the parochial system under strain in some areas and leading to a clearer demarcation between civil and ecclesiastical records. Manchester, a parish containing thirty-seven semi-independent townships, was having acute problems with its accounts by the 1790s. At Leeds on the other hand the parish co-operated with the manor and the borough to provide a more joined-up system of civic government.[35] Another development with record-keeping implications was the increasing importance in some parishes of the vestry, with its committees and paid officers. For the London (Middlesex) parish of Marylebone the vestry records go back as far as 1683.[36] At Camberwell, a Surrey parish now part of south London, a vestry clerk kept the minutes instead of the vicar from about 1700, and the parish employed a salaried surveyor of highways from at least 1781. The surviving civil parish records from before 1830 are nevertheless patchy.[37]

* * *

By the early nineteenth century there were other local bodies in the English counties besides the parishes and the county authorities themselves. Magistrates were in some places meeting in petty sessions, although formal records of their meetings are hard to come by for the years before 1800. Magistrates could also act singly, in which case they kept notebooks of the cases that came before them, and these have occasionally survived in collections of family papers. Unusually, three members of the Mosley family maintained the same justice book between 1616 and 1739.[38] Trusts were created under

---

[34] Tate, *op cit*, p7; David Sherlock, *Suffolk Church Chests*, Ipswich 2008, p1.
[35] Webb and Webb, *op cit*, pp50, 73.
[36] *Ibid*, p207.
[37] SC Humphrey, *A Guide to the Archives in Southwark Local Studies Library*, 1992, p44.
[38] Webb and Webb, *op cit*, pp388, 415–17. For the justice books of a late eighteenth-century farmer and magistrate, see BJ Davey, ed, *The Justice Books of Thomas Dixon of Riby 1787–98*, in Lincoln Rec Soc, vol 102 (2012).

local Acts to undertake and manage turnpikes, canal and navigation projects and drainage schemes. As with the much older commissions of sewers local solicitors acted as their clerks, and in some cases their records ended up in solicitors' offices.[39] Much more substantial were the archives created by the deed registries that were set up in the early eighteenth century for Middlesex and the three Ridings of Yorkshire, a belated sequel to the scheme for the enrolment of bargains and sales of two-and-a-half centuries before.[40]

By 1800 the manor had in many places lost the status that it had anciently held in local affairs. It had ceded legal and judicial functions to other bodies, and in many cases was no longer an essential element of estate management. Small manors up and down the country faded away, and their records were lost, but some larger manors not only survived but flourished, for instance where open arable fields or areas of unenclosed moor or pasture still needed to be managed. Court records for the early modern period show continuing local concerns over matters such as boundaries, roads, fences and drainage.[41] Above all the survival of copyhold tenure – tenure of property by copy of an entry in the court roll – ensured the continuance of many manorial regimes until the abolition of that form of tenure in 1922. There was a steady trend towards the use of books rather than rolls, and paper rather than parchment, but court procedure, and the types of document generated, remained very conservative. The custody of these records was still the responsibility of the stewards who held the courts on behalf of their lords, but by 1830 many of them were also local solicitors, and again it was in their offices that manorial records could have the best chance of long-term survival.

* * *

In this section it remains to consider that other medieval survival, the borough. Here the eighteenth and early nineteenth centuries

---

[39] For records of the Ancholme Drainage and Navigation, see Lincolnshire Archives Committee, *Archivists' Report 21* (1969–70), p34.

[40] Francis Sheppard and Victor Belcher, 'The Deed Registries of Yorkshire and Middlesex', *JSA*, vol 6 (1978–81), pp274–86.

[41] Brodie Waddell, 'Governing England through the Manor Courts 1550–1800', *Hist Jnl*, vol 52 no 2 (2012), pp279–315.

The Long Eighteenth Century 1700–1830 155

saw a widening gulf between the incorporated towns and cities that grew in wealth and size and those small boroughs that continued to stagnate or decline. In cities such as London and Bristol the growth of their archives prompted measures to improve their care and management. In London a room under the Council Chamber was made available in 1705 for the storage of letter books, journals and repertories, although the provision of a new muniment room had to wait until the late eighteenth century.[42] At Bristol there were financial reforms in the 1690s, and in 1751 the city's minute books were transferred from a chest to a press in the committee room at the Council House.[43] But even in the larger and better managed boroughs losses could occur. The City of London's records suffered a fire in 1786.[44] And elsewhere it was not uncommon for documents to be sent to London for production in a lawsuit and not returned. Along with these perennial hazards the eighteenth century saw a spate of unauthorised 'borrowings' by antiquarian scholars: the municipal records of King's Lynn were among those to be seriously depleted. On the other hand antiquarian interest could make custodians better aware of the value of their muniments. The work undertaken on the city of Gloucester's records in the 1720s is a case in point.[45]

Religious Archives

For the Church of England the eighteenth century was a period of relative tranquillity between the upheavals of the seventeenth and those of the nineteenth. This could provide opportunities for quiet archival progress or foster periods of inertia and neglect. At Lambeth the archiepiscopal records were concentrated in Morton's Tower and the Library, in which latter place AC Ducarel, the Librarian from 1757 to 1775, did useful sorting and listing. He

---

[42] Philip E Jones and Raymond Smith, *A Guide to the Records in the Corporation of London Record Office and the Guildhall Library Muniment Room*, London 1951, p13.

[43] N Dermott Harding, 'The Archives of the Corporation of Bristol', *Trans Bristol and Gloucs Arch Soc*, vol xlviii (1926), pp234, 239.

[44] Jones and Smith, *op cit*, p70.

[45] Dorothy Owen, ed, *The Making of King's Lynn, a Documentary Survey*, 1984, p4; Brian S Smith, 'Gloucestershire Records: the Clerks and Custodians', *Trans Bristol and Gloucs Arch Soc*, vol cv (1987), p8.

also arranged and bound the papers of Edmund Gibson, the historically minded bishop of London who died in 1748 leaving his own papers and some of Archbishop Tenison's to the Library.[46] At York the story was by contrast one of chronic muddle and shortage of accommodation. In 1776 a space was found under the minster library for a quantity of court and other records, but by 1800 it was already seriously inadequate, and in the 1830s the conditions there were described as scandalous.[47]

By the end of the eighteenth century the registrar was firmly established as the key figure in diocesan record-keeping, and he generally belonged to the same breed of lawyer that we have repeatedly encountered in this chapter. His office steadily filled with records, many now in volume form, including fee books, precedent books and deed registers. If he belonged to a well-established local law firm there could be advantages in terms of long-term storage for the records, but the contents of his office might not be safe if he died in harness. At Ely a quantity of documents was sold as waste paper following such a death, although the antiquary Samuel Peck was able to buy 189 pounds of them by weight and, in 1772, restore them to diocesan custody.[48] Another hazard, familiar from previous periods, was the tendency of records to lie around in episcopal palaces. When Ely Place was sold in 1772 and the bishop migrated to a town house in the West End of London some documents were lost, including perhaps a seventeenth-century bishop's register.[49]

During the eighteenth century the muniments of deans and chapters continued to be kept in a variety of places – in the cathedrals themselves, in chapter houses or in or near the cloisters. Cathedral dignitaries had more time for looking after their records than bishops or archdeacons, and a certain amount of useful archival work seems to have been done, but there were also examples of loss and neglect, as at St Paul's, London.[50] Among the peculiars good

---

[46] MD Slatter, 'AC Ducarel and the Lambeth MSS', *Archives*, vol iii no 18 (Mich 1957), pp97–104.

[47] KM Longley, 'Towards a History of Archive-Keeping in the Church of York', *Borthwick Institute Bulletin*, vol 1 (1975–8), p64.

[48] Dorothy Owen, *Ely Records: a Handlist of the Records of the Bishop and Archdeacon of Ely*, [1971], pviii.

[49] *Ibid*, pix.

[50] For archival work at Ely Cathedral, see Peter Meadows and Nigel Ramsay, eds, *A History of Ely Cathedral*, Woodbridge 2003, pp272–4. For London, see

progress was made at Westminster Abbey, where in 1733 Richard Widmore began a programme of cataloguing that is reflected in the arrangement of the muniments today. He was also able, in 1758, to procure four presses for the muniments that had become available when the Cottonian Library was moved from the Abbey precincts to the new British Museum in Bloomsbury.[51]

* * *

Some of the more interesting developments in religious archives at this period involved institutions that lay outside the older-established structures of the Church of England. Queen Anne's Bounty was founded in 1704 to augment the incomes of small livings, and there were commissions to build new churches for populous parishes in the early eighteenth and early nineteenth centuries. Of a less official nature were the missionary societies, which relied to a great extent on the conduct of regular overseas correspondence: their remarkably full archives were to survive to provide a rich source for twentieth-century historians. The National Society was established in 1812 to promote religious education, and by the early 1970s its archive had swelled to embrace some twelve thousand files.[52]

Those excellent record-keepers the dissenters continued to expand their archives during the eighteenth century, and from the latter part of the century they were joined by first the Wesleyan Methodists and then the Primitive Methodists. Like Old Dissent the Methodists, with their minutes, conference reports, membership lists and circuit plans, treated record-keeping as a priority. A more complicated archival history, not previously alluded to in these pages, concerns the Roman Catholics. Bishops and priests in the eighteenth century and earlier often left personal memoirs, but before the restoration of the Hierarchy in 1850 there are few

---

Nigel Ramsay, 'The Library and Archives to 1897', in Derek Keene *et al*, eds, *St Paul's: the Cathedral Church of London 604–2004*, New Haven CT and London 2004, p422.

[51] Richard Mortimer, *Guide to the Muniments of Westminster Abbey*, Westminster Abbey Rec Series no vii (2012), p5.

[52] [CJ Kitching], *The Central Records of the Church of England: a Report and Survey Presented to the Pilgrim and Radcliffe Trustees*, London 1976, p28.

surviving episcopal or parish records of a more formal nature. Religious orders that had taken refuge on the Continent after the Dissolution were obliged to return to England in the aftermath of the French Revolution in 1793. They brought some valuable records back with them, but others were lost, or ended up in Continental libraries.[53]

Other Institutional Archives

The precedent in record-keeping set by the Royal Society, described in Chapter 9, was followed in the eighteenth century by similar bodies – the Antiquaries from 1707, the Royal Society of Arts from 1754 and the Royal Academy from 1768. They benefited from a number of practical developments such as the readier availability of writing paper, the growth of the printing industry and improvements to the postal services, the last-named first in London and then, from the early eighteenth century, in the provinces.[54] These developments also encouraged a notable growth in the charitable sector, especially in the case of bodies concerned with medicine and welfare. The London hospital founded by Thomas Guy (d1724) followed an older tradition of foundations endowed with landed estates, but other charities were set up that were supported not by agricultural rents but by the contributions of their patrons and subscribers. The Bath General Infirmary was started as a charity in 1737, obtained an act of Parliament in 1739 and opened its hospital in 1742. Headed as it was by a committee, its key records were its minute books, subscription books, ledgers and letter books, and its principal record-creating officers were its secretary and treasurer. This form of organisation, the predecessor of countless others in the following decades, is exemplified in the Infirmary's well-kept archive, which in the late twentieth century remained in the possession of its successor, the Royal National Hospital for Rheumatic Diseases.[55]

---

[53] Records from Douai made their way to Ushaw, and some from St Omer to Stonyhurst.

[54] Howard Robinson, *The British Post Office: a History*, Princeton NJ 1948, pp75–100.

[55] Ann Borsay, 'Using the Records of an Eighteenth-Century Infirmary', *Archives*, vol xxi no 92 (Oct 1994), pp172–82.

Another feature of the period was the increasing number of organisations with both central and local archive-creating elements. (For the Quakers, pioneers in this respect, see Chapter 9.) The United Grand Lodge of English Freemasons has preserved its records from1723, including correspondence with and annual returns from provincial lodges from 1745. These lodges kept their own archives, and a few, from as early as the late eighteenth century, have been deposited with local libraries or record offices.[56] The Society for the Promotion of Christian Knowledge, founded as early as 1698, relied on local representatives to distribute its printed literature, and again created a substantial archive.[57]

By the middle of the eighteenth century some societies and associations founded several decades previously were in need of some archival attention. At the Royal Society John Robertson, its Secretary from 1767 to 1776, assembled the fellows' election certificates in a series of guard books, and bought back a fellows' register that had strayed from custody.[58] Outside London an antiquarian body founded in 1710, the Spalding Gentlemen's Society, soon developed a tradition of caring for its records, though it did not acquire permanent premises until the early twentieth century. Its secretary from 1713 to 1748, Maurice Johnson, maintained a copious correspondence with the Antiquaries, the Royal Society and other contacts, and he and his assistant Dr John Green spent much time arranging the resulting mass of letters and placing them in 'large, strong brown folders'.[59]

Among the older charities the eighteenth century saw some modernisation in financial record-keeping, and, as with the larger City livery companies, the more systematic creation and preservation of estate records. Some institutions, however, stuck at least in part to their antiquated ways. St John's College, Cambridge adopted the more accessible volume format for its annual accounts, but alongside them it retained until 1770 its ancient series of bursars' rolls and continued to store them in chests alongside statutes and

---

[56] Information available through the NRA.
[57] WE Tate, 'SPCK Archives', *Archives*, vol ii no 18 (Mich 1957), pp105–15.
[58] Marie Boas Hall, *The Library and Archives of the Royal Society 1660–1990*, London 1992, p14.
[59] Diana Honeybone and Michael Honeybone, *The Correspondence of the Spalding Gentlemen's Society 1710–1761*, Lincoln Rec Soc, vol 99 (2010), ppxxiv–xxv and Appendix 3.

legal papers.⁶⁰ Less and less needed for administrative purposes, some of the older records of these academic bodies began to attract scholarly attention. At St John's, Oxford William Dereham, its President from 1748 to 1757, worked on the college records.⁶¹ At Eton the older records were examined in the 1720s by that well-known antiquary Tom Martin of Palgrave, and then moved from the bursar's office to a new library in the Fellows' Quadrangle.⁶² In contrast, however, to such well-endowed institutions many small local charities were prone to neglect and failure during the eighteenth and early nineteenth centuries, and their records consequently disappeared into oblivion, unless preserved among parish records or in a solicitor's office.

Estate and Business Archives

The institutional landowners already encountered in this chapter – the Church, the older colleges and charities – all benefited from the agricultural improvements of the period, and particularly those of the years between 1760 or so and 1815. But it was the great private estates that were in the best position to take advantage of or directly to stimulate them; and it was they too whose archives most clearly reflected their growing wealth and power. The leading aristocratic families of England (some of which also held large estates in Wales, Scotland and Ireland) consolidated their pre-eminent economic and social position through the operation of primogeniture and strict settlement, and the increasingly bulky legal documents thus generated took their places on the shelves of aristocratic muniment rooms such as those of the Seymour dukes of Somerset, the Leveson-Gowers of Trentham (Staffordshire), later dukes of Sutherland, and the Cavendish dukes of Devonshire.⁶³ As well as more elaborate deeds

---

⁶⁰ Malcolm Underwood, 'The Defences of a College: the Law's Demands and Early Record Keeping in St John's College, Cambridge', in Ralph Evans, ed, *Studies in Memory of Trevor Aston*, Woodbridge 2004, p245.

⁶¹ Robin Darwall-Smith and Michael Riordan, 'Archives for Administrators or Archives for Antiquarians? A History of Archive Cataloguing in Four Oxford Colleges', *JSA*, vol 30 no 1 (Apr 2009), p105.

⁶² Information kindly supplied by Penny Hatfield and Eleanor Hoare.

⁶³ See HMC *Principal Family and Estate Collections*, Guides to Sources ... 10 and 11, 2 vols London 1996, 1999, *sub* Cavendish, Percy, Seymour, Sutherland-Leveson-Gower and Wyndham.

and legal papers they kept more detailed leases and agreements, more thorough and accurate estate particulars and surveys, and, inevitably, more correspondence. A late eighteenth-century innovation was the wet-process letter book, a method of keeping copies of outgoing letters in volume form that was invented by James Watt around 1780.[64] To such series of estate records could be added in some cases papers to do with home farms, woodland management, urban development and the exploitation of minerals. The development of large urban landholdings, such as those of the Russells, Portmans and Grosvenors in London, necessitated their own estate offices and archives.

To manage all these aspects of land management and wealth creation the roles of the land agent and the solicitor expanded and became more specialised. The chief legal official became the confidential adviser to the family, the forerunner of Dickens's Mr Tulkinghorn; and in place of the old structure of reeves, bailiffs and receivers there emerged the powerful figure of the head agent, controlling a number of local agents on the family's different properties. At Trentham the process can be followed between 1690 and 1740, while at Boughton, the Northamptonshire seat of the dukes of Montagu, there was a chief agent and accounting officer from 1720.[65] This division of responsibility was reflected in a separation of the legal records in the muniment room from the working records of the estate that the agent kept to hand in his own domain. Their exact locations, however, varied according to local circumstances. At Melbourne Hall (Derbyshire) and Badminton House (Gloucestershire) free-standing pavilions were built for the muniments.[66] At Holkham, the Norfolk seat of the Cokes, earls of Leicester, a separate building combining estate office and muniment room was erected near the splendid new Hall in 1759–60, but later this was abandoned in favour of offices in part of the Hall itself.[67]

---

[64] Michael Cook, 'Towards a History of Record Technologies: the Damp-Press Copying Process', *JSA*, vol 32 no 1 (Apr 2011), pp35–49. It was taken up by solicitors as well as land agents.

[65] JR Wordie, *Estate Management in Eighteenth-Century England: the Building of the Leveson-Gower Fortune*, London 1982, pp23–30; PH Mackay and DN Hall, *Estate Letters of the Time of John, 2nd Duke of Montagu 1709–39*, Northants Rec Soc, vol xlvi (2013), pxxxiii.

[66] For Badminton, see Brian S Smith, *op cit*, p10.

[67] Christine Hiskey, *Holkham: the Social, Architectural and Landscape History of a Great English Country House*, Norwich 2016, pp233, 249, 328.

In some houses the losers by these arrangements were the records of domestic management. These had been simplified since the days of the large baronial household, and the office of head steward was replaced by two figures of humbler origin, the butler, in charge of the male servants, and the housekeeper, in charge of the women. The series of general household accounts gave way to the more modest wages books and cellar books, which found a natural home neither in the muniment room nor in the estate office. They tended to be passed from one senior servant to another, or cleared out during bouts of spring-cleaning, and are often missing from the surviving country house archives of today.

For some estates the preferred site of the principal muniment room was not in or near a country house but in the London town house, as with the earls Spencer and the dukes of Norfolk. This reflected the fact that the chief legal agent was now a London solicitor, who found it convenient to use the muniment room of his client as an adjunct to his own office. Another variant is represented by the dukes of Northumberland (the successors to the Percy estates of the dukes of Somerset), whose Middlesex seat at Syon House was near enough to London to make it a suitable place to keep the muniments. In 1809 the second Duke built a new free-standing evidence room there, next to the early seventeenth-century one noted in Chapter 7, and had it furnished with handsome mahogany cupboards, shelves and drawers.[68]

The muniments kept in country houses were not immune from loss or damage. Some houses were re-ordered internally, with consequent disturbance to the records. Thoresby Hall, the Manvers seat in Nottinghamshire, suffered a destructive fire in 1746. Unenlightened records management could also present a hazard. Around 1800 various bundles in the muniment room at Wollaton Hall (Nottinghamshire) were docketed 'illegible' or 'of no value', and at a similar date household papers in the Northumberland archive were marked 'of no use: destroy', although in both cases the condemned documents survived.[69] Well-built estate offices such as that of 1737 at Trentham could be places for the orderly preservation

---

[68] Information kindly supplied by Christopher Hunwick, archivist to the Duke of Northumberland.

[69] HMC *Manuscripts of Lord Middleton*, 1911, pv; GR Batho, ed, *The Household Papers of Henry Percy, Ninth Earl of Northumberland (1564–1632)*, Camden 3rd S, vol xciii (1962), pxx.

The Long Eighteenth Century 1700–1830   163

of records, but elsewhere piles of non-current records in the recesses of estate offices could fall victim to clear-outs and bonfires.[70]

* * *

In the eighteenth century the City of London continued to dominate the world of commerce and finance, though increasingly challenged by places such as Bristol, Liverpool and Manchester. The Bank of England, dealing as it did with chartered companies and the government itself as well as private clients, was building up an important archive by the mid-eighteenth century, including minutes of its Court of Directors and papers of successive Governors and Secretaries as well as accounting records.[71] Other banks remained private partnerships rather than joint stock enterprises, and continued to keep the kinds of document previously described.[72] Alongside the banks, however, there grew up a major insurance industry including, in London, such firms as the Hand-in-Hand, Sun, Westminster, Phoenix and Royal Exchange. Like the banks, these firms were notable producers of ledgers and other records.[73]

Among the creators of industrial records pride of place must be given to the brewers. By 1700 there were already two hundred common brewers in London, and in the following decades the London porter breweries included some of the largest industrial enterprises in England, with record-creating capacities to match. Typical constituents of the brewer's archive were partnership records, accounts with employees and customers, production records and papers relating to brewing premises and public houses. By 1800 a leading business of this kind 'might be maintaining at least thirty regular accounting books at any one time'.[74]

---

[70] For Trentham, see Wordie, *op cit*, p40.

[71] John Orbell and Alison Turton, *British Banking: a Guide to Historical Records*, Aldershot 2001, p3; HMC *Annual Review 1990–1*, pp35–7.

[72] See Chapter 9.

[73] HAL Cockerell and Edwin Green, *The British Insurance Business: a Guide to its History and Records*, Sheffield 1994, pp5 *et passim*.

[74] Lesley Richmond and Alison Turton, eds, *The Brewing Industry: a Guide to the Historical Records*, Manchester 1990, p28 (introduction by Prof Peter Matthias).

Outside London the Industrial Revolution produced some major archives. In iron-founding and manufacturing the pioneers included the Darbys of Coalbrookdale, a family influenced in its record-keeping by its Quaker affiliation: it was already keeping detailed cash books and stock books in the 1730s.[75] Somewhat later an impressively complex archive was created by the great industrial and engineering business founded on the partnership of Matthew Boulton (d1809) and James Watt (d1819).[76]

When a family business turned itself into a partnership a range of documents had to be created – partnership deeds and associated papers, profit and loss accounts, and deeds and papers relating to jointly owned assets or premises. More thorough accounts would need to be kept: when the Cromptons of Derby turned their country bank into a partnership they took on a clerk to keep the cash books.[77] In the case of an expanding industrial business, records of production, supplies and wages would be necessary. Yet, especially for the years before 1780, the survival rate for such archives is low. A business could be destroyed in short order by a down-turn in trade, the collapse of a market on which it depended or a falling-out among the partners. Occasionally records were abandoned in a derelict building, as in the case of the Arkwright mill at Mellor (Derbyshire), to await rescue by business historians of a much later era. More usually premises were destroyed by fire or rebuilt to meet the demands of the next generation. This was true even of the large breweries, which suffered archival losses despite an often impressive continuity of ownership and management.[78]

Many businesses remained *family* businesses, and where the family survived, even if the business did not, there was a chance that the business archive might survive with it. The Henley family were shipowners at Wapping in the late eighteenth and early nineteenth centuries. They turned themselves into country landowners but

---

[75] See Barrie Trinder, *The Industrial Revolution in Shropshire*, London and Chichester 1973.

[76] WKV Gale, *Boulton, Watt and the Soho Undertakings*, Birmingham nd; Tim Proctor, 'Two Men of Industry: the Soho Firms of Matthew Boulton and James Watt, as revealed by the archives of Soho', *Business Archives*, no 88 (2004), pp13–30; NRA 14609, 9497, 22549.

[77] AC Littleton and BS Yamey, *Studies in the History of Accounting*, London 1956, p268.

[78] Richmond and Turton, *op cit*, p24.

preserved 116 wooden boxes of business papers in the attics of their house at Waterperry, near Oxford, for nearly a century and a half before they were deposited in the National Maritime Museum at Greenwich.[79]

But what of the many small businesses, those of professional men, farmers, small merchants, shopkeepers and others, that also flourished at this period? Such enterprises often ended with the lives of their founders, if not before, and families of the middling sort tended not to occupy the same house or business premises for more than one or two generations. Survivals, such as the memorandum books of Thomas Turner, a mid-eighteenth-century Sussex shopkeeper, are consequently very rare.[80] Farming records for the period before 1830 are particularly scarce, due in part to the fact that so many farmers were tenants rather than owner-occupiers, and hence not anchored for very long in one place, but also no doubt to the fact that they were in any case not dedicated record-keepers.[81] London was home to innumerable individual and small family enterprises, yet even there the survivals are meagre. In 1990 the Guildhall Library held only about forty account books, letter books or small groups of papers dating from before 1800.[82]

One exception to this dismal tale, however, concerns the records of attorneys or solicitors. A number of firms surviving today can trace their origins back to the late eighteenth century, and of these a few have preserved letter books and bill books from that period. In addition, moreover, to keeping the records of what may be called the firm's own business, many solicitors took on a wide assortment of clients for whom they might draw up conveyances, wills, partnership deeds and other documents. These papers, together with the relevant correspondence, were kept in boxes relating to those clients, and were regarded as the property of the

---

[79] Simon Ville, 'The Henley Collection', *Business Archives*, no 51 (Nov 1985), pp45–51.

[80] David Vaisey, ed, *The Diaries of Thomas Turner 1754–1765*, Oxford 1984, pp354–6.

[81] But for an unusual survival of farming records from the late eighteenth century, part of a collection of family papers, see Richard Olney, *Farming and Society in North Lincolnshire: the Dixons of Holton-le-Moor 1741–1906*, Lincoln Rec Soc Occasional Series no 2 (2018), pp185–90.

[82] Joan Bullock-Anderson, *A Handlist of Business Archives at Guildhall Library*, 1989.

clients rather than that of the firm. Solicitors' attics and basements thus became archive repositories that could represent rich sources for the historian, and in many cases it is these records, rather than the firms' own business records, that in modern times have been deposited in local record repositories.

The Personal and Family Archive

'Henceforth,' wrote Jonathan Swift in London on 9 September 1710, 'I will write something every day to MD [his symbol for friends in Dublin], and make it a sort of journal; and when it is full I will send it whether MD writes or no.'[83] In other words, he was planning to write a journal in letter form, and he continued to send it off to Dublin in instalments during his three-year sojourn in the English capital. The flexibility of the Augustan epistolary form was taken a stage further by that great letter-writer Horace Walpole. He arranged for the letters that he sent to Sir Horace Mann over many years to be returned to him at intervals for copying and binding into volumes.[84] Another phenomenon of the period was the rise in popularity of the travel journal, a testimony to the greater leisure and mobility now enjoyed by members of the middling sort.[85]

Horace Walpole, the son of a prime minister, was conscious that his correspondence would have some interest for posterity, and this was especially true of those who themselves had prominent public careers. As the eighteenth century progressed greater numbers of politicians, diplomats, generals, admirals and others kept the private correspondence relating to their official duties. For some it might be necessary to defend their conduct after they left office, although there were cases when it might be more prudent to destroy documents than to keep them.

For a personal archive in the process of formation the most usual place of storage at this date was a lockable drawer underneath the writing surface of a desk. For larger quantities of papers, in bundles

---

[83] Swift's *Journal to Stella*, Everyman edn 1924, p4.

[84] WS Lewis et al, eds, *Horace Walpole's Correspondence with Sir Horace Mann Vol 1*, London 1955, pxlii.

[85] See Robin Gard, ed, *The Observant Traveller: Diaries of Travel in England, Wales and Scotland in the County Record Offices of England and Wales*, London 1989.

The Long Eighteenth Century 1700–1830   167

or volumes, one could use a cabinet or cupboard. Swift recorded in letter VII of his *Journal to Stella* that he put incoming letters into 'the letter partition of my cabinet'. Horace Walpole kept the returned originals of his letters to Mann in a cabinet in his London house but the volumes of transcripts in a cupboard at Strawberry Hill. In the early nineteenth century Evelyn's diaries were discovered in 'the ebony cabinet in the billiard room' at Wotton.[86]

As for posterity, if one did not direct one's papers to be destroyed, or in the rare case of a civil servant to be sent to the State Paper Office,[87] the problem of what to do with them fell into the lap of one's heirs and executors. Some families were not archivally minded, but others took pride in preserving the papers of earlier generations, rather as they might look after the ancestral monuments in the parish church.[88] In some cases a dynasty had been founded by a statesman or military commander whose papers were preserved as a memorial to his career and public service: thus the Cecil papers at Hatfield were followed a century later by the Marlborough papers at Blenheim. Among gentry families seventeenth-century figures such as Sir Ralph Verney, Sir William Dugdale and John Evelyn continued to exert archival influence from beyond the grave.[89]

Sometimes later generations showed too much interest in the family papers rather than too little. One historian writes of middle-class family archives 'often purposely shaped by self-appointed guardians'.[90] Around 1700 there was 'something of a vogue among gentry women' for 'preserving parts of a family archive, of their own or an earlier generation, by copying original letters and documents into family commonplace books'.[91] Volumes such as diaries had

---

[86] Lewis *et al, op cit*, pxlii; F Verney, ed, *Memoirs of the Verney Family*, 4 vols n.p. 1892, i.xi–xii, quoted in Susan E Whyman, *Sociability and Power in Late Stuart England: the Cultural World of the Verneys 1660–1720*, Oxford 1999, p5.

[87] For such a bequest – a chestful of official papers – see JC Sainty, 'A Huguenot Civil Servant: the Career of Charles Delafaye, 1677–1762', *Huguenot Soc Proceedings*, vol xxii (1970–6), p411.

[88] See Eric Ketelaar, 'The Genealogical Gaze: Family Identities and Family Archives in the 14th to 17th Centuries', *Libraries and the Cultural Record*, vol 44 no 1 (2009), pp9–28.

[89] For Verney, see Whyman, *op cit*, p5.

[90] Susan E Whyman, *The Pen and the People: English Letter Writers 1660–1800*, Oxford 2009, p168.

[91] Frances Harris, 'The Letterbooks of Mary Evelyn', *English Manuscript Studies*, vol 7 (1998), p206.

some chance of preserving their documentary integrity, although they could be edited and censored. Letters were more vulnerable to being re-ordered and weeded.

Unlike the middle classes the landed aristocracy had the advantage of a comparatively stable environment for records in their country houses. Some indeed became repositories for the papers of relatives and connexions who lacked such facilities themselves. But such houses were not always safe archival havens. With the muniment room often out of bounds for papers of a more personal nature, the obvious alternative storage area was the library, but there bound volumes of correspondence or papers could end up being mistaken for books, and even disposed of accidentally in a library sale. For less presentable records there was always the attic, provided that its roof was in good repair. In 1826 Sir Harry Verney came upon 'a wainscoted gallery' at the top of his house at Claydon full of boxes of estate and family papers.[92] In the late eighteenth century the attics of Wotton House were reputed to contain trunksful of Evelyn papers, from which the maids were allowed to help themselves to kindling for lighting the fires.[93]

* * *

The eighteenth-century antiquarian scholar kept correspondence and notebooks in the usual way, but he also had what he called his collections – the notes, transcripts, pedigrees and other documents that embodied the fruits of his researches, and that could form the materials for a publication.[94] But in addition to, or mingled with, these papers might be original documents obtained during the course of his work. Some of these had been acquired when they had already strayed from their archival contexts, but others, less happily, might have been lifted from those contexts by the antiquary himself. Francis Blomefield, the historian of Norfolk, discovered the Paston papers in Lord Yarmouth's muniment room, and was largely responsible for their subsequent chequered history.

---

[92] Whyman, *Sociability and Power*, p5.

[93] Simon Adams, 'The Papers of Robert Dudley, Earl of Essex: 1, the Browne–Evelyn Collection', *Archives*, vol xx no 87 (Apr 1992), p75. Scrap paper could also be used for sewing patterns and in baking and preserving.

[94] See HMC Guide to *Papers of British Antiquaries and Historians*, px *et passim*.

Even in this case, however, it can be argued that had it not been for his intervention that priceless fifteenth-century collection might not have survived at all.[95]

Antiquarian collections once formed did not, of course, always remain intact. Particularly from the mid-eighteenth century some of the more valuable ones were sold and broken up. Documents or groups of papers might reappear in other collections, but others might disappear altogether. A few collections, however, made their way into institutional custody. In 1753 the British Museum was established by royal charter, its foundation collections of manuscripts including the Cottonian Library, still needing much repair after the fire of 1731, and the remarkable collections of Robert Harley, second earl of Oxford, and Sir Hans Sloane. For those who had stronger ties with the University of Oxford, or who fell out with the British Museum, there remained the refuge of the Bodleian Library, whose most notable acquisition in the early nineteenth century was a substantial tranche of Richard Gough's collections.[96]

---

[95] Norman Davis, ed, *Paston Letters and Papers of the Fifteenth Century Vol 1*, Oxford 1971, ppxxivff.
[96] *Papers of British Antiquaries and Historians*, pp83–4.

III

The Age of the Archivist 1830–1980

The century and a half between 1830 and 1980 was a period of momentous change in England, politically, economically, socially and culturally. Its population continued to grow and became predominantly urban and industrial rather than rural and agricultural. It acquired a literate working class; aristocracy gave way to democracy; and the State became ever more powerful. All these changes had an impact on the types of archive formed, as well as on their sheer volume. New archives came into existence as bureaucracies burgeoned at national and local levels, and as societies and organisations of all kinds proliferated, while the archives of long-standing institutions, if they survived, had to adapt themselves to new requirements and working methods.

These changes were reflected in the types of document that made up the average archive and in the way that it was managed. As a result the archive of 1930 was less attractive in appearance than its predecessor of a century before. Handsomely bound volumes of minutes and accounts were now less in evidence than untidy files and bundles of papers, and these gatherings were more likely to be stored in tin boxes and metal filing cabinets than wooden receptacles. Handwritten letters featured less than typewritten ones, and printed items formed a more conspicuous part of the whole. After 1930 there were further and yet more rapid changes, as new technology made itself felt. Microfilming came into its own during the Second World War as a way of making security copies, and later as a means of making copies of documents available to historians while protecting the originals. By the mid-1960s the possibilities of computers were being taken increasingly seriously, although their main impact on the world of archives would be after 1980.

In 1830 England remained an unenlightened country as far as standards of archival care were concerned. Many of the country's most valuable archives were in private hands – repositories were very few and far between – and their very existence was in many cases unknown and unrecorded. The conditions under which they were stored were scarcely more sophisticated than those obtaining in the Middle Ages, and the creation of an archival profession was still some decades in the future. By 1980 much had changed. Repositories in which archives needing homes could be cared for had proliferated; an archival profession had finally come into being; and standards of care and management had risen greatly. Above all the country knew much more about its archival riches and valued them more highly as part of its cultural heritage, although a comprehensive framework for their protection remained far from complete.

11

Archives in an Age of Reform 1830–1900

Introduction

The Victorian period was the great age of the manuscript letter. By 1874, even before the introduction of compulsory elementary education and little more than thirty years since the start of the penny post, nine hundred million communications a year were being handled by the General Post Office (GPO).[1] By 1890 the GPO employed 100,000 people,[2] its work assisted by a railway network that now covered much of the country. This revolution was underpinned by a great increase in the manufacture of paper, much of it made from wood pulp rather than rags. UK production totalled 360,000 tons in 1877, compared with 43,000 tons in 1842.[3]

This expansion was closely linked to another Victorian phenomenon, the growth of organisations of all kinds. The bureaucracy of the GPO was itself an outstanding example. Another was the national system of poor relief created by the Act of 1834. It set up around 640 poor law unions covering the whole of England and Wales and oversaw them through a flow of letters and circulars from its London headquarters. By 1914 the Poor Law Board was holding 22,000 volumes of correspondence and over 4,000 registers.[4] Archive creation on such a scale can hardly have been envisaged even by the zealous reformers of the early 1830s.

---

[1] Howard Robinson, *The British Post Office: a History*, Princeton NJ 1948, pp366–7.
[2] *Ibid*, p425.
[3] Chambers's *Encyclopædia*, 1908 edn, 10 vols, vii.739.
[4] Paul Carter and Stephen King, 'Keeping Track: Modern Methods, Administration and the Victorian Poor Law, 1834–1871', *Archives*, vol xl no 128/9 (Apr–Oct 2014), pp31–52.

Central Government and the Public Records

Despite these general trends the central departments of government largely avoided bureaucratic gigantism before 1900. The Treasury managed to do so by delegating the day-to-day work of revenue-gathering to other bodies, such as the Boards of Excise (later Inland Revenue) and Customs. Nevertheless, it maintained its close oversight of the nation's finances, for instance by ensuring that double-entry book-keeping became the norm throughout Whitehall.[5]

The Treasury was fortunate, too, in that its purpose-built premises escaped major remodelling in the mid-nineteenth century. This was not the case with the Departments of State – the Home, Foreign and Colonial Offices – which had begun life in improvised accommodation, and which by 1830 were running into record-keeping problems as a result. It was not until the 1860s that they were provided with rather splendid new premises, near the Treasury on the west side of Whitehall. They were joined there by the newly created India Office, the successor to the Board of Control, which thus acquired much needed space for its own, much larger, archive.[6]

As in the period 1782–1830, the Foreign Office archive well illustrates the challenges faced by many government departments in the age of reform. It had its own printing office from about 1825, and from the mid-century was keeping series of confidential print. From that time also dated its adoption of the telegraph, with its obvious implications for international communications, and from 1878 it numbered telegrams in the same way as despatches. But at that date clerks were still making copies of despatches by hand: the first typewriter appeared in 1889, and the first shorthand writer in 1898. It was not until after 1900 that the registry system was thoroughly reformed and that, eventually, the practice of binding papers in volumes before sending them for permanent storage was abandoned.[7]

---

[5] Henry Roseveare, *The Treasury: the Evolution of a British Institution*, London 1969, pp137–8.

[6] Antonia Moon, 'Destroying Records, Keeping Records: Some Practices at the East India Company and at the India Office', *Archives*, vol xxxiii no 119 (Oct 2008), p117.

[7] Michael Roper, *The Records of the Foreign Office 1782–1968*, PRO 2002, pp13–14, 17–18, 41, 54.

During the first half of the nineteenth century the State Paper Office continued to fulfil its traditional function as the repository for non-current State papers, both domestic and foreign, and in 1833 it finally acquired a modern building in Whitehall in which to house them. They remained, strictly speaking, outside the sphere of the public records, but in the early nineteenth century their historical interest and value was increasingly recognised, and their subsequent fate is described later in this chapter.

* * *

In 1830, as noted in Chapter 9, there were still only two places where historians and other members of the public could examine the ancient records of the kingdom, the record offices in the Tower of London and the Westminster Chapter House. A quantity of court and other records were in temporary accommodation in the Royal Mews but were disturbed again in 1835 when the site was earmarked for the National Gallery. This time alternative storage space was found in Carlton Ride, the largely wooden structure that had previously served as a riding school for Carlton House. There some of the most important medieval records of the royal courts were to languish for another two decades and more.[8]

Meanwhile, on 16 October 1834, a very substantial portion of the Palace of Westminster was consumed by fire. The incident has been described as 'the most momentous blaze in London between the great Fire of 1666 and the Blitz', and it occurred as the result of an exercise in records management that went wrong. It had been decided to clear a room full of those now obsolete wooden documents the Exchequer tallies and to burn them in the furnaces below the chamber occupied by the House of Lords. The resulting conflagration destroyed not only that chamber but a number of the surrounding rooms and offices, including the meeting place of the Commons in St Stephen's Chapel. The fate of the parliamentary records is dealt with later in this chapter, but as regards

---

[8] *Papers and Documents Relating to the Evidence of Certain Witnesses Examined before the Select Committee of the House of Commons Appointed 'to Inquire into the Management and Affairs of the Record Commission'*, 1837, pp112–13; J Mordaunt Crook and MH Crook, eds, HM Colvin, gen ed, *The History of the King's Works Vol 6: 1782–1851*, London 1973, pp321–2, 350–1.

the public records stored in and near the Palace the destruction was less than it might have been. Many of the older records were at that date in the Royal Mews. The most valuable of those remaining at Westminster were mostly in the Chapter House, which escaped the blaze, although its custodian Francis Palgrave had some anxious hours. The new (1823–6) range of buildings to the west of Westminster Hall housed fairly recent records, but there was one major exception, the archive of the defunct Augmentations Office, which since 1793 had been stored in a room next to the Exchequer Court. Although these buildings escaped the fire it was considered too risky to leave the records in them, and many were thrown out of the windows, much as had happened in the Whitehall fire of 1619. They landed in St Margaret's Lane, and most were taken across to St Margaret's church as a temporary sanctuary, but some loose papers were trodden under foot in the chaos or spoiled by water from the fire-fighting operations.[9]

Parliament could hardly have received a clearer message about the state of the public and parliamentary archives and the ramshackle buildings in which many of them were housed, but in fact a movement for reform had already begun to gather momentum. The Record Commission demonstrated a new energy from 1831, and the following year its secretary, Charles Purton Cooper, published a plan for a new central repository.[10] Further progress was delayed by the Parliamentary Reform crisis, the fire of 1834 itself, and the parsimonious reluctance of the Treasury to consider a large building project. (According to one source it had a strong aversion to the very word 'Record'.)[11] The idea of creating a single record *authority*, however, was more attractive, especially if it involved winding up the Record Commission and re-employing its officers in the new organisation, thus avoiding the expense of pensioning them off. Lord Langdale, the conscientious and reforming Master of the Rolls, promoted the scheme, supported by the clear-sighted archivist Francis Palgrave at the

---

[9] Caroline Shenton, *The Day Parliament Burned Down*, Oxford 2012, pp174 *et passim*; Warwick Rodwell and Tim Tatton-Brown, eds, *The Art, Architecture and Archaeology of the Royal Abbey and Palace of Westminster*, 2 vols Leeds 2015, ii.245.

[10] Peter Walne, 'The Record Commissions 1800–1837', *JSA*, vol 2 (1960–4), p12.

[11] John D Cantwell, 'The Making of the First Deputy Keeper of the Records', *Archives*, vol xvii no 73 (Apr 1985), p34.

Chapter House; and the Home Secretary, Lord John Russell, took a helpful interest in it.[12]

The Public Record Office Act (only later given this short title) reached the statute book in 1838. The Master of the Rolls (MR) was duly made Keeper of the Public Records, with Palgrave as his deputy, and under them a small body of staff was created, headed by the officials in charge at the Tower and elsewhere. But two matters remained to be resolved – where and when the proposed general record office would be built, and what it would contain. They were of course closely related: the size of the repository would depend on the quantity of documents it was intended to accommodate, and that in turn depended on the number of bodies to be covered by the Act and the rate at which they transferred their older records for permanent storage.

As regards the building, the site proposed by Cooper in 1832 had been the Rolls site in Chancery Lane. That was where, under the new legislation, Langdale and Palgrave set up their headquarters, and indeed where the Public Record Office was eventually erected. But for some years that outcome remained uncertain. At one stage the Victoria Tower, in Barry's imposing new Palace of Westminster, was under consideration, before being rejected as too small. It was only in 1847 that the Rolls site was finally agreed, and between 1850 and 1858 that the new Record Office was built. It was remarkable for neither its beauty nor its convenience, but it was thoroughly fireproof . Wood was eliminated from its construction as far as possible; record storage was provided in a number of fireproof strongrooms; and in them, at the special insistence of the then MR Lord Romilly, even the shelves were of slate rather than wood.[13] The lesson of 1834 had not been forgotten.

At last England could boast a national repository, one that could provide a service both to government departments and to the public, and one that could provide a national model for archival management. But already, in the twenty years since the passage of the Act, pressures on the State to improve the way in which it managed its records had been mounting. These pressures, moreover, came

---

[12] John D Cantwell, *The Public Record Office 1838–1958*, London 1991, pp7ff; Roger H Ellis, 'The Building of the Public Record Office', in Albert EJ Hollaender, ed, *Essays in Memory of Sir Hilary Jenkinson*, Chichester 1962, pp9–10.

[13] Ellis, *op cit*, pp15–16; Cantwell, *op cit*, p156.

not from institutions whose records were traditionally regarded as public, but from the area of modern departmental records. In 1841 a large quantity of naval records had to be cleared out of a store in Deptford and was given shelter in the Tower. In the mid-1850s, due to the exigencies of the Crimean War, more naval and military records had to be stored in the Tower, but in 1858 both the Chapel of St John and the Wakefield Tower were required for other purposes, and their contents were decanted into the as yet unfinished Record Office.[14] In the 1850s the comparatively recently built State Paper Office fell victim to the redevelopment of that part of Whitehall. The British Museum put in a bid for its contents, on the grounds that they belonged more appropriately with the Museum's political collections than with the public records in Chancery Lane, but it lost the battle, and the State Papers were transferred to the Record Office in 1862.

The Master of the Rolls, meanwhile, had been confronting the question of what exactly it meant for him to have 'charge and superintendence' of records that were destined for the Record Office but had not yet reached it. How, in particular, could he prevent tranches of unsorted records being dumped on him at short notice? His hand, however, was strengthened first by informal agreements and then, in 1852, by a widely drawn if questionably worded Order in Council.[15]

* * *

Not surprisingly it became evident even before the Record Office was finished that more accommodation would be needed. For once the Treasury was in expansive mood, and the Office was extended at the Fetter Lane end in 1863–71. A further building programme was embarked on in the 1890s, this time on the Chancery Lane side, involving the destruction not only of a row of rickety houses used as record store-rooms but also of the handsome early eighteenth-century Rolls House and the venerable though much degraded Rolls Chapel. By now, however, some of the

---

[14] Rupert C Jarvis, 'The Grigg Report, II: The Public Record Office', *JSA*, vol 1 (1955–9), p12; Cantwell, *op cit*, p197; Cantwell, 'The 1838 Public Records Act and its Aftermath: a New Perspective', *JSA*, vol 7 no 5 (1984), pp277–86.

[15] Cantwell, *Public Record Office*, pp142–3.

disadvantages of the cramped site were becoming more obvious, and internally the building suffered from poor ventilation and limited natural light.[16]

The years 1860 to 1900 were nevertheless in some ways the most creative and vigorous period of the PRO during its stay in Chancery Lane, especially during the deputy-keepership of Sir Thomas Duffus-Hardy (1861–78) and the earlier part of the long tenure of Sir Henry Maxwell-Lyte (1886–1926). Work proceeded on cleaning, sorting and listing the older records, and progress was made, albeit slowly, in securing more regular transfers of more recent material from departmental registries and stores. Under an Act of 1877 it became allowable for the first time to 'weed', that is selectively to destroy, modern papers judged to be of no permanent value. Search rooms were provided for the growing numbers of those wishing to search the older records for 'literary' as well as legal reasons; fees were reduced and then abolished; and the periods during which State and other papers were embargoed were very gradually reduced. Finding aids were improved, and publications not forgotten. In 1855 Romilly secured a grant to continue the calendaring of the State Papers, and in 1857 it became possible to resume the work of the Record Commission in the form of a new series of medieval *Chronicles and Memorials*, known as the Rolls Series, although it was later decided to concentrate instead on improving the finding aids to the Office's own holdings.[17]

In other ways, however, the Record Office failed to present itself as a model of good practice. One great advantage of a general repository that brought together records from various sources under one roof was that it presented opportunities for its curators to research the history of public administration and elucidate the origins and interconnections of the various departments, as part of the process of arrangement and listing. Unfortunately it also presented opportunities for creating fresh muddles rather than resolving old ones. Palgrave and his colleague Joseph Hunter believed correctly that documents from an archive should be kept together – the doctrine of *respect des fonds* – and that their

---

[16] *Ibid*, p264; Royal Commission on Public Records, *Report* 1912, p13.
[17] Aidan Lawes, 'Publishing the Public Records 1800–2007', in Paul Brand and Sean Cunningham, eds, *Foundations of Medieval Scholarship: Records Edited in Honour of David Crook*, York 2008, p17.

arrangement in the repository should reflect where feasible the way in which they had been created and assembled in the first place. A classified guide to the records could always be produced to assist the researcher. But others in the Office believed that they could assist historians more directly by rearranging documents in date order (as with the State Papers), alphabetically (as at one stage with parliamentary petitions) or by type of document (as with various accounts from Exchequer and other sources). Thus the Stonor papers (for which see Chapter 4) were scattered through artificial classes of correspondence, deeds and accounts.[18]

Meanwhile, some unfortunate things were happening to more modern records, although in some cases PRO inspectors were able to intervene on their behalf while they were still in departmental custody. The port books (though not in their entirety), the Chancery Masters' Exhibits and the 1851 and 1861 census enumerators' returns were saved, but the parliamentary poll books for the period 1843–70 and the Insolvent Debtors' Files were not so fortunate.[19]

The greater attention paid in the Office to medieval rather than more recent records was a feature of its culture that was firmly established in the nineteenth century and that was to last well into the twentieth. The PRO hierarchy was composed of three layers: the assistant keepers, a coterie of middle-class gentlemen for whom, as one of their number was later to write, 'serious history ... gave place to frivolity and journalism about the time of the battle of Bosworth';[20] the clerks who did the bulk of the administrative work; and the workmen who got on with the 'manual' tasks of cleaning, packing and shelving the documents.[21] These class distinctions spilled over into the way in which searchers were treated. Serious students could receive invaluable expert assistance, but genealogists,

---

[18] Michael Roper, 'The Development of the Principles of Provenance and Respect for Original Order in the Public Record Office', in Barbara L Craig, ed, *The Archival Imagination: Essays in Honour of Hugh A Taylor*, Ottawa 1992, pp138–42.

[19] Cantwell, *op cit*, pp332–3.

[20] NAM Rodger, 'Drowning in a Sea of Paper: British Archives of Naval Warfare', *Archives*, vol xxxii no 117 (Oct 2007), p104. Palgrave had liked to regard the assistant keepers as 'a species of college'. They certainly resembled one in their tendency to quarrel among themselves.

[21] Cantwell, *op cit*, pp181, 231.

who were 'generally of the lower classes of society' and who could be annoyingly bent on proving claims to fortunes or peerages, were given shorter shrift.[22]

All this contributed to an inward-looking culture that affected the PRO's national role. Many records of national importance within its remit continued to be kept outside London, but the Office's chronic shortage of space meant that it took them in only if they were considered to be at serious risk. An alternative was to establish regional repositories, but this was never done, although for a time it was contemplated for Chester.[23] When Maxwell-Lyte came from outside to take up the deputy-keepership in 1886 he began by encouraging the Office to 'spread its wings', but as his long reign proceeded he became less enthusiastic about collaborating with other bodies, and in the early 1900s the Office files were still revealing 'an official attitude of Olympian detachment' to the problems of local custodians.[24] As early as the 1820s the Record Commission had been aware of the work of the newly founded French *École des Chartes* in training archivists, but the PRO failed to start a similar course within its own institution, although one such scheme in the 1890s got as far as being scotched by the Treasury.[25]

Only a few minutes' walk from the PRO lay that other great repository of manuscript records, the British Museum. As might be expected from the foregoing, relations between the two institutions were not of the closest or most cordial, and were particularly cool during the time that Sir Frederic Madden was head of the Museum's Department of Manuscripts (1837–66). And indeed there were enduring cultural differences. Unlike the Museum the PRO could not choose what records it took in: it could not reject them because they were in a filthy condition or because it thought their contents of insufficient interest. With its limited resources, moreover, once it had taken in a deposit it could not devote to it the same detailed and meticulous attention that the Museum gave to its holdings. It stored

---

[22] *Ibid*, pp40, 220; AE Stamp, 'The Public Record Office and the Historical Student: a Retrospect', *TRHS*, 4th S vol xi (1928), pp26–7. See also Philippa Levine, *The Amateur and the Professional: Antiquarians, Historians and Archaeologists in Victorian England 1838–1886*, Cambridge 1986, pp123–6.

[23] Cantwell, *op cit*, p158.

[24] *Ibid*, p311; JR Ede, 'The Record Office: Central and Local', *JSA*, vol 5 no 4 (Oct 1975), p210.

[25] Cantwell, *op cit*, p327.

them in boxes rather than bound volumes and produced *ad hoc* finding aids rather than printed catalogues with elaborate indexes. In other words, it was a record office rather than a library, although its listing methods did not always serve to underline the distinction.

* * *

Before leaving the subject of the public records it may be appropriate to deal here with a small body that was closely connected administratively with the PRO, although it was entirely concerned with non-public records. The Royal Commission on Historical Manuscripts, or Historical Manuscripts Commission (HMC), to give it its handier title, was set up in 1869 to investigate and report on a wide range of privately held archives, including those of individuals, landed families, colleges, cathedrals, boroughs and other institutions. It can be seen as the successor to the Rolls Series, the Record Commissions, and before them of parliamentary and other enquiries going back to Bernard's *Catalogi* in the late seventeenth century. Alive to the sensitivities of private owners (from the higher ranks of whom some of the Commissioners themselves were drawn), the HMC was at pains to emphasise its independence of government. It was financed by its own Treasury grant and employed its own team of inspectors. But it operated from within the PRO, its chairman was the Master of the Rolls, and its part-time secretary was one of the Office's assistant keepers.

It got off to a good start.[26] There was a positive response to its initial enquiries, and its work drew attention to some collections of the first importance, among them the Cecil papers at Hatfield and the records of the House of Lords. (The owner of the former, the third marquess of Salisbury, later prime minister, was an early and influential supporter of the HMC.) Its work was hampered, however, by the meagreness of its resources in relation to the huge task before it, and by the amateurishness, not to say the eccentricity, of some of its tiny band of inspectors.[27]

---

[26] See HMC *First Report*, 1870.

[27] See, for instance, John Cordy Jeaffreson's strange report on Miss Conway Griffith's MSS in the *Fifth Report*, to which Dr Christopher Kitching drew my attention.

Archives in an Age of Reform 1830–1900 183

❋ ❋ ❋

Of the public bodies falling outside the scope of the Public Record Office Act, perhaps the most anomalous was the India Office. It was headed from 1858 by a Secretary of State and occupied grand premises in Whitehall from 1867, but its records were never *public* records, due perhaps to the fact that it was financially independent of the Treasury. It did, however, adopt regulations for the management of its records on the PRO model following the Act of 1877. As for the records of Parliament, which had constitutional reasons for keeping its records separate from those of the Executive, they were badly affected by the fire of 1834. At that time the older records of the House of Lords were still in the Jewel Tower, which was fortunately well away from the blaze. Since 1827 a fireproof room underneath Soane's newly built Royal Gallery had been used as an overflow store. Its contents were much nearer the fire but were the subject of a well-organised salvage operation and escaped almost unscathed. They were subsequently disturbed more than once during the rebuilding of the Palace, but eventually, along with the records from the Jewel Tower, were given a new home in the Victoria Tower. The records on the Commons on the other hand suffered a major disaster in the fire: the journals mostly survived, but almost all the rest was lost. It was not until after 1900 that the archive of the Commons joined that of the Lords in the Victoria Tower.[28]

❋ ❋ ❋

Another notable feature of the Victorian period was the development of the Royal Archive as the private archive of the Sovereign. Its origins may be traced back to the emergence of Cabinet government in the eighteenth century. The king had to keep in touch by correspondence with his closest political advisers, principally the prime minister, but it was considered undesirable for him to employ a private secretary, who might act as an intermediary and become

---

[28] Shenton, *op cit*, pp183–4, 187–90 *et passim*; HMC *First Report*, Appendix, p1; Maurice F Bond, *Guide to the Records of Parliament*, London 1971; HS Cobb, 'Parliamentary Records for the Political Historian', *Archives*, vol xx no 89 (Apr 1993), pp18–24.

privy to Cabinet secrets. Any letters from the king would therefore have to be written by himself, and any letters to him kept by him without secretarial assistance. Neither George I or George II appears to have kept papers.[29] George III, George IV and William IV did so, with unofficial help from members of their households. The situation changed, however, with the accession of the young and inexperienced Victoria in 1837. At first the prime minister, Melbourne, was her guide and assistant, but the modern history of the archive really begins when she married. The efficient and meticulous Prince Albert assumed the role of her records manager, arranging her papers by correspondent and subject, and mounting them in a series of bound volumes. After his death, however, the system lapsed. The post of private secretary was eventually regularised, but by Victoria's death her archive had descended into confusion.[30]

By the mid-nineteenth century there was no doubt about the private status of the archives of the duchies of Lancaster and Cornwall. The records of the former, after a sojourn in Somerset House, had been moved to the Duchy's new offices in Lancaster Place, on the site of the Savoy. In 1869 the older records were passed to the PRO, but as a gift from the Queen.[31] After some years in unsatisfactory accommodation the Duchy of Cornwall moved in the 1850s to a new office in Buckingham Gate, near the Palace. There was no question, however, of any transfer of its older records to the PRO. Indeed the Duchy would have welcomed a chance to fill some of the gaps in its archive by a transfer in the opposite direction.[32]

During the nineteenth century the practice was maintained by foreign secretaries, diplomats and other high-ranking public servants of taking home their 'private' correspondence on leaving office. There was another category, however, of records created in public offices but later moving out of public custody, and that

---

[29] Earlier royal correspondence has to be sought among the State Papers.

[30] Sir Robin Mackworth-Young, 'The Royal Archives, Windsor Castle', *Archives*, vol xiii no 59 (1978), pp115–30. Victoria herself was 'much against destroying important letters'. In the twentieth century Melbourne's own papers were given to the Royal Archives. (*Ibid*, pp122, 126.)

[31] The PRO nevertheless regarded the *judicial* records of the Duchy as public.

[32] Royal Commission on Public Records, *Second Report, Part 1*, 1914, p15. Palgrave had failed to get both duchies included in the Act of 1838. Cantwell, *op cit*, p223.

was of documents that were either lost or deliberately stolen. A clause was included in the 1838 Bill enabling the MR to reclaim such strays, but it was removed before the Act was passed, leaving successive Deputy-Keepers in difficulties when items surfaced in auction rooms or otherwise came to their attention. It was possible to issue a warrant for their return, but only if the document or group of documents had recently left official custody and had not changed hands in the meantime. When some early modern accounts of the Royal Revels were offered for sale to the British Museum they turned out to have been removed from a cellar in Somerset House by a former clerk in the Audit Office, who was obliged to surrender them. The papers of John Cayley (formerly of the Augmentations Office), however, included some Wardrobe books, and when his collection was dispersed at auction after his death in 1834 they entered the enormous antiquarian collections of Sir Thomas Phillipps. When Maxwell-Lyte tried to reclaim them sixty years later they could not be dislodged from the hands of the trustees to whom they had passed under Phillipps's will. Only occasionally was a restoration effected, if the PRO could overcome its reluctance to make a payment.[33]

Local Government

As in Whitehall and Westminster, so in the municipal corporations of England there was radical change in the 1830s. An Act of 1835 imposed a uniform system of elected local government on the boroughs (with the exception of the City of London). They acquired new duties and powers, and the records produced, especially by town clerks and borough treasurers, increased in proportion. Ancient manorial and other officials did not completely disappear, but power shifted to new committees. At Bristol, for instance, it was the finance committee that was given responsibility for the corporation's archives, and, on a very different scale, the old Hutch Committee at Great Yarmouth was replaced by a records committee.[34]

---

[33] Cantwell, *op cit*, pp102–3, 222, 348–9.
[34] N Dermott Harding, 'The Archives of the Corporation of Bristol', *Trans Bristol and Gloucs Arch Soc*, vol xlviii (1926), p247; Paul Rutledge, 'Archive Management at Great Yarmouth since 1540', *JSA*, vol 3 (1965–9), p91.

186 *English Archives*

This did not mean that after 1835 every borough paid more attention to the preservation of its older records. In many cases the first two or three decades of the new regime were a period when more urgent matters demanded attention. In 1838 Palgrave thought that there was a good case for bringing borough records under the Public Record Office Act, since 'the Town Clerks who commonly read these documents have generally neglected them'.[35] But from the 1870s awareness of the historical value of the older municipal records increased, and where new town halls were built it became more usual to provide a fireproof strongroom for them, as at Leicester in 1878.[36] In some cases interest from the PRO and the HMC was helpful, as at Bristol and Gloucester.[37] But at the end of the century conditions in some municipalities remained unsatisfactory. At Winchester the less valuable part of the archive was reported to be housed in a (disused) water closet.[38]

Perhaps the most striking developments occurred in the great industrial and commercial centres of the Midlands and the North. Birmingham, Manchester, Liverpool, Leeds and Sheffield were among the places that took pride in their identities and histories. But this did not result in the creation of record offices on the PRO model. Rather these municipalities put their resources into free public libraries, in aid of which they were empowered under an Act of 1850 to raise a penny rate. In 1866 Birmingham established a Reference Library that soon built up an impressive collection of manuscripts relating to the borough (later city) and its hinterland, although in 1879 it received a major setback when many of its holdings were destroyed by fire.[39] Such municipal collections were closer in nature to those of the British Museum than to the archives in the Public Record Office, but in fact neither of those national institutions seems to have had much influence on local practice.

---

[35] Cantwell, *op cit*, p33.

[36] AKB Evans, 'The Custody of Leicester's Archives from 1273 to 1947', *Leics Arch and Hist Soc Trans*, vol lxvi (1992), p117.

[37] Dermott Harding, *op cit*, p247; Brian S Smith, 'Gloucestershire Records: the Clerks and Custodians', *Trans Bristol and Gloucs Arch Soc*, vol cv (1987), p12.

[38] Local Records Committee *Report*, 1902 (Cmd 1335), p74. Some small corporations had been wound up in 1882–3, their records passing to local trusts.

[39] Alfred Andrews, 'The Birmingham Reference Library', *Archives*, vol i no 5 (Lady Day 1951), p12.

***

Unlike the boroughs, the counties were not reformed in the 1830s. For another half-century, until the County Councils Act of 1888, they continued to be governed by the county magistrate in quarter sessions. But the magistrates' powers were increasingly circumscribed by the central government in London, most notably by the operation of the New Poor Law. The result was a weakening of county feeling and a low level of interest in the preservation of county records in the period 1835–70. Not many new county halls were built, and when space became short consideration was often given to the main series of quarter sessions minutes and files rather than to the mass of financial and other records. A vacant corner of the county gaol might be requisitioned, as at Devizes in Wiltshire. The Buckinghamshire magistrates chose to pass some eighteenth-century treasurers' records to the county archaeological society.[40] When Somerset did provide a muniment room in its new shire hall at Taunton in 1858 it was reserved for the 'more important documents'. The lord lieutenant, Lord Portman, told a meeting of quarter sessions that lesser items could be put in an inferior room, while 'some of the old accounts, one, two or three hundred years old, might go into the cellar. They could not destroy them, but if they were placed in safety in the room below, they would be worn out in time, and certainly prove a loss to nobody – (a laugh)'.[41]

Portman was right that the Custos Rotulorum or his deputy in archival matters the clerk of the peace had no authority to destroy the records of quarter sessions, which was a court of record. He had taken the trouble to check this with the Master of the Rolls, who had confirmed that 'it was certainly the duty of the county to find room for the records of the county, as it was his [the MR's] duty to find a place for the national records'.[42] In 1877 there was a proposal to amend the Act of that year to bring quarter sessions records into the realm of public records, but it was not proceeded with.[43]

---

[40] Maurice G Rathbone, *Guide to the Records in the Custody of the Clerk of the Peace for Wiltshire*, 1959, ppx–xi; Local Records Committee *Report*, p29.
[41] *Taunton Courier*, 30 June 1858. I owe this reference to Mr TW Mayberry.
[42] *Ibid*.
[43] Cantwell, op cit, p278; *County of Dorset: Report of the County Records Committee*, 1877. The clause was promoted by Lord Shaftesbury as lord lieutenant of Dorset.

In practice the care of the county records devolved upon the clerks of the peace, who, like the town clerks, seldom gave the archives a high priority.[44]

From the 1870s, however, the counties, like the boroughs, began to take a more consistent interest in their records. A return of 1882 showed that the number of counties with fire-resistant strongrooms had increased.[45] In 1879, for instance, Lancashire had obtained a local Act under which it built a record room with a safe-type door, steel-shuttered windows and wooden presses.[46] The HMC, although paying more attention to borough records, did report on some quarter sessions archives, and in the 1880s Middlesex employed one of its inspectors to sort and list its records, assisted by workmen lent by the PRO. It appears not to have been a very pleasant job: in his *Recollections* the inspector, Cordy Jeaffreson, 'forbore to speak of what I did and endured, in order to preserve the remnants of the Middlesex County Records from quick and utter destruction'.[47]

Under the Local Government Act of 1888 elected councils took over the administrative functions of quarter sessions, and the clerks of the new county councils became responsible for the records that these councils began to create. Quarter sessions, however, continued to function for judicial purposes, and there was a problem about what to do with their older records. It was solved in most counties by uniting the clerkship of the peace with the clerkship of the county council in one individual, and by forming a joint records committee, normally chaired by the lord lieutenant as custos rotulorum. Hertfordshire formed such a committee in 1895, Bedfordshire in 1898 and Middlesex in 1900. These three counties, all near London, received help with their records from the firm of Hardy and Page, record agents.[48] London County Council,

---

[44] 'In the past clerks of the peace have in most cases grossly neglected their custody of county muniments', wrote Herbert Fowler (*The Care of County Muniments*, 2nd edn 1928, p7), echoing Palgrave's similar opinion of town clerks a century earlier.

[45] B Wood Smith, *County Records of England*, pr 1882.

[46] R Sharpe France, 'The Lancashire Record Office', *Archives*, vol i no 7 (1952), pp45–51, quoted in Elizabeth J Shepherd, *Archives and Archivists in 20th Century England*, Farnham 2009, p97.

[47] John Cordy Jeaffreson, *A Book of Recollections*, 2 vols London 1894, ii.95.

[48] WJ Hardy (d1919), the senior partner in Hardy and Page, was the son of Sir William Hardy of the PRO and father of William Le Hardy (1889–1961), later

the successor to the Metropolitan Board of Works, took an early interest in its records, setting up a room for them in the 1890s.

※ ※ ※

The New Poor Law was only the first major reform to challenge the old system of county government and create new record-keeping bodies. Civil registration of births, marriages and deaths was introduced in 1837; sanitary authorities appeared in the rural areas, and boards of health and improvement commissions in the towns; and in 1894 a more uniform structure of rural and urban districts was created, based on poor law divisions rather than old county and hundred boundaries. These bodies continued to accumulate records until their demise in the 1970s. Also in 1894 what remained of the civil functions of the parish passed in many cases to newly created parish councils. Unfortunately the relevant documents were not consistently handed over, and a provision for the supervision of that process by the county councils proved to be largely a dead letter. Enclosure awards could be among the casualties.[49] Tithe awards too were vulnerable:[50] in one Shropshire case an award was rescued from a public house, only to be passed to the parish overseers who subsequently denied ever having received it.[51]

The Established Church

In 1900 the Church of England was still the Established Church, as it had been in 1830, but in the intervening years its wealth and privileges had been curtailed, and its venerable archives disturbed and depleted. The chief agent of change was the Ecclesiastical Commission, set up in 1836 to overhaul the organisation and revenues of the Church. Extensive alterations were made to the diocesan map of England, with the boundaries of some existing

---

part-time archivist of Middlesex and Hertfordshire. William Page founded the *Victoria County History*.

[49] Royal Commission, *Third Report*, 1919, pp13–14.

[50] Tithe awards or apportionments under the Tithe Commutation Act of 1836 replaced the payment of tithes in kind by a rent-charge.

[51] Royal Commission, *Third Report*, 1919, p25.

dioceses altered and some new dioceses created. Inevitably series of records such as benefice papers were broken up, and where the new diocesan boundaries cut across archdeaconry boundaries there was bound to be further disruption.[52] A more general disturbance was created by the Commission's assault on the Church's endowments. In order to even out the wide variations in the incomes of bishops and cathedral chapters it took over the administration of their estates, in a protracted process that stretched over more than three decades. Large numbers of locally kept records such as deeds, leases, rentals and accounts were consequently transferred to London, a movement on a scale not seen since the Commonwealth period, and lodged in the Commission's offices in Whitehall Place.[53] The implementation of this policy, however, was uneven. The diocese of Ely retained many of its older records, but at Winchester the fine series of medieval pipe rolls was included in the transfer.[54]

Just as the registration of births, marriages and deaths had become a civil responsibility in 1837, so in the 1850s the ecclesiastical courts were reduced in scope and importance, and some of their functions transferred to other bodies, with deleterious effects on the preservation of their older records.[55] Those of the Court of Arches were moved in 1857 from the neighbourhood of Doctors' Commons (themselves abolished) to St Paul's Cathedral, where they were 'left for rubbish in a well'. By the time they were retrieved and taken to Lambeth Palace in 1865 they were 'rotting and reeking with damp'.[56] Also in 1857 the Church's probate jurisdiction was ended completely. The following year the records of the Prerogative Court of Canterbury were taken to the central registry in Somerset House, and those of diocesan and other local courts were deposited in district registries. Faced with deciding what to hand over and

---

[52] Dorothy Owen, *The Records of the Established Church, excluding Parochial Records*, London 1970, p14.

[53] CE Welch, 'The Records of the Church Commissioners', *JSA*, vol 1 (1955–9), pp14–16. For the Commissioners' own records, see below.

[54] For Ely, see Owen, *op cit*, p13. The Winchester pipe rolls and some other medieval records were later deposited in the PRO.

[55] Brian L Woodcock, *Medieval Courts in the Diocese of Canterbury*, Oxford 1952, p2; Audrey Erskine, 'Ecclesiastical Courts and their Records in the Province of Canterbury', *Archives*, vol 3 no 17 (Lady Day 1957), p17.

[56] Melanie Barber, 'Records of the Court of Arches in Lambeth Palace Library', *Ecclesiastical Law Jnl*, vol 3 no 12 (1993), pp11ff.

what to keep some registrars chose to part with more records rather than fewer, resulting in 'a miscellaneous dumping of much undifferentiated court material'.[57]

Diocesan registrars found themselves with some empty shelves as a result of these changes, but nature abhors an archival vacuum, and the shelves soon refilled with files and rolls relating to benefices, faculties for church buildings, tithe apportionments and the like. Non-current volumes and files were still being stashed away wherever there was a vacant space, often in the more dilapidated parts of a cathedral close. At York a search room was provided next to the registry, in the shadow of the minster, but it was compared by Charles Dickens to 'an indifferent chandler's shop', with 'a pestilential little chimney in it' that enveloped both the documents and their readers in smoke. Following his exposé in *Household Words* something was done about the chimney, but otherwise conditions had scarcely improved fifty years later.[58] And the situation at York was by no means unique, as revealed by a committee chaired by Bishop Creighton in 1899.[59]

In the early nineteenth century bishops, like statesmen, found themselves accumulating larger personal or private archives, as distinct from the official papers kept by their registrars. Parsons, parishioners (often complaining about their parsons) and others wrote to them with increasing frequency. The conscientious John Kaye as bishop of Lincoln from 1827 to 1853 received and kept some fourteen thousand letters on parochial matters alone, 'an average of 560 for each year of his demanding episcopate'.[60] For Bishop Blomfield of London, another very burdensome diocese, there are sixty letter books for almost exactly the same period.[61] But generally the survival rate for such papers is poor. It was still usual for bishops to keep such material in their palaces, and for it to pass into the hands of executors or family members after their deaths.

---

[57] Owen, *op cit*, pp23, 28, 47.

[58] KM Longley, 'Towards a History of Archive-Keeping in the Church of York', *Borthwick Institute Bulletin*, vol 1 (1975–8), p68.

[59] This was an internal Church of England investigation, and distinct from the Local Records Committee of 1899–1902, also chaired by Creighton before his untimely death.

[60] RW Ambler, *Lincolnshire Parish Correspondence of John Kaye, Bishop of Lincoln 1827–1853*, Lincoln Rec Soc, vol 94 (2006), pxxiii.

[61] HMC *Guide to Papers of British Churchmen*; NRA 36483.

Kaye's correspondence survived because, unusually, it ended up in the custody of the diocesan registrar. Stored in 'two carriage boxes' in Bishop Alnwick's medieval tower near Lincoln Cathedral, it was transferred by a later registrar to the custody of the diocesan record office.[62]

In 1830 parish records by and large conformed to the pattern of the early modern period, with parish registers, churchwardens' accounts and overseers' papers the principal documentary components. In 1900 the parson continued to keep the registers, but the parish chest, if still in use, filled with documents of a more modern kind – fund-raising accounts and papers (compulsory church rates having been abolished in 1868), Sunday school minutes, papers relating to social and missionary activities and printed items such as parish magazines. This was particularly true of those numerous urban and suburban parishes that in many cases had not even existed seventy years before. In the older parishes, meanwhile, the records were not always well cared for, and this applied even to the registers, whose genealogical and historical value for the period before 1837 was becoming more widely appreciated. A survey conducted in 1909 found that of 772 registers starting in 1538 and known to have existed in 1831, 116 were no longer extant.[63]

The English cathedrals were as much affected as the dioceses by the legal and financial changes of the period,[64] but their clergy had more time than hard-pressed bishops and parish priests to devote if they chose to their records. Not all deans and chapters were welcoming to scholars, but at Durham, Ely, Hereford, Lincoln and St Paul's, London, to name a few, there was progress in re-shelving, rearranging and re-boxing documents, stimulated on occasion, as with the boroughs, by interest from outside.[65] As for the peculiars, those bodies existing, and sometimes exercising jurisdictions, outside the diocesan system, many were abolished in the 1840s, with consequent losses of records. But in three cases, those of

---

[62] Lincolnshire Archives Committee, *Archivists' Report 9* (1957–8), p51.

[63] Royal Commission on Public Records, *Third Report*, 1919, p16; Local Records Committee *Report*, 1902, p33.

[64] The Cathedrals Act of 1840 extended the reach of the Ecclesiastical Commissioners to deans and chapters and was followed by further legislation in 1854.

[65] See the relevant chapters by Nigel Ramsay and others in the *Histories* of these cathedrals, several of which have been published since 1990.

the collegiate foundations of Ripon, Manchester and Southwell, their archives, going back to the Middle Ages, passed to the newly founded cathedrals of those places.[66] St George's Chapel, Windsor and Westminster Abbey survived relatively undisturbed, although they lost records to the Ecclesiastical Commissioners in the 1860s. Like some of the older cathedrals they began from around the same period to take a more consistent interest in the care of their archives.[67]

By 1900 the Ecclesiastical Commissioners were themselves presiding over a formidable archive. As the managers of large and far-flung estates, including some major urban developments, they employed an army of agents, surveyors and local stewards; and they became closely involved in matters such as the creation or amalgamation of parishes, the provision of new churches and the endowment of livings. And of course a large component of the records comprised thousands of deeds, maps and other documents for individual estates, many as already noted deposited from elsewhere, and all, somewhat unhelpfully, registered in one enormous numerical series.

Institutions and Organisations

England's ancient charities, like the Church, came under the scrutiny of the reformers during the nineteenth century. The universities and colleges of Oxford and Cambridge were the subject of legislation in 1858, as were the Endowed Schools in 1869. A more general Act to regulate charitable trusts had been passed in 1853, preceded by a series of enquiries and followed by further legislation. A Charity Commission was set up, and a team of inspectors began a programme of thorough investigations, resulting in new schemes for institutions that had become increasingly anachronistic in the Victorian age. Constitutions were revised, methods of accounting modernised and new series of records started. From the middle of the century more

---

[66] See the Pilgrim Trust Survey, pr 1951.
[67] Eleanor Cracknell, 'The Archives', in Nigel Saul and Tim Tatton-Brown, eds, *St George's Chapel, Windsor: History and Heritage*, Stanbridge 2010, pp15–20; Laurence E Tanner, 'The Nature and Use of the Westminster Abbey Muniments', *TRHS*, 4th S vol xix (1936), pp49–51; Richard Mortimer, *Guide to the Muniments of Westminster Abbey*, Woodbridge 2012, pp13–14.

schools kept systematic records of their educational work, and hospitals preserved more medical records. Their older records – their title deeds, account rolls and so on – became of more historical significance than administrative usefulness, and whether or not they were cared for or neglected might depend on the interest taken in them by individual administrators or scholars. The archives of Cambridge University were particularly well looked after by two of its registrars, Joseph Romilly (1832–62) and John Willis Clark (1891–1910), but at Oxford Philip Bliss, the keeper of the university archives from 1826 to 1857, 'introduced the greatest and most far-reaching disorder', gathering in extraneous material but failing to throw anything away.[68]

Meanwhile, new charities were being created at a rapidly increasing rate. In the early twentieth century it was estimated that there were over a thousand charitable institutions in London alone, not counting small parochial charities or those administered by the livery companies, and of those over eight hundred had been established since 1800.[69] London was also home to a growing number of national bodies. One outstanding group, already introduced in the preceding chapter, was formed by the missionary societies. They were not an exclusively nineteenth-century phenomenon, but they burgeoned after 1800, and were remarkable for the richness of their correspondence files, the means that kept them in touch both with their supporters at home and with their workers in the foreign field.[70] Another group of archival significance was the professional bodies, in this case very much a nineteenth-century product. Prominent among them were the Law Society from 1824, the Royal Institute of British Architects from 1834 and the various engineering institutes. They were membership bodies, concerned with the regulation of their professions, and the papers relating to these functions formed part of their core records.[71]

---

[68] Heather E Peek and Catherine P Hall, *The Archives of the University of Cambridge: an Historical Introduction*, Cambridge 1962, pp22–3; Dorothy Owen, *Cambridge University Archives: a Classified List*, Cambridge 1988, pix; Reginald L Poole, *A Lecture on the History of the Oxford University Archives*, Oxford 1912, p28.

[69] Chambers's *Encyclopædia*, 1908 edn, iii.112.

[70] See, for instance, Henry S Cobb, 'The Archives of the Church Missionary Society', *Archives*, vol ii no 14 (Mich 1955), pp293–9.

[71] See, for instance, Lenore Symons, 'Archives and Records of the Institution of Electrical Engineers', *Archives*, vol xvi no 69 (Apr 1983), p54.

In total bulk, however, the archives of these central bodies were exceeded by those resulting from the activities of countless smaller local organisations, from political, religious and workplace associations to clubs and societies of all kinds. But individually many of these kept little in the way of records apart from minute books and accounts, and even those were seldom preserved in the longer term. They were likely to perish sooner rather than later unless passed down in the families of their creators or given to a local library or museum. Where, however, the local body was affiliated to a larger organisation the chances of survival were somewhat improved. This section ends with a consideration of three national movements, each characterised by strong links between the centre and its local and provincial supporters.

In 1851 England had 113 distinct dissenting congregations.[72] Old Dissent, principally the Baptists and Independents (later Congregationalists) had expanded since 1800, and by the end of the century there were also large concentrations of Roman Catholic and Jewish congregations, but in record-keeping terms the most impressive organisation was that of the Methodists, with their reliance on minutes, conference reports, membership lists and printed circuit plans. The total amount of paperwork further increased when the original Methodist body split into a number of separate connexions. The largest of them, however, remained the Wesleyans, who from the mid-century showed an increasing interest in the preservation of their older records.[73]

The trade union movement was undoubtedly influenced by the record-keeping culture of the Methodists, but it also had affinities with the friendly society tradition, with its meetings in public houses and its careful records of members' subscriptions and benefits. Under the oppressive Combination Acts the early unionists were wise to keep no records at all, but from the mid-nineteenth century they begin to survive in significant quantities. In the latter half of the century the movement expanded considerably, and national organisations were established, notably the Trades Union Congress in 1867.

The development of unionism and the spread of nonconformity were not unconnected with the Liberal and radical movements of

---

[72] Clive D Field, 'Preserving Zion: the Anatomy of Protestant Nonconformist Archives in Great Britain and Ireland', *Archives*, vol xxxiii no 118 (Apr 2008), p14.
[73] William Leary, 'The Methodist Archives', *Archives*, vol xvi no 69 (Apr 1983), pp16–27.

the later nineteenth century. In terms however of organised political parties it was the Conservatives who led the way. It was they who formed a national body in 1867, the Liberals following in 1874, and they who were the better record-keepers in the constituencies in the years following the Third Reform Act of 1884.

* * *

It would be surprising if, among all these expanding organisations, there had not been some who, in addition to caring for their own records, were willing to act as repositories for relevant documents created elsewhere. Among older-established institutions in London that enlarged their manuscript collections in the Victorian period were the College of Arms, Lambeth Palace Library, the Royal Society, the Society of Antiquaries, the Guildhall Library and the libraries of the Inns of Court. The newly founded professional bodies, most notably the RIBA and the engineering bodies, also took in the papers of members and other relevant material. Of those institutions founded specifically to collect books and manuscripts, the British Museum's Department of Manuscripts grew during the years 1830 to 1900 to become the leading national manuscript collection. By the end of 1875 it already held 46,000 volumes of manuscripts, and a students' room specifically for their consultation was opened in 1884.[74] In Oxford, too, the Bodleian Library significantly extended its collections, but elsewhere outside London the provision of repositories for the safe keeping of archives and manuscripts remained patchy and poor. In the cities and larger towns the public library movement offered some scope for future development, but in the counties the establishment of antiquarian and archaeological societies from the 1830s could not make up for the dearth of publicly funded repositories.

Business and Estate Archives

Many businesses already well-established in 1830 grew ever larger in the following decades, and the great iron manufacturing,

---

[74] PR Harris, *A History of the British Museum Library 1753–1973*, London 1998, p274.

engineering, textile and brewing enterprises were joined by newer ones, notably in steel, chemicals and machine tools. The growth of commerce and international trade was reflected in the expansion of banking and mercantile houses, and of railway and shipping companies. The largest of these concerns developed into veritable institutions, employing many professional and clerical people as well as shop-floor workers. It is not surprising that they accumulated records on an unprecedented scale, and that they changed in character as well as in bulk. Most importantly, a series of Acts from 1844 ushered in the age of the limited liability company, dictating to some extent what kinds of document were kept and what information was supplied to shareholders and the public at large. Company secretaries kept regular series of minutes, accountants prepared and audited annual financial statements, and registers of shareholders were maintained. While clerks in offices and counting houses were thus engaged other types of record were being created amid the noise and dirt of the workshop and the factory floor – working drawings, pattern books, engine registers and so on. One example among many is the surviving archive of Lister Brothers, of Horsfall in the West Riding, worsted spinners, founded in 1845, which contains production records and drawings as well as accounts, order books and letter books.[75]

Not all business archives could look forward to such a secure future as those of Listers. Bound volumes of minutes and accounts, needless to say, have survived better than the bulky and often somewhat rebarbative records from the factory floor. Industrial buildings were often solid and substantial, but they were subject to destructive fires, and might be abandoned if the firm failed or was taken over. In the latter case, however, the records might be transferred to the headquarters of the successor firm, as sometimes happened in the brewing and banking industries. In 1896, for instance, Barclay and Co Ltd was formed through the amalgamation of a number of country banks with Quaker connections and took care to keep their well-ordered archives.[76]

By 1900 the family firm, characteristic of the eighteenth and early nineteenth centuries, had become less common among the larger

---

[75] See Patricia Hudson, *The West Riding Wool Textile Industry: a Catalogue of Business Records from the Sixteenth to the Twentieth Century*, Edington 1975.

[76] John Orbell and Alison Turton, *British Banking: a Guide to Historical Records*, Aldershot 2001, p6.

enterprises, but, as in previous periods, business papers sometimes survived alongside more personal papers in family hands. Among the Yorkshire clothing firms Isaac Holden and Sons and RV Marriner Ltd are good examples.[77] The wealthy merchant James Morrison (1789–1857) kept both his personal and business papers: his family preserved the latter first in their London office and later on their Wiltshire estate.[78] For the smaller nineteenth-century business perhaps the best hope for its archive might be its survival among the clients' papers in a solicitor's office. In an increasingly complex world businessmen more frequently needed legal advice when setting up partnerships and dealing with executorships, insolvencies and bankruptcies. But for the great majority of the more ephemeral small Victorian businesses, from the housebuilder to the corner shop, the chances of documentary survival are slim indeed.

* * *

In 1873 the landowners of England included about 360 individuals or families holding ten thousand acres or more, owning in total about a quarter of its soil. Below them were the greater gentry, owning between three and ten thousand acres, and comprising a further 1,140 individuals or families.[79] At that date the English landed estate was still enjoying a period of unparalleled prosperity. Some of the wealthier families had become entrepreneurs in mining, quarrying, transport or urban development. Some were conspicuous consumers, building country houses and entertaining on a grand scale. Some bought sporting estates, while others improved their farm buildings and cottages. All these activities generated records but were essentially subordinate to the central business of managing their agricultural land and preserving their inheritance through ever more lengthy and sophisticated legal arrangements. The period 1830–75 can be regarded as the golden age of the estate archive, of which the core remained the deeds, legal papers, rentals, accounts

---

[77] Hudson, *op cit*.

[78] Caroline Dakers, 'The Morrison Archive', *Business Archives*, no 103 (Nov 2011), pp41–51.

[79] John Bateman, *The Great Landowners of Great Britain and Ireland*, 4th edn, repr Leicester 1971, pp501–11; FML Thompson, *English Landed Society in the Nineteenth Century*, London and Toronto 1963, pp30–2.

and estate correspondence and papers. Some accumulations of estate and family papers now covered several centuries and contained material of great historical value.[80] On the other hand it has to be said that some of the more recent documents filling the shelves of estate offices were less attractive, and less durable, than their predecessors. Manuscript estate maps were giving way to annotated Ordnance Survey sheets, rentals and accounts were now less handsomely bound, and individually drawn leases and agreements were being replaced by printed forms.

As before 1830, the main archival division was between the legal records, usually kept in a muniment room, and the estate records, normally to be found in the estate office. Both were in many cases improved or upgraded in the following decades. The ventilation of muniment rooms was improved, and some were given iron safe-type doors that may still be seen today. At many country houses, such as Trentham and Holkham, estate offices were to be found near the stables and service areas. At Holkham the new buildings erected near the house in the 1850s included a detached estate office with rooms for the agent and his two clerks but also, less typically, a substantial strongroom furnished with tin deed boxes and iron racks for the maps and plans.[81] The central records of some great estates, however, were kept not in the vicinity of the principal country house but, again as before 1830, in the London town house, as with the Cavendishes, Spencers and Fitzalan-Howards. Outlying estates might have their own sub-offices, and a solicitor in a nearby market town might also be employed from time to time. In London firms such as Farrers or Frere, Cholmeley specialised in serving landed families, and one or two came to work almost exclusively for one aristocratic client – notably Curreys for the dukes of Devonshire and Boodle, Hatfield for the Grosvenor estate. The Duke of Bedford set up a new muniment room on his Bloomsbury estate in 1841–3, reputedly the first wholly fireproof building of its kind.[82] The records of aristocratic households were, as earlier, kept generally by the butler and the housekeeper, but matters became

---

[80] See the summaries in HMC *Principal Family and Estate Collections*, Guides to Sources ... 10 and 11, 2 vols London 1996, 1999.

[81] Christine Hiskey, *Holkham: the Social, Architectural and Landscape History of a Great English Country House*, Norwich 2016, ppx, 328.

[82] *King's Works*, vi.474. It replaced an earlier building that had been absorbed into the site of the British Museum.

more complicated when the grandest families moved frequently between their various residences. The Sutherlands took their house steward with them on their travels, leaving a housekeeper at Trentham to be overseen by the estate steward there.[83]

Towards the end of the century some landowners took a greater interest in their older records. The visit of an HMC inspector could lead to the engagement of a local antiquary or other scholar to conduct more detailed work on a section of the archive, as was the case at Longleat and some Warwickshire houses. At Berkeley Castle, where the archive was exceptionally rich, cataloguing work begun in the early nineteenth century was resumed some decades later by Edward Peacock, a Lincolnshire antiquary, and then, from 1888, by Isaac Jeayes of the British Museum.[84] Jeayes built up a practice among the record-owning aristocracy, working in his own time. He was meticulous in his calendaring of individual documents, but had little respect for archival order, and was said to be expensive.

By 1900 social change and economic depression, especially in the countryside, had combined to make the large landowners of England less secure and comfortable than they had been a quarter of a century previously; but the archival consequences of their decline became more obvious after 1900, and fall to be considered in the next chapter.

Personal and Family Papers

The period 1830 to 1900 saw the receiving and keeping of letters become the distinguishing characteristic of the personal archive at almost every level of society. It is the papers of leading public figures, however, that exhibit this trend most clearly. Prime ministers in particular had an immense correspondence, partly because of the range of official business with which they had to deal but also because of the number of unsolicited letters that they received from members of the public. In the 1830s Wellington was already the recipient of correspondence of this type, and made matters worse for himself by his habit of composing tart replies. ('Field Marshal

---

[83] Pamela Sambrook, *The Servants' Story: Managing a Great Country House*, Stroud 2016, p19.

[84] David Smith, 'The Berkeley Castle Muniments', *Trans Bristol and Gloucs Arch Soc*, vol 125 (2008), pp19–25.

Archives in an Age of Reform 1830–1900 201

the Duke of Wellington is *not* the General Post Office!') Later in the century Gladstone had an even fatter postbag, making his personal archive probably the largest in English history. (Unlike Wellington he dealt very summarily with his daily pile of letters, exclaiming 'Bosh! Bosh!' as he skimmed through them.)[85] Cabinet ministers, diplomats, colonial governors and senior military and naval officers also accumulated more papers, some of them, as in the previous century, of a 'private' nature although on official business.

Whether or not these figures habitually and systematically preserved their papers depended on personal inclination but also on cultural factors. Wellington's attachment to his archive sprang from his desire to memorialise his military career. Gladstone was influenced by his mentor Sir Robert Peel, who like Gladstone himself had inherited the conscientious business habits of the successful middle classes. More typical of nineteenth-century prime ministers were Russell, Palmerston, Derby and Salisbury, men who belonged to the country-house tradition of record-keeping, with its strongly rooted custom of preserving private or semi-official political papers. During Victoria's reign, however, these men were joined in government by lawyers and literary men who were less consistent in their record-keeping habits. Some were preservers: others travelled very light indeed. Lord Chancellor Lyndhurst destroyed most of his papers, believing that there was little in his career 'to make the world desire to know anything about me hereafter'. John Morley disliked accumulations and made regular bonfires of his correspondence. Macaulay kept 'in the breast pocket of his coat the *last* letter he received from some two or three people; and then, when another came, he destroyed the former one'. The majority of Cabinet ministers, though, seem to have been keepers rather than discarders. Of 229 such ministers between 1782 and 1900 whose archives were surveyed by the HMC in 1980, no fewer than 190 or so had left identifiable collections.[86]

Around 1850 the most common ways of keeping personal papers were still either to bind them in volumes or to tie them into bundles and lodge them in boxes or desk drawers. In the second half

---

[85] RJ Olney, 'The Wellington Papers 1790–1978', *Archives*, vol xvi no 69 (Apr 1983), pp3–11; RJ Olney, 'The Gladstone Papers 1822–1977', in John Brooke and Mary Sorensen, eds, *WE Gladstone IV: Autobiographical Memoranda 1868–1894*, London (HMC Prime Ministers' Papers Series) 1991, pp118–30.

[86] HMC Guide to *Papers of British Cabinet Ministers 1782–1900*, 1982.

of the century stationers began to produce box files.[87] Cardboard thus began its long association with records management, and tin boxes became a lighter alternative to wood, although they were prone to rust if stored on damp floors. Libraries and studies remained the favoured rooms in which to keep letters and papers, but in some cases the sheer volume of material necessitated other measures. Wellington set up a muniment room at Apsley House, where his secretary arranged his papers in mahogany cupboards, and at Hawarden Gladstone designed a room, the Octagon, for his archive.

By the late nineteenth century the letter had become a familiar object rather than a treasured one, but Victorian sensibilities required that the proprieties should be observed, and that archives should be shorn of sensitive material. Hence the frequent, but less frequently obeyed, instruction 'Burn this'. Such precautions applied particularly to diaries. Gerard Manley Hopkins wrote on his, 'Please do not open this.'[88] On the other hand there was a growing interest in celebrity, reflected chiefly in the craze for autograph-hunting that took hold in the 1820s and 30s. Letters from the famous were arranged in albums or bound volumes, and were all too often censored or mutilated in the process. Leading collectors such as William Upcott and Dawson Turner acquired thousands of items, begged from their original owners, ransacked from archives or purchased at auction sales.[89] The production of biographies, another increasingly popular pursuit, not infrequently caused havoc in the personal archives to which their authors were given access. Papers were borrowed and not returned, left with a publisher (as with Morley's *Life of ... Gladstone*), or destroyed once edited transcripts had appeared in print. Another Victorian practice was the habit of returning, or requesting the return, of letters to their senders. Victoria herself reclaimed her letters to Melbourne, Russell and Disraeli. After Melbourne died Russell initiated an exchange with his late colleague's representatives, but it was untidily done,

---

[87] Henry Stone's 'patent box for the safe and orderly keeping of all letters, papers and documents' was designed to be shelved like a book and was fitted internally with a wooden bar to hold its contents in place.

[88] Lesley Higgins, 'Spelt from Hopkins's Leaves: Considering Archival Remains', *Archives*, vol 51 no 132/3 (Apr–Oct 2016), p37.

[89] ANL Munby, *The Cult of the Autograph Letter in England*, London 1962, pp26–7, 55 *et passim*.

leaving behind some of Melbourne's letters in the Russell archive and *vice versa*.

Before 1800 numerous groups of personal correspondence and papers had been collected and preserved by antiquaries, and eventually secured for posterity by being transferred to public repositories. Perhaps the last antiquary of the heroic age was William Gough, who died in 1809 leaving the bulk of his papers and collections to the Bodleian Library. In the first half of the nineteenth century some antiquaries continued to work on county histories, but after 1850 there was a decline in such activity. Country squires and country parsons with time on their hands became thinner on the ground, and new academic disciplines emerged, with specialist archaeologists and architectural historians invading the territory of the generalist antiquary. These changes were reflected in the types of archive accumulated. The antiquary had concentrated on building up collections of working papers, including original collected material, on particular topics. The papers of the modern historian were more likely to contain papers relating to publications and lectures, academic administration, and involvement in learned societies and professional bodies.

When it came to finding permanent homes for personal papers of national importance the situation in 1900 was not very different from that in 1830.[90] The leading institution remained the British Museum, whose acquisitions between 1842 and 1895 included the papers of Wellington's brother Marquess Wellesley, the political journals of Charles Greville (the brother of Wellington's secretary) and, among less Establishment figures, some of the papers of William Cobbett and Francis Place. But suitable repositories elsewhere were few and far between, and it was fortunate that in many cases the descendants of statesmen and others were able to continue to give their papers houseroom, rather than consign them to the rubbish tip or the auction room.

[90] For local authority repositories see the section on local government records, above.

12

Twentieth-Century Challenges 1900–1980

Introduction

'If English history does not matter in the least,' wrote the redoubtable Joan Wake during the Second World War, 'all this destruction does not matter, and the sooner we boil down Domesday Book to make glue for aeroplanes and use the famous "scrap of paper" to make wads for cartridges the better.'[1] Miss Wake was a native of Northamptonshire, devoted to the history and records of her ancestral county, but in many ways she was a different figure from the antiquary of the early modern period. Tireless and fearless, she campaigned locally and nationally for the protection and preservation of the country's archival heritage. At the time of the above quotation her immediate concern was with the effects of the wartime salvage drives, for which see the final section of this chapter. Taking a longer view, she was aware of the archival consequences of the decline of her own class, the landed gentry, but in some ways her work anticipated the post-war world – the world of the local record office staffed by professional archivists but also of the ever-extending reach of the State. Miss Wake was in favour of record offices – indeed she was largely responsible for founding one – but she was no friend to Whitehall bureaucracy. It is in the corridors of Whitehall, however, that this chapter must begin.

---

[1] Quoted in John D Cantwell, *The Public Record Office 1838–1958*, London 1991, p439.

Public and Other Governmental Records

Bureaucracies make records as ants make ant heaps, and the period 1900–80 saw a great increase in government bureaucracy. Departments were enlarged or created afresh to deal with health, education and social security. The State involved itself with housing and industry; and the years 1914–19 and 1939–45 created unprecedented heaps of what the armed forces called bumf. The revolution in Whitehall, however, had started some years before the First World War. In 1890 clerks were still copying letters by hand: thirty years later the typewriter and the stencilling machine held sway, with the supersession of the clerk by the typist accelerated by wartime exigencies.[2]

In 1919 the government was left with piles of records relating to the supply of men, weapons, munitions and equipment for the war effort, but there was also a more specific archival problem – what to do about the committees and commissions, nearly three hundred of them, whose functions had ended with the War itself and that lacked successor or residuary bodies. One of those exercised by it was an assistant keeper at the PRO, Hilary Jenkinson, and he referred to the loss of many of these archives in a book published in 1922 entitled *A Manual of Archive Administration, including the Problems of War Archives and Archive Making*. The book became a standard text for archive students, but its origin is clearly shown in its title, and it was published as part of the British Series of the Economic and Social History of the War.[3]

In dealing with the bumf those who worked in departmental registries faced a daunting task. They had no professional training in what would later be called records management, and in any case the average subject file was no easy matter to manage. It usually contained a mixture of correspondence, policy documents and ephemeral matter; it was written and printed on acidic paper that was creating a growing conservation problem; and it was accessed

---

[2] Barbara L Craig and Heather MacNeil, 'Records Making, Office Machines and Workers in Historical Contexts: Five Photographs of Offices in the British Civil Service c1919 and 1947', *JSA*, vol 32 no 2 (Oct 2011), pp205–20. Stencil typing is illustrated on p209.

[3] For the reference to lost records, see p117. The Official History of the War itself caused archival disturbance, by extracting documents from their contexts and filing them with the History's own papers.

through bulky drawers of index cards rather than the index books and précis books of former days.[4] The Acts of 1877 and 1898 under which weeding operations were carried out provided no mechanism for the regular assessment of files and their orderly transfer to the Record Office, and the policy for dealing with them varied from department to department.[5]

A Treasury committee considered the question of departmental records in 1908, but apparently without effect. In 1910–19 a royal commission conducted detailed investigations into departmental and other records, but its work was hindered by the First World War, and its recommendations were not implemented.[6] The Second World War yet again 'postponed the reckoning only to increase the cost'.[7] The prime minister, Churchill, himself expressed alarm at the rate with which filing cabinets in one government office were being filled,[8] and this time action followed. In 1952 a civil service committee was appointed under Sir James Grigg. It recommended that departmental files should be reviewed after five years, when much ephemeral material could be discarded, and then again after twenty-five years, at which point files deemed suitable for permanent preservation could be transferred to the PRO. In 1955 a post of records administration officer was created within the PRO to liaise with departmental record officers, and the civil service rolled up its sleeves and tackled its paper mountain with renewed vigour: in 1956 alone 3,500 tons were destroyed.[9]

* * *

[4] Cantwell, *op cit*, p450; Randolph Cock and NAM Rodger, *A Guide to the Naval Records in the National Archives of the UK*, London 2008, p15. I owe the point about acidic paper to Dr Hallam Smith.

[5] Cantwell, *op cit*, pp346, 503. Weeding of papers from 1660 onwards was permitted under the Act of 1898.

[6] *Ibid*, pp375–6, 382–4. See also below for the commission's views on national policy.

[7] GH Martin, 'The Public Records in 1988', in GH Martin and Peter Spufford, eds, *The Records of the Nation: the Public Record Office 1838–1988*, the British Records Society 1888–1988, Woodbridge 1990, p21.

[8] Cantwell, *op cit*, p465.

[9] Paul Rock, '"The Dreadful Flood of Documents": the 1958 Public Record [*sic*] Act and its Aftermath', *Archives*, vol li no 132/3 (Apr–Oct 2016), p68.

The question of departmental records was closely connected with the constitution of the PRO, and the Grigg committee went on to propose a major reform. But before discussing the resulting legislation it is necessary to consider the development of the PRO itself in the first half of the twentieth century. The momentum described in Chapter 11 was not well maintained after 1900. The Master of the Rolls was now too busy as a judge to have a great deal of time for Record Office matters, and there was a lack of dynamic leadership in the Office itself. During the 1920s strict economies were imposed – for a number of years the Deputy-Keeper's annual report was duplicated rather than printed – and the Second World War brought further demands on a reduced staff. When Kenneth Timings joined it in 1947 his first impression was of 'drabness, dirt and dust, and a sense of disillusionment among my senior colleagues'.[10] Space had run out at Chancery Lane, and various 'limbo' repositories had been acquired for records awaiting archival attention, first at Cambridge, then at Canterbury, and later, when Canterbury had become too dangerous a place in 1942, in a disused prison at Shepton Mallet (Somerset). After the War a more satisfactory store was eventually opened at Hayes, and in 1951 a branch repository and search room for modern records (never a great success) was established at Ashridge in the Chilterns. This was in response to the increased public demand for, and availability of, recent records, but it was still the older records that claimed most archival attention at Chancery Lane.[11] By 1958 the Office presided over forty-six-and-a-half miles of shelves there and at Ashridge, with a further one hundred and twenty miles' worth that might reach the Office in the future.[12]

It was against this background, and having sidelined the elderly and difficult Jenkinson, that Grigg and his committee formulated their proposals for reforming the PRO. They recommended that responsibility for it should be transferred from the MR to a government minister, thus bringing it within the departmental structure of government. The Public Records Act as passed in 1958 appointed the Lord Chancellor, with his relevant legal responsibilities, to that position, and created an advisory council, chaired by the MR, to advise him on archival matters. The Act also

[10] Quoted in Cantwell, *op cit*, p455.
[11] The provision of handwritten transcripts of extracts from Domesday Book for legal purposes long remained part of the duties of an assistant keeper.
[12] Cantwell, *op cit*, p493.

Twentieth-Century Challenges 1900–1980 209

defined more clearly what were and what were not public records, by the simple expedient of declaring that public records were those declared to be such either in the Act itself or in statutory instruments to be issued under it. It introduced a fifty-year rule governing public access and empowered the Lord Chancellor to appoint approved local repositories for public records, a provision whose consequences are discussed in the next section of this chapter. As for records management, the Act did not lay down hard and fast rules but confirmed the role of the executive head of the PRO (now called the Keeper rather than the Deputy-Keeper) in overseeing the work of selecting records for permanent preservation. Jenkinson had retired in 1954, and, as we have seen, progress had already been made by the time the Act came into force.

The Act of 1958 thus dealt with anomalies that went back to the earlier legislation of 1838, but unlike its predecessor it was not a Public Record *Office* Act, and left unanswered the question of accommodation. The pressures on space, both for records and for readers, continued to grow, and by the late 1960s it was acknowledged that a new building was necessary. It was finally opened in 1978, on a not ideally accessible site at Kew (Surrey). Catering initially for modern records, the site eventually replaced Chancery Lane altogether.

* * *

Of the major archives remaining outside the scope of the 1958 Act the one closest to the seat of government in Whitehall was that relating to the British empire in India. When that empire came to an end in 1948 the India Office archive, along with the extensive manuscript collections in its library, had to find a new home. They were moved first to a carefully adapted office building in Blackfriars in the 1960s, and then, in 1982, to the British Library.[13]

At Westminster the records of the House of Lords continued to be housed in the Victoria Tower, and in the early twentieth century, as already noted, the Clerk of the Commons began to transfer his records to that repository. Just after the Second World War a

---

[13] For the Blackfriars Road building, see the article by Joan Lancaster in *Archives*, vol ix no 41 (Apr 1969), pp2–10. The residuary body for the India Office was the Foreign (and Commonwealth) Office.

record office for both Houses was formally established there. The Tower was converted into a modern repository, with adequate fire protection and air-conditioning, in 1958–61.[14]

Queen Victoria's death in 1901 left her household with the problem of what to do with her bulky personal archive, a problem that was compounded a few years later by the death of Edward VII. One difficulty was where to draw the line between the papers concerning matters of State and those relating to the private life of the monarch, not all of which it might be judged desirable to keep.[15] The solution, adopted in 1914, was to create a repository for the royal archive at Windsor Castle. Its custodian, the Registrar, reported to the Royal Librarian, who in turn was responsible to the Private Secretary. The place chosen was the Round Tower, like the Victoria Tower at Westminster a late example of a type of repository with an ancient pedigree.

The private archive of the Sovereign could now be properly managed, but the existence of the Round Tower repository also attracted records from outside sources. The most important deposit was of the papers of George III and George IV, which the Duke of Wellington had acquired as the latter's executor, and which had been kept for several decades at Apsley House, the Duke's London house. (William IV's papers had mostly been lost or destroyed after his death.) Another significant addition to the holdings of the Round Tower came from the public records. In 1921 the ancient offices of Lord Chamberlain and Lord Steward ceased to be political appointments, and it was decided that their records should henceforth be part of the Royal Archives.[16]

Local Government

Since 1889 the English shires had had a more modern form of government, the county councils. In the early twentieth century

---

[14] Maurice F Bond, *Guide to the Records of Parliament*, London 1971; HS Cobb, 'Parliamentary Records for the Political Historian', *Archives*, vol xx no 89 (Apr 1993), pp18–24.

[15] In fact most of Edward VII's personal papers were not retained. (Sir Robin Mackworth-Young, 'The Royal Archives, Windsor Castle', *Archives*, vol xiii no 59 (1978), p124.)

[16] The records of the Master of the Horse, however, had seemingly never been public records.

these authorities became increasingly busy, with departments for highways, education, social services and planning. They all generated records: it was reckoned that by 1923 Bedfordshire County Council had accumulated in a little over thirty years four times the quantity of the county's quarter sessions records going back to 1650.[17] When the counties took over bodies such as school boards, in 1902, or the Poor Law unions, in 1929, they also took on responsibility for their records, although these were not always quick to reach county council custody.[18] By the 1930s storage problems were becoming acute. During that decade a number of counties erected rather imposing new shire halls, with basement rooms where files and deed bundles could be stored, but that did not necessarily encourage better records management. In the early 1950s non-current records could still be found 'pushed into odd corners' of buildings scattered around the county's estate.[19]

By the 1960s the English county council had reached maturity as an archive-creating institution, but from that decade it was threatened with disruption and upheaval. The Local Government Act of 1972 abolished or amalgamated some counties, and created new metropolitan authorities in Lancashire, Yorkshire and elsewhere. There was more redrawing of the administrative map at district level, with the old rural and urban districts merged into new district authorities. The archival fall-out was considerable, with 'truck loads of records discarded by the outgoing authorities'.[20]

In many shire counties, however, the county council could by this time call on the services of an office within its own structure, the county record office. In most parts of England it was a post-Second World War phenomenon, but its origins can be traced back to the late nineteenth century, when the creation of county councils stimulated interest in the preservation of quarter sessions records. In 1889 WPW Phillimore, a publisher and the principal founder of the British Records Society,[21] concocted a scheme for

---

[17] G Herbert Fowler, *The Care of County Muniments*, 2nd edn London 1928, p53.

[18] Lilian J Redstone and Francis W Steer, eds, *Local Records: their Nature and Care*, London 1953, p134.

[19] *Ibid*, pp136–7.

[20] See also below for the effect of legislation on record offices.

[21] Founded in 1888, The British Records Society published indexes, abstracts of wills and similar genealogical and historical aids, but also became involved in editing records for publication.

county repositories. The matter was taken up by a departmental committee on local records that reported in 1902, favouring a network of county record offices rather than a system based on local libraries. But this did not result in legislation, and nor did the royal commission of 1912–19, which favoured a mandatory scheme for local authority records. In the 1920s, however, the introduction of regulations for the protection of manorial documents created an important precedent. A list of local repositories was drawn up to which the Master of the Rolls could direct manorial records in need of safe custody, but it was a very motley collection. As it stood in 1934 it contained one county record office, that for Bedfordshire (for which see below), one city record office, that for Bristol (founded in 1924), and nine city or county muniment rooms, but the total of fifty-five repositories otherwise consisted of twenty-six municipal libraries and a disparate group of university libraries, archaeological societies and the like.[22]

The first county muniment room to call itself a record office was Bedfordshire's, in 1923. It was largely the work of Dr Herbert Fowler, a retired academic zoologist and keen local historian, who had taken the chair of the county's records committee in 1913 and had built up a record service with the help and encouragement of Hilary Jenkinson from the PRO. It was a small beginning in a small and relatively uncomplicated county, but it had a wide influence, assisted in 1923 by the publication of Fowler's book on *The Care of County Muniments*.[23] Before 1939 only a few other counties followed Fowler's example. (His *protégé* FG Emmison became the first county archivist of Essex in 1939, with headquarters in new county buildings.) But expansion rapidly followed after 1945. By 1948 twenty-nine English counties possessed a record office, and there were five more by 1956.[24] By 1970 only two counties, the West

---

[22] The list was printed by Joan Wake in *How to Compile a History and Present Day Record of Village Life*, 3rd edn Northampton 1935.

[23] Patricia Bell and Freddy Stitt, 'George Herbert Fowler and County Records', *JSA*, vol 23 no 2 (2002), pp249–64. In emphasising the need for trained archivists, Fowler helped to confirm the modern usage of the word. See also Margaret Procter, '"What's an Archivist?" Some Nineteenth-Century Perspectives', *JSA*, vol 31 no 1 (Apr 2010), p21.

[24] FG Emmison and Irvine Gray, *County Records*, Historical Association 1948; *List of Record Repositories in Great Britain*, British Records Association 1956.

Riding of Yorkshire and, for very different reasons, Rutland, had no record office.

The county record office served its authority in rather the same way as the PRO served the national government, yet there were significant differences. County councils were not obliged to set up record services, and they came into existence as the result of a variety of local initiatives.[25] Record offices in some ways resembled the British Museum rather than the PRO, in that they accumulated collections of local archives from private as well as official sources, although it was not until 1962 that they were given statutory authority to do so.[26] Where local record offices differed from the British Museum, however, was in the extent of their human and financial resources. Many were underfunded and understaffed, and led a make-do-and-mend existence in stark contrast with the well-upholstered traditions of Bloomsbury.

Associated with the rise of the local record office was the rise of the archival profession. In 1947 a graduate diploma in archives administration was founded at University College, London, in large part through Jenkinson's instrumentality. In the same year a similar course was set up at Liverpool University, and between 1947 and 1980 archivists were also trained at the Bodleian Library.[27] Perhaps unsurprisingly this did not result in uniformity of practice on the French model. Just as record offices had diverse origins, so their cataloguing and other customs varied. Some followed the PRO model, others a library-based tradition. (The first county archivist at Worcester had been trained at Birmingham Reference Library and favoured the Dewey decimal system for archival references.) When the archivists came together in 1947 to form a professional association it was initially called the Society of Local Archivists.

---

[25] For the role of county committees, see Melinda Haunton, 'County Committees to County Record Office? The National Register of Archives and the Growth of the County Archive Network', *Archives and Records*, vol xxxiv no 1 (2013), pp15–16.

[26] This was the result of an MP (and HMC commissioner) seizing the chance to bring forward a private Member's bill. Hon Nicholas Ridley, 'The Local Government (Records) Act 1962: its Passage to the Statute Book', *JSA*, vol 2 (1960–4), pp288–92. Some county archivists, notably Felix Hull in Kent, provided a records management service for their authorities. See Elizabeth J Shepherd, *Archives and Archivists in 20th Century England*, Farnham 2009, p83. Others tended to concentrate on their holdings of private archives.

[27] Shepherd, *op cit, passim*.

And in the 1950s it debated issues such as whether the doctrine of *respect des fonds* should be applied to family archives that covered more than one county.[28] Following the 1958 Act it became possible for locally generated public records to be deposited locally, and county offices were among those designated for their reception. This meant more frequent, though not necessarily more friendly, contacts with Chancery Lane.[29]

Despite these drawbacks the 1950s were the heyday of the county record office. In the 1960s life became more difficult, as demands from readers, especially genealogists and graduate history students, increased, and as cataloguing backlogs lengthened. Locally there was increasing competition from other repositories, particularly university libraries ambitious to build up research collections. And nationally talk of local government reform began to alarm the archivists. The Act of 1972, and its fall-out, only confirmed their fears. Even in counties relatively unaffected by major boundary changes some county archivists found themselves moved down the administrative hierarchy or transferred from the chief executive's department to one concerned with libraries and 'leisure'.[30]

* * *

In the years 1900–45 there was only slow progress in the preservation and care of borough archives. A few of the larger urban authorities established record offices – Bristol, as mentioned, was a pioneer in 1924 – but in general the older records remained in borough muniment rooms and the more recent in town hall basements. Many boroughs had public libraries,[31] but there was seldom close co-operation between town clerk and borough librarian. Norwich, unusually, saw a partnership with the City Library. At Leicester, even more unusually, the city and the county museum got together. After 1945 there was a new possibility, an arrangement between

---

[28] See *Archives* 1956–8, *passim*.

[29] They received no subvention from the Treasury for this service. For the PRO's relations with local record offices, see JR Ede, 'The Record Office: Central and Local', *JSA*, vol 5 no 4 (Oct 1975), p210; Michael Roper, 'The Public Record Office and the Profession', *ibid*, vol 10 (1989), pp126–7.

[30] See the HMC's annual *Secretary's Reports* for this period.

[31] See above, Chapter 11.

the borough and the county record office. The county could offer to help with borough records left *in situ*, to accept records on deposit, or even, as in East Suffolk, to establish a joint service.[32] But boroughs were sometimes suspicious of empire-building at County Hall, and might need to be persuaded that the county archive service was a friend rather than an 'insatiable octopus'.[33] Between borough librarians who presided over local history collections and county archivists such suspicions might be reinforced by differences in culture and professional training.

In 1972 some boroughs joined larger authorities, while others ceased to exist as record-creating institutions, and in some cases residuary bodies were set up to look after their now redundant archives. The non-metropolitan counties became responsible for borough libraries, and in theory at least the county record office could involve itself with their manuscript holdings. In the metropolitan counties on the other hand library services were made a second-tier or district responsibility. In places such as Birmingham, Manchester, Liverpool, Sheffield and Leeds, all with major collections, it could be difficult to secure co-operation between city and county.[34]

* * *

As with the boroughs, other local authorities and institutions had more opportunity after 1945 to seek archival advice, or to make deposits of non-current records. (For diocesan and parish records see the next section of this chapter.) In other cases, however, notably the county police forces, retention of records by the originating authority was the almost universal practice. Problems arose particularly when institutions were abolished and their functions taken over by other bodies. The old authorities, in winding up their affairs, did not have the fate of their record-filled basements at the front of their minds, and the new bodies had even less interest in them, as happened with the district council records in 1972.

---

[32] For Suffolk, see Derek Charman, 'The Ipswich and E Suffolk Record Office', *Archives*, vol iv no 21 (1959), pp18–28.

[33] Felix Hull, speaking at a symposium on archive services and smaller repositories. *Archives*, vol iv no 24 (Mich 1960), p193.

[34] HMC *Secretary's Reports*, 1973–4, p8; 1974–5, p9.

216   *English Archives*

Manorial records were a special case. When copyhold tenure was abolished in 1922 many manorial courts ceased to have any *raison d'être*, but their records might still need to be consulted by former copyholders and others. The Act of 1922 made no provision for them, but under an amending Act of 1924, based on a permissive Act of 1897, the Master of the Rolls was empowered to create a register of manorial documents, and, as we have seen, to direct them to approved repositories for safe keeping.[35] This was a timely intervention at a period when the break-up of landed estates was causing the loss and dispersal of manorial and other records. After 1945 the MR could add more county record offices and professionally run libraries to his list of repositories, but the older ones retained their approved status, adding to an already complicated archival map.

The Established Church

All had not been well with the state of English diocesan records at the close of the nineteenth century, and little progress was made in the early years of the twentieth. When around 1915 the newly appointed registrar at Lichfield investigated the records that he had inherited he found some of them in a decaying building that had begun life as an episcopal banqueting hall in the 1660s but had more recently been a racing stables, though at least the jockeys' lockers were handy for storing papers.[36] In 1929, however, the Church passed a Measure to allow the establishment of diocesan record offices, with the agreement of registrars. The first office of this kind was opened in 1935 for the substantial and important archives of the diocese of Lincoln. The cathedral's Exchequer Gate, a dry but draughty medieval building long occupied by the diocesan registrar, was adapted for the purpose, and a young Lincolnshire-born but Oxford-educated scholar, Kathleen Major, became the first diocesan archivist. In the 1930s dioceses had even less spare money than usual for such schemes, but fortunately the Pilgrim Trust, founded

---

[35] For the approved repositories, see above. In 1959 a clause was added to the Manorial Documents Rules prohibiting the export of manorial documents. Rules for tithe records, similar to those for manorial documents, had been issued in 1936 and again in 1946–7.

[36] The Pilgrim Trust Survey of Ecclesiastical Archives, TS 1951, *sub* Lichfield.

in 1930, took a particular interest in ecclesiastical records, and was able to support the cost of both the conversion of the building and (for the first few years) the archivist's salary.[37]

Work at Lincoln and elsewhere was interrupted by the War, the destructive effects of which are discussed at the end of this chapter. Soon after it ended the Pilgrim Trust, in anticipation of a flood of grant applications, initiated a thorough survey of ecclesiastical records.[38] By the time it was completed, in December 1950, more help was fortunately at hand in the shape of local authority record offices. Eight county offices had already received diocesan appointments, and by 1970 the majority of England's forty-three dioceses had made some arrangement for the professional care of their older records, although not all could provide adequate catalogues or cater for readers on a regular basis.[39]

It was not only diocesan records that found their way into record offices after 1945. Concerns over the care of records in parish custody had not diminished in the early twentieth century, but from 1929 it was possible for incumbents to deposit registers and other documents for safe keeping in approved repositories. Not all, especially those at an inconvenient distance from the appointed record office, chose to do so, but archidiaconal hands were strengthened by a further Parochial Registers and Records Measure in 1978. In two cases major groups of former diocesan and other ecclesiastical records were also transferred to local record offices. Pre-1858 probate records were disgorged from district registries, and the Ecclesiastical (from 1948 the Church) Commissioners began to make local deposits of deed bundles and other documents relating to ecclesiastical estates.

The implications for the archival map were not, however, as tidy as this might suggest. At Lincoln the diocesan record office merged with the county service in the late 1940s. At Gloucester on the other hand the older diocesan records were to be found in the city library, while the Church Commissioners made a deposit in

---

[37] London Metropolitan Archives, Pilgrim Trust records, LMA 4450/A/04/009, 4450/C/03/034.

[38] Pilgrim Trust Survey. The chief investigator and compiler was Margaret Midgley.

[39] Dorothy Owen, *The Records of the Established Church, excluding Parochial Records*, London 1970, Appendix; Robert Somerville, 'Diocesan Record Offices', *Archives*, vol ii no 11 (Lady Day 1954), pp138–9.

the county record office, although later the county archivist was able to bring them together. At Leicester the county museum was the diocesan repository, but the probate records went to the newly established county record office. At Southwell the repository for the Nottingham diocesan records was the Chapter library, but the county record office in Nottingham held tithe, probate and Church Commissioners' records, and the Nottingham archdeaconry records went to Nottingham University Library. Where county arrangements could not be made a university might come to the rescue, as at Cambridge (for the diocese of Ely), Durham, Oxford and York.

The cathedrals were less willing to part with their records. At the time of the Pilgrim Trust report in 1951 twenty-three large cathedral archives were still *in situ*. During the following three decades the picture changed only slowly, and where facilities were provided for students they tended to be in cathedral libraries rather than local record offices. Westminster Abbey and St George's Chapel, Windsor also continued to look after their own records, the former with the help of a major grant from the Pilgrim Trust.[40]

Despite its policy of local deposits the Church Commissioners' own archive continued to grow. It was supplemented by the records of other bodies that they had taken over, including those of the early nineteenth-century Church Building Commission and what remained of the archive of Queen Anne's Bounty.[41] By 1970 the Commissioners were presiding over three miles of shelving at their London headquarters on Millbank, but they employed no professionally qualified staff and provided no adequate facilities for readers.[42]

The central organisation of the Church of England was also expanding, in the shape of bodies such as the General Assembly (later General Synod) and the Central Board of Finance. Then there were satellite organisations such as the National Society for the promotion of Church schools, whose archive included some twelve thousand files by the early 1970s.[43] Traditionally the only repository

---

[40] The Westminster Abbey grant in fact preceded that to Lincoln.

[41] See GFA Best, *Temporal Pillars: Queen Anne's Bounty, the Ecclesiastical Commissioners, and the Church of England*, Cambridge 1964.

[42] [CJ Kitching], *The Central Records of the Church of England: a Report to the Pilgrim and Radcliffe Trustees*, London 1976, p20.

[43] *Ibid*, p28.

available to take in the redundant records of such bodies was Lambeth Palace Library. Its holdings came to include archives such as that of the early eighteenth-century Commission for Building Fifty New Churches, but by 1970 it had run out of space, and the Church Commissioners, responsible for it since 1866, placed restrictions on new accessions. Since 1891, however, there had been an alternative in Church House, Westminster, which hosted some of the Church's independent organisations, including the National Society. A report presented to the Pilgrim and Radcliffe Trustees in 1976 saw Church House as initially the most feasible site for a new and properly funded Records Centre, but with Lambeth Palace as its ultimate destination if funding could be secured to extend the accommodation there.[44]

Institutions and Organisations

The older institutions such as colleges and other foundations continued to follow their own archival courses in the early twentieth century, with periods of change alternating with periods of stagnation. At Winchester College the bursar listed the manorial documents following his retirement in 1927, and later his assistant tackled the deeds 'in accordance with the methods laid down by the British Records Association'.[45] At New College, Oxford on the other hand neglect was the order of the day. When around 1970 the archivist Francis Steer examined the deed boxes, cardboard boxes and parcels into which the contents of the presses had overflowed he found almost everything covered with a layer of dust that had been 'undisturbed for a great many years'.[46] New College seems to have been more typical of the period than Winchester.

Two factors underlay these variations. The pressure to modernise and meet new challenges resulted in a lack of attention to traditional archival housekeeping. At Cambridge University, for instance, the

---

[44] A new library building in the grounds of Lambeth Palace was completed in 2020.

[45] Sheila Himsworth, *Winchester College Muniments: a Descriptive List*, 2 vols Chichester 1976, 1984, i.xv (introduction by John Harvey).

[46] Francis J Steer, *The Archives of New College, Oxford: a Catalogue*, Chichester 1974, pxii; Jennifer Thorp, 'Archives', in Christopher Tyerman, ed, *New College*, London 2010, p99.

retirement of John Willis Clark as registrar in 1910 was followed by a period in which 'the expansion of the university brought a corresponding increase in the business of the registrar's office, and modern methods took precedence over ancient'.[47] The second factor was simply a lack of money, particularly in the inter-war years.

The period after 1945, by contrast, saw more light shed on these muniments, and much dust and grime removed in the process. As with the Church of England, there was an immediate need for repair and reconstruction following the damage directly inflicted by the War, but there was also a growing appreciation of the value of at least the older records, and rising standards of care. Institutions saw more clearly what needed to be done, and professional help was more readily to hand. At Winchester it 'became evident that the historical study of archives was entering on a new phase', and a comprehensive catalogue of the archive was begun, assisted by a Pilgrim Trust grant.[48] In 1949 the Royal Society appointed an archivist, again with help from the Pilgrim Trust. Between 1952 and 1972 enquiries about the archive grew from two or three a month to two or three a day.[49] Among the wealthier London livery companies the Stationers paid more attention to their archive than before the War, and they too appointed a professional archivist. At Cambridge University proper strongroom accommodation was provided in 1947, and the following twenty-five years saw the advent of a professional archivist and the eventual transfer of the collection to the university library. At Eton College the archival work of Noel Blakiston of the PRO was followed by the appointment of an archivist in 1966.[50] Not all institutions, however, moved at the same pace. Among the Oxford and Cambridge colleges a professional archivist was still a rarity in 1980. For smaller institutions there were advantages in depositing material in a library or record office. That was the course followed, for instance, by a number of the smaller London livery companies, which transferred material to the Guildhall Library.

---

[47] Heather E Peek and Catherine P Hall, *The Archives of the University of Cambridge: an Historical Introduction*, Cambridge 1962, p23.

[48] John H Harvey, 'Winchester College Muniments', *Archives*, vol v no 28 (1962), p207.

[49] Marie Boas Hall, *The Library and Archives of the Royal Society 1660–1990*, London 1992, p55.

[50] Information kindly supplied by Penny Hatfield.

Post-war changes in education, medicine and public health also had their impact on record-keeping. Ancient constitutions were revised, and new series of records begun. St Bartholomew's Hospital was among the older hospitals to survive the creation of the National Health Service, and to retain its records in its own custody. By 1975 it had acquired a full-time archivist to look after not only the older muniments but also the medical records that had survived from the early nineteenth century and the departmental records that had been transferred to the Archives since 1963. Records of hospitals that closed in the late 1940s were of course at risk, but some were luckier than others. Those of the Lock Hospital and Rescue Home, well-kept since its inception in 1746, passed to the Paddington Group Hospital Management Committee, which in 1953 deposited them with the Royal College of Surgeons.[51]

* * *

Organisations and movements that had originated in the nineteenth century reached maturity in the twentieth, but that brought its own archival problems. In the trade union movement, for instance, small unions were absorbed in larger ones. In some cases this resulted in the preservation of archives, but in others the smaller union lost its premises and often its records with them. When the National Union of Railwaymen was formed in 1913 the records of one of its constituent bodies, the United Pointsmen's and Signalmen's Society, disappeared without trace.[52] Among the nonconformists there were similar mergers, as congregations shrank and chapels closed. When the Methodists were reunited in 1932 there were losses particularly of Primitive Methodist records at district level.[53] More recently formed archives were also among those undergoing vicissitudes in the inter-War period. A survey of Liberal Party records conducted in the early 1970s attributed their meagre survival partly to 'the

---

[51] Nellie JM Kerling, 'Archives', in VC Medvei and John L Thornton, eds, *The Royal Hospital of St Bartholomew 1123–1973*, London 1974, pp299–307; Lesley A Hall, 'Sex in the Archives', *Archives*, vol xxii no 93 (Apr 1995), pp2–3.

[52] Philip S Bagwell, 'Sources for the History of British Trade Unionism and Industrial Relations', *Business History*, no 56 (Nov 1988), p2.

[53] William Leary, 'The Methodist Archives', *Archives*, vol xvi no 69 (Apr 1983), pp16–27.

frequency with which the party has moved headquarters', but partly to 'the divisions within the party after 1916'.[54] In the Roman Catholic Church record-keeping at diocesan level had been slow to mature, and in 1940 records were still being kept in cupboards in the bishop's house in many cases.[55]

As with the older-established institutions, more progress was made in the post-war years. The Methodists began to pay more attention to their archives in the 1950s, although more thoroughgoing work, leading to deposits in the John Rylands Library at Manchester and in local record offices, had to wait until the 1970s. After 1945 more Roman Catholic bishops appointed archivists, though they were often priests with no archival training. By 1980, however, deposit in a record office had become an acceptable alternative. Interest in the preservation of trade union records went back to the 1890s, when Sidney and Beatrice Webb gathered some up during the course of their researches and deposited them in the library of the newly founded London School of Economics. In the 1970s and 80s many more such records, including those of the Trades Union Congress down to 1960, found a home in Warwick University's Modern Records Centre.[56] The archive of the Labour Party was catalogued by the HMC between 1967 and 1973, and that of the National Union of Conservative and Unionist Associations was transferred to the Bodleian Library from the late 1970s.

The plight of records kept at local or branch level is illustrated by a recent study of Conservative constituency party records. Non-current minute books were often relegated to cupboards, attics, basements or even sheds, from which they were later discarded along with 'the junk, unsold jumble, broken typewriters and mouldering posters from elections long past'. A dirty volume with a broken binding might not stand out from the surrounding rubbish, and even if recognised and cursorily examined might

[54] Chris Cook *et al*, eds, *Sources in British Political History 1900–1951 Vol 1: a Guide to the Archives of Selected Organisations and Societies*, London and Basingstoke 1974, p146.

[55] See eg Robin Gard, 'The Archives of the Diocese of Hexham and Newcastle', *Catholic Archives*, vol 19 (1999), pp24–41.

[56] EJ Hobsbawm, 'Records of the Trade Union Movement', *Archives*, vol iv no 23 (Lady Day 1960), pp129–37; Alistair Tough, 'Trade Unions and their Records', *Archives*, vol xix no 83 (Apr 1990), pp136–7.

be thought too old to have current usefulness but too recent to have much historical interest. Nevertheless, a number of such volumes and other party records have found their way to local repositories.[57]

Estate and Business Archives

The decline of the landed aristocracy, begun in the late nineteenth century, accelerated in the early twentieth. Estate and family archives could be rendered highly vulnerable, particularly when estates were sold and houses given up. Muniments might be destroyed during a sale if no longer needed for proving title, and estate records might be left to decay in deserted offices. A number of country houses were abandoned during a spate of sales following the First World War. In 1921 the Grenville family sold the contents of their huge mansion at Stowe (Buckinghamshire), including manuscripts from the evidence room, Gothic Library and letter room.[58] There was more loss and destruction after the Second World War, when many owners gave up the struggle to live in their unheated, understaffed and often badly damaged or neglected houses.[59]

Considerable though the archival losses were, they affected the gentry more than the magnates. The latter not infrequently had assets that were not tied to the fortunes of agriculture – their archives can reflect their investments in minerals, transport or urban development – and if they sold land it was more likely to be outlying properties than core estates. Some of the grandest houses remained in family occupation, and if London houses were given up the records kept there could be concentrated at the principal seat. Thus those at Norfolk House were transferred to Arundel Castle, and those at Devonshire House to Hardwick and later to

---

[57] Stuart Ball, 'National Politics and Local History: the Regional and Local Archives of the Conservative Party', *Archives*, vol xxii no 94 (Apr 1996), pp27–59.

[58] JV Beckett, 'The Stowe Papers', *Archives*, vol xx no 90 (Oct 1993), p193.

[59] Caroline Seebohm, *The Country House: a Wartime History 1939–45*, London 1989; Roy Strong *et al*, *The Destruction of the Country House*, London 1974; Giles Worsley, *England's Lost Houses*, London 2002. And for the wider context, see David Cannadine, *The Decline and Fall of the British Aristocracy*, rev edn 1992.

Chatsworth.[60] Among the heads of the leading landed families were some who took a personal interest in their archives – men such as the seventh earl Spencer, the fourth Lord Leconfield and the ninth duke of Rutland.[61] Lord Spencer was of the firm opinion that family archives such as his should be retained 'wherever possible ... in the houses to which they belong'.[62] And if sales of chattels were required from time to time it was usual for the records to be among the last to be parted with. By 1980 a number of owners were employing full-time archivists. And abandoned servants' quarters could prove suitable for conversion to record storage.

On occasion landowners did dispose of their archives, or parts of them. But before 1945 their options (apart from simply abandoning them) were limited. They could sell them at auction, as the Grenvilles did in 1921, or they could sell or give them to an institution. Few repositories, however, had the money to buy them or the facilities to house and catalogue them. The British Museum in theory had both, but it seldom concerned itself with the contents of muniment rooms, and in the area of family papers it was inclined to pick and choose, leaving a residue to fend for itself. After 1945 the situation changed. More repositories were in a position to accept large tranches of family and estate records, and among them were the county record offices. They had little or no money for purchases, and before 1980 there was no very substantial public fund available to assist private treaty sales, but many collections were deposited on long-term loan.[63] The understanding – written agreements were unusual – was that the material in question would be listed and made accessible, under restrictions where necessary, to students. This suited both owners and repositories, although later it could lead to problems. It also led in some cases to the fragmentation of an archive,[64]

---

[60] The Spencer papers were similarly removed from Spencer House to Althorp: see Lord Spencer's articles in *Archives*, vol ii no 10 (Mich 1953), pp76–8, and the *Bulletin* of the National Register of Archives, no 13 (1964), pp21–6.

[61] For the Duke of Rutland see Catherine Bailey, *The Secret Rooms*, London 2012.

[62] *Archives*, vol ii no 10 (Mich 1953), p78.

[63] The British Museum modified its policy to facilitate co-operation with local repositories. See *Archives*, vol i no 3 (Lady Day 1950), p46.

[64] For the Portland papers, for instance, see RJ Olney, 'The Portland Papers', *Archives*, vol xix no 82 (Oct 1989), pp78–87.

or to the fossilisation of an arbitrary division between the deposited and retained parts of it.

* * *

In the area of business records the twentieth century saw the decline of the heavy coal-fired and steam-powered industries that had characterised the Victorian era, and the rise of lighter industries such as those around electrical engineering and food production. Such changes were bound to lead to losses of records, and nationalisation caused further disruption and destruction, although coal-mining archives fared better than railway ones. As the newer industries matured, however, their records could become a source of corporate pride, and the approach of a centenary could prompt the preparation of a company history and the eventual appointment of an archivist, often attached to a publicity department.[65] By 1980 new ideas of records management offered some hope to beleaguered custodians of business records, but 'retention schedules' could in practice mean destruction schedules, and some managers were seduced by new technology into thinking that the microfilm and later the computer removed the obligation to retain original documents.[66]

As with estate records, however, the loss of business records would have been far greater had not their historical value come to be better appreciated. This was one archival area where historians led the way. Economic history became a popular subject after the First World War, and business records also came to be recognised as an important source for social history. In the early 1920s George Unwin, working on his book *Samuel Oldknow and the Arkwrights*, and alerted by the distribution of some eighteenth-century weavers' pay tickets by an enterprising boy scout to 'casual passers by', decided to explore Arkwright's derelict cotton mill at Mellor (Derbyshire). When he and his companion reached the top floor they found 'a great number of letters, papers, account books and other business records of every kind and size, covering the whole floor of a large room and partly hidden from sight by several

---

[65] Old catalogues, posters, photographs, etc were useful for advertising purposes.
[66] See *Business Archives*, no 25 (Jan 1967) for the virtues of microfilming, and no 40 (June 1974), where it is stated that 'people are at last finding out that computing is for everyone'.

inches of dust and debris'.[67] Discoveries such as this prompted the formation of a Council for the Preservation of Business Archives in 1934. After the War it enlarged its activities, and changed its name to the Business Archives Council in 1952. It believed in the importance of survey work, and of maintaining good relations with the sometimes sensitive and wary owners of businesses. Archives deemed to be at risk were monitored, and when they were threatened with destruction or dispersal efforts were made to steer them into suitable repositories, involving negotiations with owners, liquidators and archivists.[68]

In the post-war archival world there were more local record offices willing to take in business records, but a notable feature of the period was the development of specialist collections within libraries and other institutions. For textile firms the Brotherton Library at Leeds and the Goodchild Collection at Wakefield gathered records relating to the Yorkshire clothing industries, while the John Rylands University Library of Manchester catered for the Lancashire cotton spinners, including appropriately enough the records of Rylands and Sons covering the years 1742 to 1969.[69] Railway records could find a home in the Railway Museum at York, and shipping records in the Merseyside Museums. The records of small businesses, however, remained highly vulnerable, although some found their way into local libraries and record offices, perhaps through a member of the owner's family or a former employee.

The records of small businesses could also survive among clients' papers in a solicitor's office, as noted in Chapter 11. These legal firms were also small businesses in their own right, and by the mid-twentieth century some had archives spanning over a century. Some solicitors developed an historical interest in the contents of their attics and basements.[70] Others were keen to alleviate their storage problems by making deposits in local record offices, and many did so in the years following the Second World War, although,

---

[67] Quoted by Peter Matthias in 'The First Half-Century: Business History, Business Archives and the Business Archives Council', *Business History*, no 50 (Nov 1984), p3.

[68] GN Clark and Eileen Power were among the leading pre-War figures.

[69] HMC *Guide to the Records of Business and Industry: Textiles and Leather, sub* Rylands.

[70] See eg Reginald L Hine, *Confessions of an Uncommon Attorney*, 3rd edn London 1946.

as already noted, these deposits usually consisted of clients' papers rather than bill books, letter books and other records relating to their own businesses.[71]

Personal and Family Papers

The twentieth century saw the democratisation of the personal archive, with the keeping of documents in drawers, cupboards or boxes under the bed more common at all levels of society. This was accompanied by a relative decline in the importance of the manuscript letter, accompanied and assisted as it was by the increased accessibility of the telephone. Personal archives included more typed and printed items, giving them a more miscellaneous character and a more utilitarian appearance. The decline of the letter, however, was temporarily halted by the Second World War, when postal communication was encouraged, and when telephone calls were not only more expensive but less reliable.[72]

At the beginning of the century statesmen such as Balfour, Asquith and Lloyd George were still maintaining voluminous archives, including correspondence of a semi-official nature. But, again, the letter increasingly sat beside the telegram, the bundle of speech notes or the text of a lecture or broadcast. The large archive of Winston Churchill, with its inextricable mixture of public, semi-public and private correspondence, preserved by its creator at least partly for literary purposes, was a latter-day representative of a tradition that went back to Gladstone and Peel.

As with the records of the great estates, the personal and family papers of the major landed families faced an uncertain future in the twentieth century. Houses such as Hatfield or Petworth might maintain the tradition of preserving family papers *in situ* and might be able to provide homes for the papers of relatives less able to accommodate them. But it was not always possible to retain large collections of nineteenth-century political papers. The British Museum was the obvious choice for the papers of Peel and

---

[71] In September 1953 the BRA put on an exhibition to show the range of documents that could be found in solicitors' offices. Jenkinson wrote the introduction to the *Catalogue*.

[72] The keeping of diaries, another wartime feature, was encouraged by Mass Observation.

Gladstone, but they put a strain on the cataloguing systems of even that august institution. After 1945 there were more repositories willing to consider archives of this kind, including some university libraries and even some local authority repositories.[73] For those collections that remained in the custody of their originating families the hazards did not diminish in the twentieth century. Documents could suffer from damp in unheated rooms or outhouses, and those on acidic paper and held together with metal clips or staples were especially at risk. Even fire hazards changed rather than retreated: smoking became common, and electrical wiring, particularly in the early days, could be as dangerous as candles.

As for the papers of antiquaries, the British Museum, the Bodleian Library and other repositories continued to acquire groups of papers that had passed through the hands of nineteenth-century antiquarian collectors. The greatest of these was Sir Thomas Phillipps, who used a tower on the top of the Cotswolds and later a house in Cheltenham in which to house the many thousands of manuscripts that he accumulated. They had a regrettably untidy fate, being dispersed by his trustees in a great series of sales between 1886 and 1980.[74]

Towards a National Policy for Archives

The public records had come under a well-established system of regulation by 1900, as described in Chapter 11. For the Victorians, however, it was a very different matter to infringe the rights of private property, for instance by sending government inspectors to poke around in private muniment rooms. When the HMC was set up in 1869 it emphasised that it would examine private papers and publish the results of its investigations only with the consent of the owners. It was a commission of enquiry, not a regulatory body, and so it remained in the twentieth century. The period 1900–80, however, saw two major changes. One concerned the geography, so to speak, of English archival provision, already touched on in this chapter: the other concerned changing public perceptions of the role of the State.

By 1980 the map of England was dotted with record repositories, many of which had not existed in 1900. London, already the

---

[73] For the availability of suitable repositories, and of public funds to assist the purchase of collections, see the next section of this chapter.

[74] See ANL Munby, *Phillipps Studies*, 2 vols London 1971.

home of national repositories, now hosted a number of specialist collections of archives and manuscripts. Outside London the county record office movement was paralleled by a great expansion of other repositories. The spread of free municipal libraries has already been described, and had been well under way by 1900. In the twentieth century the most striking development was perhaps the growth of libraries attached to the newer universities, designed to provide research material but also to enhance the prestige of their parent institutions. In total, as one observer pointed out in 1960, England had a higher density of repositories than any other country except Belgium and Switzerland.[75]

This growth in provision meant that, in theory at least, owners of archives had a much enlarged choice of where to deposit them safely, and that orphaned archives also had a better chance of finding appropriate homes. In practice the position was less satisfactory. The coverage of the country as a whole was uneven: in some areas there was competition between rival institutions, but some categories of specialist archives were poorly served or not catered for at all. It was argued by some that limited resources were being too thinly spread, and that fewer but better equipped and staffed record offices would benefit archives and readers alike. This led to the idea that there might be a case for a framework of national oversight and regulation. There was, in other words, a case for the government inspector after all.

Alongside these concerns relating to archives in public or institutional custody there were others relating to those remaining in private hands. The belief gained ground that, like buildings or works of art, they could be a vital part of the national heritage, and as such equally deserving of protection. Archives were being broken up or sold abroad from early in the century, and anxieties increased during the Second World War. With the reach of the State extending in so many directions, it no longer seemed outrageous that archives, like historic buildings, might be inspected and 'listed'. Furthermore, could not the tax system be tweaked to encourage owners to offer papers in lieu of estate duty, or sell them by private treaty to approved repositories rather than cast them on the open market? Progress was indeed made in some of these directions, as the following paragraphs relate.

---

[75] GRC Davis, 'Some Home Thoughts for the English Archivist from Abroad?' *Archives*, vol iv no 23 (Lady Day 1960), pp176–7.

As already noted, the PRO routinely inspected public records outside its own custody. From the late nineteenth century the records held by county councils were also acknowledged to be of public importance, though not coming under the Public Records Act, and historians were becoming increasingly interested in locally and privately held collections of personal, family and business records. The local records committee of 1899–1902 and the royal commission of 1910–19 both favoured a national network of local authority record offices funded by local taxation but regulated by a team of inspectors based at the PRO. The royal commission wanted to see compulsory rather than permissive legislation to bring this about, but in the straitened circumstances of the 1920s there was no enthusiasm in Westminster or Whitehall for such a thoroughgoing measure. As we have seen, however, the manorial legislation of 1924 provided a limited precedent for the statutory regulation of one class of private records.[76]

During the inter-war period the PRO and the HMC suffered from cuts in their budgets, and an attempt by the latter to conduct a survey of locally held records on a county basis was aborted,[77] while county authorities were similarly hampered on the archival front. It was against this background that the British Records Association was founded in 1932. It originated in a movement among the archaeological and record societies, led by the British Records Society, but was also supported by Jenkinson from the PRO and Fowler in Bedfordshire. It aimed to bring together the three main interest groups in record-keeping matters – owners, custodians and users – but it was also an attempt to build stronger links between national and local interests, and to provide the kind of leadership that was lacking from the relevant national bodies. As Maurice Bond wrote in 1962, it was 'a private society to remedy official inaction'.[78] Equally ambitiously, it became directly involved

---

[76] See the section on local government archives in this chapter.

[77] In Northamptonshire Joan Wake opposed the scheme, not wishing to alarm her owners by donning the mantle of a government inspector. The only county to complete its survey was Bedfordshire.

[78] Maurice F Bond, 'The British Records Association and the Modern Archive Movement', in Albert EJ Hollaender, ed, *Essays in Memory of Sir Hilary Jenkinson*, Chichester 1962, p71. See also Richard Olney, 'The BRA – a Potted History', in *The British Records Association 1932–1992: Jubilee Essays*, London 1992, pp5–11.

in records preservation, taking over the work begun a few years earlier by the British Records Society in rescuing records at risk and distributing them to appropriate repositories. To do this a semi-autonomous Section of the Association was set up, with the dedicated Ethel Stokes doing much of the work.[79]

During the Second World War the BRA sustained and even increased its activities, launching a campaign to prevent the destruction of valuable records as 'salvage', and discussing what should be done about archives once the war was over.[80] Jenkinson led the way in producing a plan that incorporated many of the planks of what would later be called a national archives policy – a national archives council chaired by the Master of the Rolls, employing an inspectorate and supported by a national register of archives; a network of county (and some borough) record offices obliged to care for their own authorities' archives and empowered to take in diocesan and private records; a scheme to list or schedule private archives, the most important of which would receive statutory protection; and regulations to control the export of manuscripts.

A committee was set up under the Master of the Rolls, which continued its deliberations for some time after the War, but only one of its proposals bore immediate fruit, and that was one that did not require legislation. In 1945 a National Register of Archives was established, at first operating independently but later becoming a key function of the HMC. After giving up an attempt to rely on the archaeological and record societies, its first director, Lt-Col GEG Malet, set up committees of volunteers in the counties, and this led not only to a flow of archival information but also in some cases to the creation of a local record service.[81] The Public Records Act of 1958, like its predecessor of 1838, was not concerned with

---

[79] Roger Ellis, 'Records Preservation from BRS to BRA', in *Jubilee Essays*, pp16–30; Oliver D Harris, '"The Drudgery of Stamping": a Physical History of the Records Preservation Section', *Archives*, vol xix no 81 (Apr 1989), pp3–17; Penelope Baker, 'Back-Bone or Burden: the Role of the RPS in the BRA', *Archives*, vol liii no 136 (Apr 2018), pp27–44. For Miss Stokes, see Elizabeth Shepherd, 'Pioneering Women Archivists in England: Ethel Stokes (1870–1944), Record Agent', *Archival Science*, vol xvii (2) (June 2017), pp75–94.

[80] Post-war planning was of course a widespread phenomenon of the war years. For salvage, see also the next section of this chapter.

[81] For Col Malet, see the obituary by RL Atkinson in *Archives*, vol i no 8 (Mich 1952), pp3–6. See also Haunton, *op cit*.

private records, but as already indicated it led to closer links with a growing number of local repositories: by 1975, 155 had been approved as places to hold public records. The 1958 Act also led, in the following year, to the issue of a new royal warrant for the HMC, which became the recognised advisory body for all records outside the Act. It acquired its first full-time secretary and moved out of the PRO into its own office a little farther up Chancery Lane.[82] It also assumed day-to-day responsibility for the Manorial Documents Register, and maintained close relations with the British Records Association. Between 1945 and 1980 there were other positive developments. In 1952 a system of export controls was created; an Act was passed in 1962, as already noted, to regularise the holding of private collections by local authority record offices; a provision in the 1973 Finance Act enabled manuscripts to be offered to the nation in lieu of estate duty (later inheritance tax); and in the same year a scheme, administered by the Victoria and Albert Museum, was launched to assist repositories to purchase manuscripts.

These measures, useful in themselves, could also have served as building blocks for an overarching structure of measures for the protection of archives, but by 1980 that structure had not materialised. There were a number of political and practical reasons for this. The professional archivists were not a large body, and not over-familiar with the workings of Whitehall. It was even more difficult to assemble a body of interested MPs, and to secure parliamentary time for legislation. It made strategic sense to form alliances with a wider group of professional bodies and organisations in the heritage world, but here too there were difficulties. Archivists did not always see eye to eye with librarians and museum curators, and they were in any case much the smallest body of the three. It also made sense to enlist the support of both the owners of manuscripts and their users – that army of historians both professional and amateur. But, as the BRA knew from experience, it was hard to engage the owners, and historians all too often disagreed among themselves on questions such as the benefits of regional as opposed to county or borough services.[83]

---

[82] Roger Ellis was on permanent loan, so to speak, from the PRO. His successor in 1972, Godfrey Davis, formerly of the British Museum, was the first Secretary from an outside institution.

[83] The BRA was poorly supported by historians, Sir Frank Stenton being a notable exception.

The archivists needed also to work closely with both the PRO and the HMC. As we have seen, however, relations between the PRO and local repositories could lack cordiality. (The first professionally qualified archivist was appointed to the staff of the PRO only in 1979.) The HMC had much closer links with local record offices, but it had not been established to act as a pressure group, and when it advised the government it did so behind the scenes, giving rise from time to time to misunderstanding and frustration among the archivists. Furthermore, despite their historical links, the HMC's role was very clearly differentiated from that of the PRO, and it reported to a different government department. The PRO remained under the Lord Chancellor, whereas the HMC, after a long period of direct Treasury support, found itself linked to a succession of government bodies or departments concerned with the arts and the national heritage.

Then there were a number of more practical issues. Which bodies should be represented on the proposed national archives council, and to which arm of government should it report? How easy or difficult would it be to devise a system for 'listing' pre-eminent archives? After all, archives, more easily than buildings, could change shape, move around or even disappear from official view entirely. If a dedicated inspectorate were needed, how much would it cost, and who would foot the bill? At a more fundamental level lay the fact that England, in contrast with France, was a decentralised State, in which it was difficult to co-ordinate national and local action. There was felt to be something un-English about a Ministry of Archives. As an assistant keeper in the British Museum's Department of Manuscripts (and later Secretary of the HMC) put it in 1960, 'the English, it goes without saying, have no respect for ideologies or bureaucracy'.[84] The nearest England had come to adopting a *dirigiste* scheme for its archives had been in the exceptional circumstances of the Second World War.

Losses in the Second World War

The Napoleonic, Crimean and First World Wars all had their impact on English, and in particular English governmental, archives, but the effects of the Second World War were on a different scale. England was not invaded in 1940 and was spared the widespread

[84] GRC Davis, *op cit*, p177.

devastation inflicted on parts of Europe, but there was much damage, particularly as a result of the campaigns of the *Luftwaffe*, and the post-War consequences were considerable. The worst direct damage was in London: maps prepared at the time show huge concentrations of destruction in and near the docks, around St Paul's Cathedral and in the area later comprehensively rebuilt as the Barbican Centre. But outside London there were areas of devastation in the coastal ports from Dover and Southampton to Bristol and Liverpool, and in cities such as Coventry and Exeter targeted by the Baedeker raids. It could, though, have been even worse. Important concentrations of historic buildings – and archives – in places such as Oxford and Cambridge were spared, and in the countryside many areas were relatively or completely unscathed.

Archival losses were caused not only by the destruction of the buildings in which they were housed but also very often from the fires that followed or from the water used to extinguish them. In total, however, more damage to records was probably caused by disturbance and neglect. Even when they were removed to places of greater safety they could deteriorate rapidly if not regularly checked for signs of damp. Another hazard was the campaign to collect and recycle unwanted papers for the war effort – the so-called salvage drives – although some were rescued through the efforts of the British Records Association and others.[85]

Before the war thought had already been given to the protection of the great national collections, and at the outbreak of hostilities quantities of records were moved out of London. Some of the PRO's holdings, including Domesday Book, were despatched to Shepton Mallet prison. Other records from Chancery Lane went to country houses and other temporary repositories: at Belvoir Castle the Duke of Rutland was given the rank of honorary assistant keeper in recognition of his custodial responsibilities.[86] Many manuscripts from the British Museum found a home at the National Library of Wales. The most treasured documents from the House of Lords Record Office were deposited in the Bodleian

---

[85] J Hurstfield, *The Control of Raw Material*, History of the Second World War, United Kingdom Civil Series, London 1953, *passim*. It can be noted here that waste paper and parchment, often from attorneys' offices around the London law courts, had supplied a thriving recycling industry as far back as Dickens's day.

[86] Cantwell, *op cit*, pp427–8, 440; Caroline Shenton, *National Treasures: Saving the Nation's Art in World War II*, London 2021, pp94–5.

Library, but bulky records such as the acts of parliament were despatched to a country house in Hampshire, from which they returned at the end of the war 'covered in mould and mildew'.[87]

Local authorities had also taken precautions with regard to their older records,[88] but there were some major losses, for instance of probate records at Exeter and tax records at Liverpool. The impact of the war on the records of the Church of England are better documented, thanks to the post-war survey carried out by the Pilgrim Trust. Diocesan records were lost in significant quantity at Canterbury and Coventry, and on a lesser scale at Lambeth, Gloucester and Norwich, while the archives at Ely, Exeter and Hereford suffered when they were moved. At Salisbury the cathedral's copy of Magna Carta was removed from the library to the diocesan registrar's strongroom in the Close, where it was 'locked inside a rough wooden box along with other treasures'.[89] The Manchester collegiate records were left where they were, and the muniment room was lucky to escape only with broken windows, but the workmen responsible for repairing them 'left cigarette ends and dead matches on the floor', as the Pilgrim Trust investigator recorded.[90] At Westminster Abbey the most valuable records were sent to the National Library of Wales, and others were taken by the archivist to his Hampshire cottage where he could work on them undisturbed, but the chapter clerk contributed his recent files to the salvage drive, leaving a gap in the archive for the years 1900–39.[91]

Over the country as a whole the losses of records relating to businesses and organisations must have been heavy, but the surviving evidence is patchy. In London, for which more information is available, the livery companies were among the institutions most severely hit. The Stationers had removed their most valuable records, but those that remained were badly damaged.[92] The small archive of

---

[87] Shenton, *op cit*, p207.

[88] For Bedfordshire, see *Archives*, vol i no 1 (Lady Day 1949), p15.

[89] Shenton, *op cit*, p209. The Lincoln Magna Carta spent the war in the USA, latterly in Fort Knox.

[90] Pilgrim Trust Report, 1951, *sub* Manchester.

[91] Richard Mortimer, *Guide to the Muniments of Westminster Abbey*, Woodbridge 2012, p17.

[92] Robin Myers, *The Stationers' Company Archive: an Account of the Records*, Winchester and Detroit 1990, ppxxx–xxxi. There was water damage from the firemen's hoses, and some records were 'thrown away in the resulting chaos'.

the Worshipful Company of Cooks was comprehensively incinerated, along with its poor box, Master's ivory mallet and beadle's staff.[93] Among the Inns of Court the archive of Gray's suffered a major disaster. The Unitarian archive at Essex House was thought to have been lost when the building was demolished by a flying bomb in 1944, but it was later discovered in its basement strongroom, damaged by heat and water but protected from total destruction by the metal trunks in which it was stored. It was rescued and transferred, in some confusion, to Dr Williams's Library.[94] Among the larger businesses the National Provincial Bank required each branch to prepare duplicates of its records and send them to another branch at a distance for safe keeping, but such elaborate precautions must have been unusual.[95] Around St Paul's many records of the book trade must have been lost, along with vast stocks of the books themselves. The losses among the records of London solicitors must also have been considerable, not helped by the tendency of firms to store them in basements that could be flooded.

Few country houses suffered direct hits in air raids, but in many the muniments suffered damage from neglect or disturbance. On a much smaller scale many personal archives were lost. At a flat in West Hampstead, badly damaged in the Blitz, the casualties included a desk containing a marriage certificate, a fire insurance policy and all the letters from a wife to her husband: such losses must have been replicated very widely.[96] As in previous emergencies, going back at least to the seventeenth century, the idea of burying valuables, including manuscripts, had a certain currency. Chips Channon asked his gardener to bury his diaries in the churchyard at Kelvedon (Essex) – 'Perhaps some future generation will dig them up' – while down in Wiltshire Miss Talbot at Lacock Abbey buried her 1225 exemplification of Magna Carta at a spot known only to herself and her coachman. Fortunately it came to no harm.[97]

---

[93] Heather Creaton, *Sources for the History of London 1939–45*, London (BRA Archives and the User no 9) 1998, p78.

[94] Peter B Godfrey and GM Ditchfield, 'The Unitarian Archives at Essex Hall', *Archives*, vol xxvi no 104 (Apr 2001), p59.

[95] Creaton, *op cit*, p78.

[96] Juliet Gardiner, *Wartime: Britain 1939–1945*, London 2004, p298.

[97] *Ibid*, pp170–1; Nicholas Vincent, *Magna Carta: Origins and Legacy*, Oxford (Bodleian Library) 2015, p137.

Postscript

During the last four decades English archives have been subject to many changes. What is more, the pace of those changes has accelerated. The situation, however, is an uneven one: there have been both gains and losses.

To note first the gains, one significant advance is that the nation's archives have become more widely recognised as an integral and important part of its heritage. More money has become available from the public purse for the acquisition of outstanding collections and for their conservation and cataloguing. It has become rare for such archives to be broken up in the auction room or sold abroad. Standards for the accommodation of records have risen greatly, and more collections are now housed in well-designed modern buildings. Many more private archives, moreover, are now looked after by professional curators, and there have been advances in the storage and management of modern records. Computer technology has played an important part not only in records management but in making archival material quickly and easily available to a wider public.

Other developments, however, have been less benign. The publicly funded archive sector has suffered from budgetary cuts, with inevitable consequences for staff and services. Administrative changes have not always helped. And hard times have had a direct impact on archives in private hands, with more collections now at risk of loss or destruction than for many years past. Local record offices lack the resources to take in large numbers of them, and the national coverage of specialist repositories remains partial and uneven.

As stated in the Introduction, it would have been inappropriate to describe these developments in detail in the present volume. To do them justice would have required a book in itself, and one with the benefit of a longer historical perspective than that available to the present author. In two respects, however, it is hoped that the present volume may have some contemporary relevance.

The first is connected with the word archive itself, and what it means in general parlance. In the late twentieth century the French philosopher Jacques Derrida wrote that 'We no longer know very well what we are saying when we say "archive".'[1] Since then the word has been more and more loosely used, until it can now mean almost any collection of documentary or other material. It is hoped, however, that in studying archives over an extended period this volume may help to re-focus attention on their essential and defining features.

Secondly, there is the perennial question of relations between the archival and historical communities. Although misunderstandings can still arise, it is good to record that there is now more, and more fruitful, contact between the two professions. And although those professions are separate and distinct, no one, *pace* Sir Hilary Jenkinson, would now argue that the same individual cannot be both an historian and an archivist.[2] After all, interrogating the history of an archive should inform both the work of the historian in assessing its evidential value and the work of the archivist in deciding how best to arrange and catalogue it.

Dealing with archives, whether as curator or user, will never be unproblematic. As one wise historian has written, 'Records speak only when they are spoken to, and they will not talk to strangers.'[3] But perhaps this book may help to further the conversation.

---

[1] *Archive Fever: A Freudian Impression,* English translation Chicago 1996, p91.

[2] For Jenkinson's statement that 'the Archivist is not and ought not to be an Historian', see his *Manual of Archive Administration*, Oxford 1922, p106.

[3] CR Cheney, in *Medieval Texts and Calendars,* Oxford 1973, quoted in Simon Keynes, *The Diplomas of King Aethelred 'The Unready' (978–1016)*, Cambridge 1980, pxv.

Select Bibliography

This is a limited selection of the published sources consulted in the preparation of this volume. It includes general studies in archival history and guides to particular classes of record, but excludes works concerned with individual archives. (See also the *Note on Sources* in the Introduction.)

Anglo-Saxon Charters, ed SE Kelly *et al*, eds, 20 vols, London and Oxford (British Academy) 1973–2021.

Aston, Trevor, 'Muniment Rooms and their Fittings in Medieval and Early Modern England', in Ralph Evans, ed, *Lordship and Learning: Studies in Memory of Trevor Aston*, Woodbridge 2004.

Ayloffe, Sir Joseph, *Calendar of the Ancient Charters, and of the Welch and Scottish Rolls, now remaining in the Tower of London ...*, London 1774.

[Bernard, Edward], *Catalogi librorum manuscriptorum Angliae et Hiberniae, in unum collecti, cum indice alphabetico*, Oxford 1697.

Brown, Warren C *et al*, eds, *Documentary Culture and the Laity in the Early Middle Ages*, Oxford 2013.

Cantwell, John D, *The Public Record Office 1838–1958*, London 1991.

Clanchy, MT, *From Memory to Written Record: England 1066–1307*, 3rd edn Chichester 2013.

Cock, Randolph and Rodger, NAM, *A Guide to the Naval Records in the National Archives of the UK*, London (IHR and TNA) 2008.

Cook, Chris *et al*, *Sources in British Political History 1900–1951 Vol 1: a Guide to the Archives of Selected Organisations and Societies*, London 1975.

Corens, Liesbeth, Peters, Kate and Walsham, Alexandra, eds, *The Social History of the Archive: Record-Keeping in Early Modern Europe*, Oxford (*Past and Present* Supplement 11) 2016.

——. *Archives and Information in the Early Modern World*, Oxford (British Academy Proceedings 212) 2018.

Davis, GRC, *Medieval Cartularies of Great Britain: a Short Catalogue*, 2nd edn, ed Claire Breay *et al*, London (BL) 2010.

Daybell, James, *The Material Letter in Early Modern England: Manuscript Letters and the Culture and Practice of Letter-Writing 1512–1635*, Plymouth 2012.

Delsalle, Paul, *Une histoire de l'archivistique*, Quebec 1998; English edn tr Margaret Procter, published as *A History of Archival Practice*, London 2017.

Field, Clive D, 'Preserving Zion: the Anatomy of Protestant Nonconformist Archives in Great Britain and Ireland', *Archives*, vol xxxiii no 118 (Apr 2008), pp14–51.

Foster, Janet and Sheppard, Julia, *British Archives: a Guide to Archive Repositories in the United Kingdom*, 3rd edn London 1996.

Foulds, Trevor, 'Medieval Cartularies', *Archives*, vol xviii no 77 (Apr 1987), pp3–35.

Fowler, G Herbert, *The Care of County Muniments*, 2nd edn London 1928.

Hallam, Elizabeth M, *Domesday Book through Nine Centuries*, London 1986.

Harmer, Florence E, *Anglo-Saxon Writs*, 2nd edn Stamford 1989.

Harvey, PDA, *Manorial Records*, rev edn London (BRA Archives and the User no 5) 1999.

Head, Randolph C, 'Documents, Archives and Proof around 1700', *Historical Jnl*, vol 56 (2013), pp909–30.

Hiatt, Alfred, *The Making of Medieval Forgeries: False Documents in Fifteenth-Century England*, London and Toronto 2004.

Historical Manuscripts Commission, *Guide to the Location of Collections Described in the Reports and Calendars Series*, Guides to Sources for British History 3, London 1982.

——. *Papers of British Cabinet Minister 1782–1900*, Guides to Sources ... 1, London (HMSO) 1982.

——. *Surveys of Historical Manuscripts in the United Kingdom: a Select Bibliography*, 2nd edn London 1994 (with supplements in the HMC's Annual Reviews to 2002–3).

——. *Archives at the Millennium: the Twenty-Eighth Report of the Royal Commission on Historical Manuscripts*, London 1999.

——. *Principal Family and Estate Collections*, Guides to Sources ... 10 and 11, 2 vols London 1996, 1999.

——. *Papers of British Antiquaries and Historians*, Guides to Sources ... 12, London 2003.

Hudson, Patricia, *The West Riding Wool Textile Industry: a Catalogue of Business Records from the Sixteenth to the Twentieth Century*, Edington 1975.

Hunter, Michael, ed, *Archives of the Scientific Revolution: the Formation and Exchange of Ideas in Seventeenth-Century Europe*, Woodbridge 1998.

Jenkinson, Hilary, *A Manual of Archive Administration, including the Problems of War Archives and Archive Making*, Oxford 1922.

[Kitching, Christopher], *The Central Records of the Church of England: a Report and Survey Presented to the Pilgrim and Radcliffe Trustees*, London 1976.

——. *Archives: the Very Essence of our Heritage*, Chichester (for the National Council on Archives) 1996.

Kumin, Beat A, *The Shaping of a Community: the Rise and Reformation of the English Parish c1400–1560*, Aldershot and Brookfield VT 1996. (For churchwardens' accounts.)

Littleton, AC and Yamey, BS, eds, *Studies in the History of Accounting*, London 1956.

Local Records. *Report of the Committee Appointed to Enquire as to the Existing Arrangements for the Collection and Custody of Local Records ...*, Cmd 1335, 1902.

McKisack, May, *Medieval History in the Tudor Age*, Oxford 1971.

McKitterick, Rosamund, ed, *The Uses of Literacy in Medieval Europe*, Cambridge 1990.

Martin, Geoffrey H, 'The Origins of Borough Records', *JSA*, vol 2 (1960–4), pp147–53.

Matthews, William, *British Diaries: an Annotated Bibliography of British Diaries Written between 1442 and 1942*, Berkeley CA and London 1950.

Moir, Martin, *A General Guide to the India Office Records*, London (BL) 1988.

Mullett, Michael, *Sources for the History of English Nonconformity 1660–1830*, London (BRA Archives and the User no 8) 1991.

Mullins, ELC, *Texts and Calendars: an Analytical Guide to Serial Publications*, London (RHS) 1958, with *Supplement* 1983. (Publications of national and local record societies.)

Munby, ANL, *The Cult of the Autograph Letter in England*, London 1962.

Olney, RJ, *Manuscript Sources for British History: their Nature, Location and Use*, London (IHR) 1995.

Orbell, John and Turton, Alison, *British Banking: a Guide to Historical Records*, London 2001.

Owen, Dorothy, *The Records of the Established Church, excluding Parochial Records*, London (BRA Archives and the User no 1) 1970.

Pilgrim Trust. Survey of Ecclesiastical Archives, Report, unpublished typescript 1951.

Popper, Nicholas, 'From Abbey to Archive: Managing Texts and Records in Early Modern England', *Archival Science*, vol 10 (2010), pp249–66.

Posner, Ernst, *Archives in the Ancient World*, Cambridge MA 1972.

Procter, Margaret, 'Life before Jenkinson: the Development of British Archival Theory and Thought at the Turn of the Twentieth Century', *Archives*, vol xxxiii no 119 (Oct 2008), pp140–61.

——. 'What's "an Archivist"? Some Nineteenth-Century Perspectives', *JSA*, vol 31 no 1 (Apr 2010), pp15–27.

Public Record Office. *Annual Reports of the Deputy Keeper of the Public Records*, 1838- .

——. *Guide to the Contents of the Public Record Office*, 2 vols 1963 (and subsequent editions).

Public Records. *Reports of the Select Committee of the House of Commons on the State of the Public Records of the Kingdom ...*, 1800. (See also below, Record Commission.)

——. *Reports of the Royal Commission on the Public Records*, 1912–19.

Rawcliffe, Carole, 'Passports to Paradise: How English Medieval Hospitals and Almshouses Kept their Archives', *Archives*, vol xxvii no 106 (Apr 2002), pp2–22.

Razi, Zvi and Smith, Richard, eds, *Medieval Society and the Manor Court*, Oxford 1996.

Record Commission. *Reports from the Commissioners ... Respecting the Public Records of the Kingdom*, 1800–1819.

Redstone, Lilian J and Steer, Francis W, eds, *Local Records: their Nature and Care*, London 1953.

Richmond, Lesley and Turton, Alison, *The Brewing Industry: a Guide to Historical Records*, Manchester 1990.

Roper, Michael, 'The Development of the Principle of Provenance and Respect for Original Order in the Public Record Office', in Barbara L Craig, ed, *The Archival Imagination: Essays in Honour of Hugh A Taylor*, Ottawa 1992, pp134–53.

——. *The Records of the Foreign Office 1782–1968*, Kew (PRO Handbooks no 33) 2002.

Sabapathy, John, *Officers and Accountability in Medieval England 1170–1300*, Oxford 2014.

Sawyer, PH, *Anglo-Saxon Charters: an Annotated List and Bibliography*, London (RHS) 1968.

Shepherd, Elizabeth J, *Archives and Archivists in 20th Century England*, Farnham 2009.

Smith, David M, *Guide to Bishops' Registers of England and Wales: a Survey from the Middle Ages to the Abolition of Episcopacy in 1646*, London (RHS) 1981.

Stenton, FM, *The Latin Charters of the Anglo-Saxon Period*, Oxford 1955.

Thomas, FS, *Notes of Materials for the History of Public Departments*, printed London 1846.

Tite, Colin GC, *The Manuscript Library of Sir Robert Cotton*, London (BL) 1994.

Tollerton, Linda, *Wills and Will-Making in Anglo-Saxon England*, York and Woodbridge 2011.

Vincent, Nicholas, *Magna Carta: Origins and Legacy*, Oxford (Bodleian Library) 2015.

Whyman, Susan E, *The Pen and the People: English Letter Writers 1660–1800*, Oxford 2009.

Williams, Caroline, 'Understanding Collections at Risk', *Archives*, vol liii no 136 (Apr 2018), pp45–69.

Woolf, Daniel, *The Social Circulation of the Past: English Historical Culture 1500–1730*, Oxford 2003.

Woolgar, CM, ed, *Household Accounts from Medieval England*, 2 vols Oxford (British Academy Records of Social and Economic History, New S xvii, xviii) 1992, 1993.

Yeo, Geoffrey, *Record-Making and Record-Keeping in Early Societies*, London 2021.

Index

Only the more substantial references to persons and places have been indexed. Phrases such as 'archive of' or 'records relating to' are omitted. Some pages contain more than one reference to the same person, place or subject.

abstracts of title xiv, 112
accounts and accountants 28, 29, 30, 31, 41, 64, 72, 73, 84, 111, 112, 137, 159, 163, 174
   estate and business 49, 77, 112, 197
   government, central *see* Exchequer; Treasury
   government, local *see* boroughs; counties; parishes
   monastic 47–8, 67
   personal 116, 139
   see also day books; journals, financial; ledgers; vouchers
act books xiv, 47, 64, 86, 127
Admiralty *see* Navy
aeraries xiv, 68
Agard, Arthur, Deputy-Chamberlain of the Exchequer 104, 118
agents, land or estate 75, 112, 136–7, 161
   see also estate offices
Alfred, King 18
almshouses 70–1
   see also hospitals
antiquaries 113, 117–19, 140–1, 155, 168–9, 200, 203, 228
archdeacons and archdeaconries 63, 97, 190, 218
Arches, Court of 142, 190

archival profession 181, 206, 213
archive, definition of xiv, 1–2, 238
   see also evidences of title; muniments
archivists xiv, 2, 28, 36, 108, 110, 126, 135, 140, 212–25 *passim*, 232–3, 238
   see also archival profession; keepers of records
arks xiv, 36, 86
armariola xiv, 84, 85, 86
   see also cupboards; presses
attics 108, 122, 146, 165, 166, 168, 222, 226
attornies *see* solicitors
Augmentations, Court, later Office, of 54, 55, 91, 94, 95, 97–8, 146, 147, 176
Augustine, Saint 10, 12

bags 37, 84, 87, 98, 102, 115n59
banks 137, 163, 197, 236
   Bank of England 163
Baptists 133, 195
basements, cellars and vaults 146, 166, 187, 211, 222, 226, 236
Bath and Wells, diocese of 62, 97, 109
Bath General Infirmary 158
Bec Abbey, English manors of 42

246 *English Archives*

Bedfordshire 188, 211, 212, 230n77
Bernard, Edward, cataloguer 140, 182
Birmingham Reference Library 186, 213
bishops 16–17, 25, 45–6, 62, 63, 96, 109, 122, 128, 190, 191
Black Death 62
Bodleian Library *see* Oxford
book-keeping *see* accounts and accountants
boroughs 43–4, 58–61, 107–8, 124, 154–5, 185–6, 214–15
see also town clerks; town halls
box files 202
boxes, tin 202
Bray, Sir Reginald, royal servant 54, 55
brewers 163, 164, 197
Bristol, city of 65, 107, 155, 185, 186
record office 212
British Museum, later British Library, Department of Manuscripts 5, 119, 128, 169, 178, 181–2, 186, 196, 203, 209, 213, 224, 227–8
British Records Association 219, 230–1, 232, 234
British Records Society 211n21, 230, 231
Browne, John, Clerk of the Parliaments 131
Browne's Hospital, Stamford (Lincolnshire) 71
Brudenell family, of Deene (Northamptonshire) 113, 125n19
buckram 102, 115
bulls, papal xiv, 33, 52, 100
Burton Abbey (Staffordshire) 23, 25n1, 94
Bury St Edmund's Abbey 13, 78–9, 93
Business Archives Council 226
businesses 10, 77, 114–15, 137, 163–6, 196–8, 225–7

Cabinet ministers 200–1
see also Prime Ministers
Cabinet records 144, 181n4, 183–4
cabinets 101, 125, 126n24, 138, 167
see also filing cabinets
calendars xiv, 52, 144, 179, 200
Cambridge
castle 41
colleges 69
Corpus Christi College 93, 118
King's College 42n20, 70
Magdalene College 140
St John's College 110–11, 159–60
University 70, 83, 111–12, 135, 193–4, 219–20
University Library 218, 220
Canterbury
archbishopric, province and diocese 46, 63, 85, 96, 235
Christ Church Cathedral Priory 11n3, 12, 13, 14–15, 23, 28–9, 47, 48, 66, 67
St Augustine's Abbey 11n3, 12, 13, 33n27
see also Prerogative Court of Canterbury
cardboard 81, 202
cartularies ix, 23, 26–7, 50, 58, 66, 67, 68, 75, 92, 93–4, 112n49, 118, 123n11
castles 34, 40–1, 44, 50, 59, 72–3, 124, 125
see also London, Tower of; Windsor Castle
catalogues 5, 135, 150, 182, 213, 228, 238
cathedrals
monastic 26, 28–9; *see also* Canterbury; Durham; Ely; Norwich; Winchester; Worcester
secular 16, 26, 64; *see also* Lincoln; London, St Paul's Cathedral; Salisbury; York
post-Reformation 109–10, 122, 123, 128, 131–2, 156, 190, 192–3, 218

Cavendish family, dukes of
 Devonshire 137, 160, 199
 see also Hardwick Hall
Cecil family, marquesses of Salisbury
 101, 116, 182, 201
 William, Lord Burghley, Treasurer
  131
census enumerators' returns 180
Chamber, Royal 54
Chancery 19, 36–7n, 40, 51–4, 55, 87,
 102–3, 149
 see also Lord Chancellors;
  Master of the Rolls; patent
  rolls; Rolls House and Chapel
chantries 68, 95, 97
chapels and meeting houses 28, 33,
 40, 59, 60, 68, 107, 112, 134, 135
Chapter clerks 47
charities 67–8, 70–1, 110, 158, 193
 see also almshouses; colleges;
  hospitals; schools
Charles I 125–6
charters xv, 10–11, 13, 15, 17, 23, 26,
 34, 58, 66, 68, 79
chests 28, 33, 36, 60, 65, 68, 70, 74,
 81–7 *passim*, 101, 104, 105, 110,
 111, 112, 136n29, 137, 147, 152–3,
 159, 192
 see also arks; coffers; hutches;
  standards
chirographs xv, xvii, 22, 31, 36
Church (of England) 10–17, 25–9,
 45–9, 62–7, 96–7, 109–10, 122,
 155–7, 189–93, 216–19, 235
Church Commissioners *see*
 Ecclesiastical Commissioners
Church courts 46, 63, 96, 109,
 190
 see also Arches, Court of;
  Prerogative Court of
  Canterbury
Churchill, Sir Winston, Prime
 Minister 207, 227
churchwardens 64–5, 97, 192
Cinque Ports 61

Clifford, Lady Anne, Countess of
 Dorset 116, 125
coffers xv, 33n27, 39n12, 86, 99, 101
Coke family, earls of Leicester 113,
 161, 199
Coke, Sir John, Secretary of State
 102, 121
College of Arms 71–2, 117, 119, 142,
 196
colleges and collegiate churches
 67–70, 84, 95, 193, 219
commonplace books 138, 167
Common Pleas, Court of 35, 55, 145
Commons, House of 55, 127, 131, 148,
 175, 183, 209
Commonwealth and Protectorate
 126–7, 132
computers 225, 237
conservation 149, 206, 237
copyhold tenure 77, 154
 see also manors
Cornwall, Duchy of 56, 61, 124, 184
coroners 41
correspondence *see* letters
Cotton, Sir Robert, manuscript
 collector 11n3, 118, 126n27
Cottonian Library 11n3, 119, 125,
 140, 147, 157, 169
Council of the North 99, 122
counties 40, 99, 105–6, 150–2, 187–9,
 210–13, 215
counting houses 115
country houses 76, 113–14, 124, 162,
 168, 198–9, 223, 236
county councils 188, 210–13
county halls *see* shire or county halls
courts, ecclesiastical *see* Church
 courts
Creighton, Mandell, bishop of
 London 191
Cromwell, Thomas, statesman 91,
 98
cupboards 76, 84–6, 91n1, 104, 162,
 167, 222
 see also armariola

Customs and Excise 130, 142, 174
Custos Rotulorum 57, 105, 151, 187, 188
custumals xv, 43, 44, 58

damp, effects and dangers of 83, 84, 85, 114, 153, 190, 202, 228
Danelaw 15
David of London, clerk and diplomat 34
day books 77, 114
deans and chapters *see* cathedrals, secular; cathedrals, post-Reformation
deeds xv, 68, 76
   see also charters; indentures
desks, writing 116, 138, 166, 201, 236
despatches xv, 145, 174
diaries 138–40, 202, 227n72, 236
   see also journals
dioceses 16, 25, 45, 62–3, 93, 96–7, 109, 122, 156, 189–90, 216–17, 235
   see also bishops
diplomas xv
diplomatic xv, 140
dissenters *see* nonconformists
dissolution of the monasteries *see* religious houses, dissolution of
dockets xv, 131
Dr Williams's Library 134, 236
documents, definition of xv, 2
Domesday Book 21, 25, 29, 30, 39, 83, 141, 148, 208n11, 234
Downing, Sir George, Secretary of the Treasury 129
Ducarel, AC, Lambeth Palace Librarian 155–6
Dugdale, Sir William, antiquary 125, 140, 167
Dunstan, saint 13, 15
Durham
   cathedral priory 13, 47, 48, 66–7, 84n13, 93
   University 218

East India Company *see* India, records relating to
Ecclesiastical (later Church) Commissioners 189–90, 192n64, 193, 217–18
Ecole des Chartes 181
Edward the Confessor 20
electronic technology *see* computers
Ely
   bishopric and diocese 109, 132, 156, 190, 218
   cathedral priory 13–14, 67, 93, 128n34
enclosure awards 151, 189
English, written 75
   see also Old English, documents in
enrolment xv, 32, 36, 37n3, 99, 105
entry books 106, 129, 130
   see also minute books
estate offices 161, 162, 199, 223
estates, landed 13–14, 22–3, 34, 42, 47–8, 49–50, 56, 61, 63, 72–5, 110, 112–14, 122–3, 128, 136–7, 158, 159, 160–3, 190, 193, 198–200, 216, 223–5
   see also agents, land or estate; extents; manors; maps, estate; rentals; surveys
Eton College 42n20, 70, 95, 160, 220
Evelyn, John, diarist 139, 167, 168
evidence rooms *see* muniment rooms
evidences of title xv, 10, 91, 100
   see also charters; deeds; muniments
Exchequer 21, 29–32, 37, 39, 40, 51, 52, 53, 98, 103–4, 121, 129, 145, 149
   Deputy-Chamberlains of 32, 83, 104; *see also* Agard; Le Neve
   Exchequer of Receipt 30, 32
   Treasury of Receipt 30, 33, 36, 52, 101, 104, 147

exemplification xv, 11
Exeter
    cathedral 64
    city 108
    diocese 63
export of manuscripts 229, 231, 232, 237
extents xv

faculties 96, 191
family archives 1, 50, 75, 76, 94, 116, 139, 167–8, 198, 199, 227
farming records 14, 165
Fastolf, Sir John 76
feudal records 75, 98
files xv, 62, 150, 157, 206
    see also box files; filing cabinets; subject files
filing cabinets 207
final concords 36
finding aids 66, 85, 108, 141, 146, 179, 182
    see also calendars; cartularies; catalogues; indexes; inventories
fines, feet of *see* final concords
fire hazards and precautions 15, 26, 27, 56, 63, 78, 104, 124, 141–2, 146, 147n14, 155, 162, 164, 175–6, 177, 183, 186, 188, 197, 199, 228, 234
    see also London, Fire of; Westminster, Palace of; Whitehall, Palace of
Fitzalan-Howard family, dukes of Norfolk 49, 162, 199, 223
Fitz Nigel, Richard, Treasurer 30, 31
Foreign Office 145, 174
forgeries, medieval 11, 26
formularies 11
Fowler, Dr Herbert 212, 230
Fox, George, Quaker 134
Freemasons 159

gatehouses 53n7, 58, 70, 72, 104, 144, 146, 216
General Post Office 99, 126, 130, 142, 158, 173
Gladstone, WE, Prime Minister 201, 202, 228
Glastonbury Abbey 15, 20, 43, 94
Gloucester
    county record office 217–18
    diocese 217–18
gospel-books 11n3, 13, 14
government, central
    Anglo-Saxon 12, 17–21, 25
    medieval 29–33, 35–40, 51–5, 87
    early modern and modern 91–2, 97–9, 101–5, 121–2, 126, 127–8, 129–31, 143–50, 174–82, 184–5, 206–9
government, local
    Anglo-Saxon 21–2
    medieval 40–4, 56–62
    early modern and modern 99–100, 105–8, 150–5, 185–9, 210–16
guard books 159
guildhalls 58, 59, 108
guilds 43–4, 60, 97

Halesowen (Worcestershire) 44
hanapers xv, 37, 87
Hardwick Hall (Derbyshire) 114, 223
    see also Cavendish family, dukes of Devonshire
Hardy and Page, record agents 188
Hemming, monk and archivist 27, 28
Henley family, shipowners 164–5
Henry VIII 54
historians 117, 140–1, 203, 214, 225, 230, 232, 238
    see also antiquaries
Historical Manuscripts Commission (HMC) 5, 182, 186, 188, 200, 201, 228, 230, 231, 232
Holkham (Norfolk) *see* Coke family, earls of Leicester

hospitals 60, 68, 70, 95–6, 158, 194, 221
Hotot, Thomas, of Clopton (Northamptonshire) 50
households 34, 49, 72–3, 116, 162, 199–200
Hubert Walter, archbishop of Canterbury, Justiciar and Chancellor 36, 37, 41n17, 46
hundreds and hundred rolls 41, 105
hutches xv, 82, 108

indentures xvi
  see also chirographs
indexes and index books 150, 207
India, records relating to 115, 137, 145, 174, 183, 209
information technology see computers
Inns of Court 72, 119, 142, 196, 236
institutions, civil and non-governmental 67–72, 110–12, 135–6, 158–60, 193–6, 219–23
Interregnum see Commonwealth and Protectorate
inventories 68, 73, 104, 106
Ipswich, borough of 43, 44, 59

Jenkinson, Sir Hilary, Deputy-Keeper of the Public Records 206, 208, 209, 212, 213, 227n71, 230, 231
Josselin, Rev Ralph, diarist 139
journals xvi
  financial xvi
  parliamentary 55, 131, 148, 183
  personal 134, 138, 166, 203
  see also diaries
Justices of the Peace 57, 105, 150, 151, 153n38
  see also Petty Sessions; Quarter Sessions

keepers of records 2, 37, 98, 101, 143, 144, 146
King's Bench, Court of 35, 55, 104, 145, 147
Kirton-in-Lindsey (Lincolnshire) 61
Knights Hospitallers 67, 78
Knights Templar 40, 53, 67

Lacock Abbey (Wiltshire) 113, 236
Lakenheath, John, monk and archivist 78
Lambarde, William, lawyer and archivist 106, 117
Lambeth Palace 63, 96, 125, 155, 190, 235
  Library 109, 119, 125n22, 127, 155–6, 196, 219
Lancaster, Duchy of 55, 72, 74, 184
  see also Savoy, palace and hospital of (London)
landbooks see charters
leases 13, 15, 136, 161, 199
ledgers xvi, 77, 114, 137, 163
Leicester, borough of 43, 44, 124, 186
Le Neve, Peter, Deputy-Chamberlain of the Exchequer and archivist 140
letter books xvi, 34, 130, 135, 158, 161, 165, 191, 197, 227
letters and correspondence 20, 36, 38, 67, 77, 98, 112, 115–16, 125, 131, 134, 138, 159, 161, 166, 168, 173, 183, 184, 191, 200–1, 227
  see also letter books; letters patent; writs
letters patent xvi, 36, 110
  see also patent rolls
Leveson-Gower family, earls Gower and dukes of Sutherland see Trentham
libraries and librarians 73, 101, 134, 136, 160, 168, 202, 209, 212, 214, 216, 232
  borough 186, 212, 213, 214, 217
  cathedral 218, 220

Index 251

university 214, 218, 222, 226, 229
  see also British Museum; Cotton,
    Sir Robert; Lambeth Palace,
    Library; London, Guildhall
    Library; Manchester, John
    Rylands University Library;
    Oxford, Bodleian Library
Lieutenancy, clerks of 151
Lincoln
  bishopric and diocese 45, 62, 63,
    97, 109, 216, 217
  cathedral 25, 46, 64, 132
livery companies see London
locks 28, 65, 66, 68, 82–3, 84, 99, 110,
  115
London 65, 125, 163, 165, 194, 228–9
  City of 21, 44, 58, 59, 95, 107, 108,
    141–2, 155, 163
  County Council 188–9
  diocese 191
  Fire of 132, 141–2
  Guildhall Library 165, 196, 220
  livery companies 60, 71, 96, 142,
    159, 220, 235–6
  St Bartholomew's Hospital 70, 95,
    96, 221
  St Paul's Cathedral 16, 125, 132,
    156, 190
  Somerset House 147, 149, 184, 185,
    190
  Tower of London 38, 40, 52–3,
    85, 103, 121, 126, 130, 140, 141,
    148–9, 175, 178
  town houses 73–4, 199
  war damage (1939–45) 234,
    235–6
  see also Rolls House and Chapel;
    Savoy, palace and hospital of;
    Temple, The
Longleat House (Wiltshire) 94, 131,
  200
  see also Thynne family
Lord Chancellors 36, 37, 38, 208
  see also Waynflete, Willam;
    Wykeham, William

Lords, House of 55, 103, 127, 148,
  175, 182, 183, 209–10, 234–5
  see also Parliament, Clerks of the;
    Westminster, Palace of
Lords Lieutenant 105, 151
  see also Custos Rotulorum;
    Lieutenancy, clerks of

Mabillon, Jean, French scholar and
  archivist 140
magistrates see Justices of the Peace
Magna Carta 118, 236
Malmesbury Abbey (Wiltshire) 92
Manchester
  collegiate church 95, 193, 235
  John Rylands University Library
    222, 226
Manorial Documents Register 212,
  216, 232
manors and manorial records 42–3,
  49, 61–2, 67, 77, 123, 154, 212, 216,
  232
maps, estate 112, 116, 199
Master of the Rolls 54, 177, 178, 182,
  187, 208, 212, 216, 231
Maxwell Lyte, Sir Henry, Deputy-
  Keeper of the Public Records 178,
  181, 185
merchants 71, 75, 77, 114, 165, 198
  see also guilds; London, livery
    companies
Methodists 157, 195, 221
methodizers 143, 144, 146, 150
microfilm 225
Middlesex 188
minute books 60, 105, 115, 129, 130,
  133, 134, 135, 143, 197
missionary societies 157, 194
monasteries see religious houses
muniment rooms xvi, 3, 46, 48–9,
  64n50, 66, 67, 68–9, 70, 83, 85, 92,
  111, 113–14, 155, 160–2, 168, 187,
  199, 202, 212, 224, 235
  see also strongrooms
muniments xvi, 3, 12, 92

National Archives, The (TNA) 5, 95, 103
  see also Public Record Office
National Archives Council 233
national policy for archives 228–33
National Register of Archives 5, 231
  see also Historical Manuscripts Commission
National Society 157, 219
Navy 99, 126, 130, 143n3, 145, 178
Nicholas, Sir Edward, Secretary of State 128
nonconformists 132–5, 157, 164, 195, 221
  see also Baptists; Methodists; Society of Friends
Norman Conquest 25
North of England, loss or destruction of records in 15, 25, 43, 65, 66
Norwich
  cathedral priory 66, 76, 84, 93, 110
  St Giles's Hospital 95–6

obedientiaries, monastic 47, 48n38, 93
Old English, documents in 13n7, 21, 22–3
order books xvi, 151n26
ordinances xvi, 43, 60
Ordnance, Board of 99, 126, 130, 149
overseers of the poor 106, 152, 189, 192
Oxford 125
  Bodleian Library 5, 119, 125, 128, 140, 169, 196, 203, 213, 222, 228
  colleges 69
  Corpus Christi College 111
  Magdalen College 70, 86, 111
  Merton College 43, 69, 84n15
  New College 69, 135, 219
  The Queen's College 71
  University College 135
  University 70, 83, 111, 135, 193, 194

palaeography xvi
Palgrave, Francis, Deputy-Keeper of the Public Records 176, 177, 179–80, 184n32, 186
paper 61, 62, 67, 75, 87, 116, 154, 158, 168n93, 206, 228
papyrus xvi, 9, 11
parchment xvi, xviii, 11, 37, 42, 61, 62, 154
parishes and parish churches 64–6, 83, 97, 99, 106, 107n23, 122, 124, 127, 152–3, 189, 192, 217
  see also churchwardens; overseers of the poor; registers, parish
Parker, Matthew, archbishop of Canterbury 92, 93, 109, 118
Parliament 55, 121, 122, 125, 141, 148, 183
  Clerks of the Parliaments 55, 127, 131
  see also Commons, House of; Lords, House of; Westminster, Palace of
Paston family, of Norfolk 75–6, 86, 168
patent rolls 36
Peace, Clerks of the 57, 105, 151, 188n44
Peasants' Revolt (1381) 62, 63, 69n67, 77–9
peculiars
  ecclesiastical 192–3
  royal see Westminster Abbey; Windsor Castle, St George's Chapel
Pells, Clerks of the 37, 55–6
Pepys, Samuel, civil servant and diarist 138, 139, 140, 142
Percy family, earls and dukes of Northumberland 73, 112, 113, 116, 162
personal papers 1, 34, 115–17, 118, 138–40, 166–7, 198, 200–3, 227–8
  see also accounts, personal; diaries; journals, personal; letters and correspondence

Peterborough
  abbey 13, 15, 25n1, 27, 47, 48, 50, 67, 93–4
  cathedral 93, 100, 123
Petty Sessions 153
Phillipps, Sir Thomas, collector of manuscripts 185, 228
Pilgrim Trust 216–20 *passim*
pipe rolls 31, 37
political parties 196, 221–2
Poor Law 173, 211
  see also overseers of the poor
prerogative, royal 52, 54, 98, 104
Prerogative Court of Canterbury 127, 142, 190
presses xvi, 97–8, 102, 103, 104, 105, 111, 132, 149, 157, 219
Prime Ministers 144, 200–1
printed documents 145, 158, 159, 174, 192, 199, 227
Privy Council 55, 98, 130, 144
Privy Seal 38
probate 127, 217, 218
  see also Prerogative Court of Canterbury; wills
Prynne, William, archivist 126, 141
Public Record Office (PRO) 38, 54, 128, 177, 178–81, 182, 185, 186, 207, 208–9, 230, 233, 234
Public Record Office Act (1838) 177, 185
public records xvi, 57, 76, 77, 121, 128, 150, 174–82, 184n31, 187, 209, 210, 214
  see also government, central; National Archives, The; Public Record Office
Public Records Act (1958) 208–9, 214
  see also National Archives, The; public records
pyx xvi, 33
  see also Westminster Abbey, Chapel of the Pyx
pyxides xvi, 84, 86, 87n29

Quakers *see* Society of Friends
Quarter Sessions 57–8, 150–1, 187
Queen Anne's Bounty 157, 218

record, courts of xvii, 2, 42, 98, 121, 187
Record Commission 150, 176, 181
record offices xvii, 226, 230
  county 211–13, 216, 224, 231
  diocesan 217
records
  definition of xvii, 2, 10
  management of 2, 175, 184, 206–7, 209, 211, 213n26, 225
Reculver Abbey (Kent) 11
Reformation, the 95–7
registers xvii, 26n4, 31n20, 34, 55, 60, 64, 86, 93, 98, 99, 106, 107, 131, 173, 197
  bishops' 45, 62, 109, 156
  of deeds 112, 156
  of leases 110
  parish 99–100, 127, 152–3, 192
  see also registrars
registrars (or 'registers') xvii, 111–12, 122, 127n29, 156, 220
  diocesan 45, 62, 109, 127, 191, 192, 216
registration, civil 189
registries 145, 154, 174, 190, 206, 217
religious houses 10–15, 20, 23, 24, 26, 28–9, 34, 47–9, 66–7, 78, 84
  dissolution of 22, 54, 91–5, 110, 117, 158
rentals 48, 112, 198, 199
repair *see* conservation
repertories xvii
respect des fonds, doctrine of xvii, 179, 214
Restoration of the monarchy (1660) 127–8, 129
Ripon (Yorkshire), collegiate church 95, 193

Rochester
  bishopric 63–4
  Bridge Trust 96
rolls 31, 36–7, 42, 45, 86, 111, 154, 159
  see also enrolment; Master of the Rolls; patent rolls; pipe rolls
Rolls House and Chapel 54, 103, 149, 177, 178
Roman Catholics 157–8, 222
Royal Archives, Windsor Castle 183–4, 210
Royal Commission on Historical Manuscripts see Historical Manuscripts Commission
Royal Household 19, 30, 184
  see also Chamber, Royal; Wardrobe, Royal
Royal Mews 148, 175, 176
Royal Society 135–6, 139n45, 159, 196, 220
Russell family, dukes of Bedford 94, 136–7, 199

sacristies 28
St Albans Abbey 67, 78, 79
St Bartholomew's Hospital see London
sales of manuscripts 118, 156, 169, 185, 202, 203, 223, 224, 228, 229
Salisbury Cathedral 46, 85–6, 127, 132, 235
salvage drives, wartime 205, 234
Sandwich (Kent), borough of 58–9, 107–8
Savoy, palace and hospital of (London) 70, 74n84, 184
schools 193–4, 211
  see also Eton College; Winchester College
scrinie xvii
scriveners 137
seals and seal matrices xvii, 19, 26, 30, 77, 83, 84, 124
  sealing wax 37n4
  see also Privy Seal

Secretaries of State 101, 102, 126, 128, 130–1, 144, 145
  see also Foreign Office
secretaries, personal and private 75, 98, 115–16, 131, 183–4
Selden, John, jurist and antiquary 117, 121, 123, 125
Sessions Houses 106
  see also shire or county halls; town halls
Sewers, Commissions of 106–7
Sherborne Abbey (Dorset) 27
sheriffs 19, 21, 31, 40–1, 57, 105
shire or county halls 151, 187, 211
skippets xvii, 83n11, 87
Smythe, John, of Bristol, merchant 114, 115
Society of Antiquaries 135, 136, 158, 196
  Elizabethan 118
Society of Friends (Quakers) 134–5, 164, 197
solicitors 112, 150, 154, 156, 161, 165–6, 198, 199, 226–7, 236
Somerset House (London) 147, 149–50, 184, 185, 190
Southampton 58, 59, 71
Southwell (Nottinghamshire), collegiate church 95, 193, 218
Spalding Gentlemen's Society 159
Spencer family, earls Spencer 162, 199, 224
Stafford, Edward, third duke of Buckingham 74, 86–7
standards xvii, 82, 113
Stapledon, Walter, Treasurer and bishop of Exeter 52, 85
Star Chamber, Court of 55, 98, 102, 122, 145–6
State Paper Office 101, 104, 118, 130–1, 144, 145, 149, 167, 175, 178
  see also Secretaries of State
State Papers 99, 101, 126, 128, 144, 178, 184n29
  Keepers of 101, 130, 144

statutes 70, 71, 109, 110–11
Stokes, Ethel, record agent and archivist 231
Stonor family, of Stonor (Oxfordshire) 57, 76, 180
Stratford-upon-Avon (Warwickshire) 60
strongrooms 73, 81, 148, 186, 199, 235
studies 73, 76, 125, 202
subject files 143, 206–7
surveys, estate 29, 49, 58, 112, 136, 161
Syon Abbey (later Syon House) (Middlesex) 86, 95, 113, 162
see also Percy family

tallies xvii, 31–2n, 175
tax records 21
telegrams 174, 227
telephones 227
Temple, The (London) 40, 51, 53, 142
terriers xvii, 58
  glebe 109
Thurloe, John, Secretary of State 126, 128
Thynne family, marquesses of Bath 94
tills xvii, 84
tithe awards 189, 216n35
towers 63n48, 69–70, 72–3, 74, 111, 113, 228
  see also London, Tower of; Westminster, Palace of, Victoria Tower; Windsor Castle, Round Tower
town clerks 44, 59, 61, 186, 214
town halls 58–9, 186, 214
  see also guildhalls
town houses 73–4, 114, 162, 199, 223, 224n60
trade unions 195, 221, 222
Treasurers, royal 29
  see also Cecil; Fitz Nigel; Stapledon

treasuries 14, 28, 32, 46, 48, 63, 76, 82, 83, 109–10
  royal 20, 30, 32, 40
  see also Treasury, HM
Treasury, HM 129–30, 143, 174, 176, 181, 182
  First Lords of see Prime Ministers
treaties 20, 33, 101, 141
Trentham (Staffordshire) 160, 161, 162, 199, 200
Twyne, Brian, archivist 111, 135
typing and typewriters 174, 206, 222, 227

vasa 85n18
vellum *see* parchment
Verney family, of Claydon (Buckinghamshire) 167, 168
vestries and vestry meetings 28–9, 46, 93, 152, 153
Victoria, Queen 184, 202, 210
visitations 62, 109
volumes 26, 31, 45, 62, 64, 71, 86, 92n5, 97n27, 101, 111, 114, 122, 154, 156, 159, 166, 173, 174, 184, 201
  see also act books; cartularies; commonplace books; day books; diaries; entry books; indexes and index books; journals; ledgers; letter books; minute books; registers
vouchers xviii, 31

Wake, Joan, archival campaigner 205, 230n77
Wakefield (Yorkshire) 61
Wallingford (Berkshire) 44, 59
Walpole, Horace, fourth earl of Orford 166, 167
Wardrobe, Royal 20, 38–9n, 52, 185
Wards and Liveries, Court of 98, 122, 146, 147

wars
- Anglo-Saxon and medieval 14, 30, 39, 50, 51–2, 63, 74
- Civil War (1642–8) 56, 93, 121–6, 141
- Napoleonic 145, 150
- Crimean 178
- First World 205, 206, 207, 223
- Second World 205, 206, 207, 217, 220, 223, 227, 229, 231, 233–6

Warwick
- borough 107
- collegiate church 68, 86
- University Library 222

Watt, James, industrialist and inventor 161, 164

wax tablets 10

Waynflete, William, Chancellor and bishop of Winchester 69–70

weeding 38, 138, 179, 207

Wellesley, Arthur, first duke of Wellington, Prime Minister 200–1, 202, 203, 210

Wells, Hugh of, bishop of Lincoln 45

Westminster Abbey 33, 47, 48–9, 66, 67, 77, 83, 86, 94, 157, 193, 218, 235
- Chapel of the Pyx 33, 52, 104, 141
- Chapter House 103, 104, 122, 141, 145, 146, 147, 148, 149–50, 175, 176

Westminster, Palace of 30, 32, 39, 53, 56, 98, 129, 141, 145, 147–8, 177
- fire (1834) 32, 175–6, 183
- Hall 30, 53, 55, 103–4, 147, 148, 176
- Jewel Tower 103, 148, 183
- Victoria Tower 177, 183, 209–10
- see also Parliament; Star Chamber

Whitehall, Palace of 98–9, 101–2, 129, 143, 145, 174, 175
- fires 102, 130, 176

Whitgift, John, archbishop of Canterbury 110

Whittington, Richard, merchant 71, 96

William I 21, 25, 29

Williamson, Sir Joseph, Keeper of State Papers 130

wills 15, 22, 110, 112
- royal 20, 32, 33n27
- see also probate

Wilson, Sir Thomas, Keeper of State Papers 101, 118

Winchester
- bishopric 23, 41, 63, 190
- borough 186
- cathedral 15, 66, 123
- College 69, 95, 111, 129, 220
- St Cross Hospital 71, 96
- see also treasuries, royal

Windsor Castle
- Aerary 68–9, 85
- Round Tower 210
- St George's Chapel 42n20, 68, 71, 95, 193, 218
- see also Royal Archives

Worcester
- bishopric 45
- cathedral 13, 27, 83

Wressle Castle (Yorkshire) 73

writs xviii, 31, 32
- royal 19, 36

Wykeham, William, Chancellor and bishop of Winchester 69

Yarmouth, Great (Norfolk), borough of 108, 185

York 39
- archbishopric 45, 63, 128, 156, 191
- cathedral 25
- city 59, 60
- Merchant Adventurers 60
- St Leonard's Hospital 70–1, 95
- St Mary's Tower 92–3, 124
- University 218